To Nick

Congratulations on your 21st Birthday

Love

Sid, Jill,
Luke & Simon

13.4.92

£3

KT-405-589

DECORATORS' · DIRECTORY · OF
STYLE

DECORATORS' · DIRECTORY · OF
STYLE

JOCASTA INNES

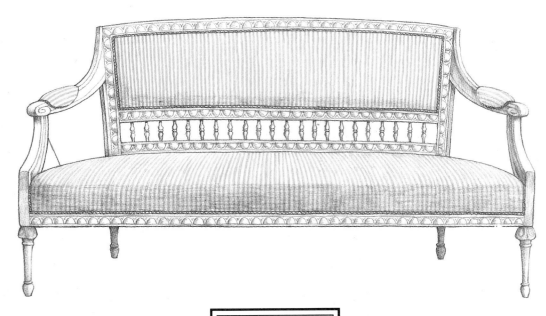

WHSMITH
EXCLUSIVE · BOOKS ·

CONTENTS

Editor: Dorothea Hall
Art Editor: Caroline Dewing
Production: Richard Churchill

Produced exclusively for
W. H. Smith and Son Limited
by Marshall Cavendish Books Limited,
58 Old Compton Street,
London W1V 5PA

© Marshall Cavendish Limited 1987

ISBN 0 86307 798 6

All rights reserved

Typesetting 10/11pt Frutiger Light 45
by Litho Link Ltd., Welshpool,
Powys, U.K.

Printed and bound by L.E.G.O. S.p.A.
Vicenza, Italy

INTRODUCTION

Style is undoubtedly a keyword of the Eighties. As an expression of individualism, of a stance that says 'I'm not drowning but waving' (to paraphrase Stevie Smith), style is an aspiration shared by everyone concerned with making their mark on the contemporary scene, from the young punks whose farouche style is a way of life, or the young designer producing one dimensional teapot or broken glass tables in the hope of attracting attention, to the professional interior decorator who makes a living imposing style on other peoples' rooms and belongings. Style sells things from tea cups to soap operas. 'Get in a stylist', says the home editor looking for an expert set dresser to humanize photographs of new kitchen units. 'It just needs re-styling', is the verdict of the marketing expert called in to beef up a worthy product whose sales are slipping. The prodigious success of television programmes like Dallas is as much, indeed probably more, to do with the style they put over as with the ramifications of the storyline.

What style is about in all these contexts is that urge to differentiate, to stand out from the crowd. Distinctiveness, in the sense of being different, is a meaning singled out by the Oxford English Dictionary, which also quotes fashionableness as an attribute of style. Translated into interior decorating terms, style is a 'look' which is immediately recognizable, at least to people with an eye for such things as the shape of a pelmet or the texture of walls and fabrics. The look may be associated with one particularly influential designer, with a certain place or region, or with a historical period.

Most people can summon up a mental image if you say 'Adam' to them, or that matter, 'Provençal' or 'Tudor'. The images may not be entirely accurate, but the fact that the mental screen throws up a picture proves that the style has registered, as an aesthetic happening with some special characteristics special enough to constitute a distinct style is an enquiry which runs through all the section of this book.

The *Decorators' Directory of Style* is not a treatise on aesthetics. Its aims are altogether more practical; to provide a visual reference for a selection of styles that are old, new and in-between, and which are of special interest to people today. There is no need to justify the choice of these styles that are most appealing to contemporary taste from the wealth of possibilities: it is what people have done ever since they began looking for inspiration or novelty, in the creations of the past, or in those from other cultures. The proof that our selection reflects current predilections is that versions of them turn up over and over again in glossy magazines,

and in the homes of friends and acquaintances. They represent the 'looks' that people find congenial, and people being as multitudunously various in every possible respect, it follows that our selection is truly catholic. There are grand styles, humble styles, soft and meltingly pretty styles, austere and hard edged styles.

Our twenty-two styles are not likely to surprise you individually, because if you had not met them before they would not have achieved the status of a recognized style. But what is new about the concept of this book is the idea of taking these different looks out of their glossy magazine context, where they lose some impact from being surrounded by less characterful effects, and bringing them all together under one cover. The effect of being able to flip from one to another, making comparisons, is not only exhilarating, it is instructive. Almost without realizing it, the contrasting and instant comparing leads to a sharpening of one's perceptions, and teaches one about style itself, what it is and what it is not.

Pictures tell this particular story vividly, but they cannot tell it all. The practical aim of this book goes beyond simply providing a set of images. The accompanying text and artwork takes each style apart for the reader, moving from general information about the historical and social background, (like the fact that the use of indigenous fruit woods for making Biedermeier furniture was due to the shortages caused throughout Europe by the Napoleonic campaigns) to a detailed profile of how the style looked and worked and was used, and finally homing in on close-ups of the small but significant details which are often what put the stamp of uniqueness on any particular style, be it American Country, English Country House or Greek Island. The appropriate furnishings are described, also how they might have been grouped in the heyday of that particular style; suitable colours and materials for walls, fabrics, floor coverings are mentioned, and special attention is given to such things as door furniture, lighting, window coverings and the choice of (or absence of) ornaments.

If someone wanted to use the book like a catalogue, in the spirit of 'Lets find a style we like' and wanted to carry it through to the letter, the guidelines are there. But on the whole we do not anticipate that modern readers would, or could, adopt a style lock, stock and barrel, unless there were persuasive reasons for doing so. The sort of antiquarianism, or purism, which cannot tolerate a nineteenth-century lamp in an otherwise eighteenth-century room, is a cult of perfection which is liable to prove prohibitively expensive in a decade when fewer and fewer good things seem to be hunted by more and more people. It is much more likely that someone attracted to a particular look or period, and living in suitable or neutral surroundings (there is not much point in going completely against the grain of the architecture, such as trying to do a Minimalist thing in cob-and-thatch cottage), may incorporate some of a style's distinguishing and attractive features, to add colour and personality and bring the place to life.

The style of our times is decidedly 'eclectic,' which is an elegant way of saying choosy though it is not infrequently interpreted as meaning anything goes. Eclecticism is our style because it meets our needs and opportunities. Few people can afford to limit themselves to a particular style, unless it is among those innovatory ones which are not yet sought after and highly priced. Mostly our effort goes into finding ways of welding a heterogeneous assortment of possessions into an overall scheme which looks pleasing and works for us. Calling this eclecticism is making a virtue of necessity, but for all that it is no bad training in the basic skills of homemaking. Eclecticism as a definite style seems to be most successfully practised in America, where designers and like minded people use it as a solution to the problem of dignifying essentially characterless living spaces, without trying to convert them into museum pieces. By mixing fine antiques with modern classics, for instance, characterful old armoires with glass and steel tables, and by taking intelligent liberties with antiques (such as covering eighteenth-century chairs with white linen or converting a marble capital into a sofa table) they have evolved a look which reconciles past and present, and polished wood with plate glass. The effect is both refreshing and inspiring, but it is perhaps more of a 'look' in the sense of being unfixed and transient, than a style, which needs a core of consistency, if it is to crystallize over the years into an aesthetic phase which can be classified, investigated, and raided by later generations who have suddenly learned how to see what was sitting there all the time.

Styles do have a way of seeming more clear-cut and all-of-a-piece the further back they are in time. This may to some extent be the result of hindsight, of being able to see the wood for the trees. The essential style of that time or place having crystallized out of the contemporary confusion of divergent trends. One could argue that every age in its turn felt itself to be eclectic, either mixing past with present, or experimenting with new inventions or fashions. I think there was a homogeneity about earlier styles which gave them a definite character, and

was applied more consistently through all the components that furnished a domestic interior.

Interior styles, until as recently as mid-Victorian times, were more intimately connected with exterior architecture than they are now, in an age when high rise flats of a uniform exterior design may be furnished with antiques and Georgian basements converted into hi-tech offices. Architectural styles, of their very nature, evolved slowly, and to begin with innovations tended to be adopted by a rich and aristocratic élite. Because the societies we are considering were hierarchical and tradionalist, the successfully established aristocratic style tended to filter down through different levels of society, influencing builders, tradesmen and craftsmen and creating standards and precedents. Ideas of excellence in building, furniture making, decorative painting and embroidery, gradually travelled through the wealthier classes, from the epi-centres of fashion out to the provinces, percolating down so that the miller's wife might be storing her linen in a chest, or serving her food on platters of a cruder make, but still retaining a kinship in shape and decoration with the elegant artefacts which the local châtelaine might have acquired a decade or two earlier, and her own metropolitan cousins a decade or two before that.

When one historical style imposes itself as pervasively as did the Georgian style in Britain (and to some extent the United States), there appeared to be a family relationship in style between almost everything produced for over a century. The explanation for this must be that the style itself offers a rich vein of inspiration and that it both meets the needs and echoes the spirit of the times. To people living in the anarchical style of the late twentieth century there is something awesome about the consistently high standards of design and workmanship which went into products of the Georgian age. The smallest article, a silver teaspoon or an inlaid tea caddy, partook of the same refinement and integrity of approach which gives us, at another level, the elegance of a Georgian terrace, or the bowspring tautness of a Chippendale chair. Though everything built or made appears to conform to generally accepted standards or proportion and suitability, the result is neither monotonous nor tame. Rather the reverse. Working within an agreed frame of reference seems to stimulate creativity; few artefacts from this period are as profoundly moving perhaps as works from more romantic, anarchic or individualistic times, but on the other hand they are rarely freakish and their calm appropriateness never palls — all is dignified, orderly and harmonious.

INTRODUCTION

The source of inspiration which sustained the Georgian age, as well as the one before it, and to some extent lingered on into subsequent eras (so that mid-Victorian villas often exhibit classical details, like pillared porticos) was the one which has proved the most powerfully influential of all in the history of aesthetic ideas – the classical ideal of proportion, which was evolved by the ancient Greeks and rediscovered with ardour and excitement by the enlightened spirits of the Renaissance.

It is neither new, nor uncreative, to refer back to the past for models and inspiration. People have been doing so throughout history, possibly because past styles have an air of being resolved, which is helpful to artists and designers floundering in a sea of uncertainties. You can 'see round' an established style, and borrow from it elements that accord with work in hand, without slavishly copying or being untrue to the spirit of your own times. Of course many revivalists have been guilty of both, with a consequent loss of vitality. This aspect of style, the working with influences from the past or from foreign cultures, is one which runs through all human creative work – literature, art, architecture and music – including interior decoration, which tends to follow on from architectural developments.

The classical Greeks were influenced by the ancient Egyptians, the Romans by the Greeks, and Renaissance artisans by – in effect – all three. The intellectual ferment of the Renaissance stimulated a Neo-classical movement which lasted on and off for several centuries, and indeed, is still being re-interpreted today (under the guise of Post-Modernism). At every stage, fashion also had its say, instigating a breakaway movement in search of the novel, the exotic or the frivolous. The vogue for chinoiserie which produced so much delicious pastiche in the seventeenth and eighteenth centuries, or the lighthearted Gothicizing by such eighteenth-century arbiters *elegantiorum* as Horace Walpole and William Beckford, who borrowed motifs from medieval ecclesiastical carving and reinterpreted them in plaster, are reactions of this sort.

By the middle of the nineteenth century the pace of this antiquarian foraging through the past seems to have accelerated. Instead of one powerful source of inspiration evolving slowly and consistently there were many styles to choose from, hence the extraordinary diversity of Victorian architecture. On the one hand the gothic camp, led by architects like William Burges, promoted a return to medieval forms overlaid with an almost Byzantine wealth of ornament, while on the other architects like Norman Shaw devised a building style, making much use of red brick and white stone, influenced by the costly domestic Neo-classicism of the time of Queen Anne. But if these were the dominant styles of the late nineteenth century, many styles of less lasting influence came and went; the Pre-Raphaelites, the Aesthetic Movement, Art Noveau, the craze for Italianate villas in prosperous suburban streets, a vogue for towers with pepperpot roofs in the French Château style. Fashion had become a decisive influence, propagating and consuming new ideas much more rapidly and voraciously in what was becoming a democratic consumer society than confined to the aristocratic milieux where standards of taste and elegance had previously been formulated. This was the advent of the idea of style as a pastiche, a 'look' that could be grafted on to the exterior of a conventional building type, or given to the interior, with the help of suitable properties.

Our own situation, a century or so later, seems comparable to that of the late nineteenth century. Whereas the late Victorians had finally shaken off the constraints of Neo-classicism, we have finaly freed ourselves from the constraints of more than half a century of Modernism. There is a feeling of liberation and experiment in the air. Architects and interior designers seem to be trying on new styles like hats. We have seen Hi-Tech, Post-Modernism and Romantic Pragmatism in architecture, and in interior design, every conceivable nuance of style from Minimalist to full blown Romantic, from hard edged Hi-Tech to intriguing Gustavian, from 'real' cottage to the extravagant fakery of entire rooms painted out in trompe l'eoeil vistas of Tuscan valleys in the heart of Kensington.

All this can be enlivening and fun, a flourish of individualism in the blankly impersonal face of the computer and micro-chip age, but it is also more than a little confusing. People are keenly aware of the importance of style, they are spending more money than ever before in the hope of acquiring it, but there is something paralysing about finding oneself in such a noisy market place, being buttonholed by plausible style peddlars advocating first this, then that fantasy. It is all very well being advised to relax, and do your own thing, but how is one to discover which thing is authentically one's own, and how much will the process of arriving at the right decision cost in terms of expensive mistakes? For most people, the solution to decorating problems in their homes is not to seek to break new ground in design, or to follow a blueprint from the past to the letter. They want guidelines, a sort of inspirational peg to hang it all on. This is where a directory of styles like this one becomes relevant and useful. By browsing through a gallery, of decorating and furnishing styles from past and present, one is made extremely conscious of what combines to make a collection of objects in a given space gell together with the resulting aesthetic consistency and thematic pleasure that one instinctively recognizes as 'style'.

The nursery of each person's individual style is almost always their first independently owned, or rented, living space. If you are the sort of person to whom such things are of interest, you will be bursting with ideas on what will make your bedsit or shared flat into a paradise. Some people's nature is to start by working off years of resentment of bourgeois parental notions of good taste, in a burst of decorating shock tactics. Black walls sprayed with slogans from an aerosol paint can seem pretty incendiary until one meets dozens more in the same post-holocaust style. Also the glamour of punk gothic surroundings can curdle unpleasantly, even threateningly, when the occupant is confined to bed for several days with a lowering illness. A few massive misjudgements at the start are quite useful, because there is some truth in the idea that one learns more from one's mistakes, than one's successes. The theory being that when young people make pretty and civilized rooms they are simply copying a formula laid down by their parents, and their horizons will not stretch to admit new ideas and influences as they grow older. The rebel who questions and flouts inherited standards may gradually return to the fold, but will not be content to transmit them passively but will actively re-interpret standards and precedents. This, of course, is valuable because it is the re-shaping of old ideas, always in danger of ossifying through perfection, that gives them new life for new times.

Most people have an inkling of the style of interior to which they are naturally drawn to, even if they would be hard put to define it precisely. The choice has to do with such things as temperament, age, income and aspirations. One would like to encourage people to go for the look they long for, as being the one that must express them best. But to work, and look good, the style you adopt or adapt has to take into account brute facts as well as delicious fantasies. The character of the place itself is a major fact. Where this is very pronounced, it could be a waste of time, effort and money, to go against it, or to suppress it. Towering Edwardian rooms with ornate fireplaces and massive doors and windows are not going to respond to the cosy cottage treatment, though they might be greatly cheered by a scheme

based on some of the elements we associated with Provençal manors and farmhouses, or made very gracious with chintzes and a profusion of rugs, needlework, cushions and pictures that one associates with not too stately country houses. Given a stark Minimalist look, they could be dramatic, as in the space-age bedroom we have featured, but the drama has to be very well thought out if it is not to miss the mark and end up looking like an operating theatre or a set for *Waiting For Godot*.

Minimalism, it should be said, is one of the hardest styles to bring off convincingly. People who suppose that it must be the ideal solution to setting up house on a shoestring may not have observed that while there may be very little on show what little there is is always choice, hard to find or very expensive.

The most successful interiors are usually the ones which respect the architecture and period style of the place enough to convey understanding, but not so far that the place acquires the stiff, 'touch-me-not' correctness of a museum set piece. Ideally, a successful room celebrates a rapport between occupier and occupied, and style here implies sensitivity to what is already there and a willingness to draw it out. No reader of this book would be so barbarous as to hammer sheets of plywood and hardboard over eighteenth-century panelled wainscoting, and doors, and then paper over these with woodchip paper. But 'well-meaning' people do still box in balusters to save cleaning, cover stone flags with vinyl flooring, replace pretty eighteenth- and nineteenth-century sash windows with plate-glass, 'tidy' over cracked ceiling plaster with polystyrene tiles, carve chunks out of decorative plasterwork to admit pipes and wires, and perpetrate other solecisms and misdemeanours under the name of 'improvement'. It is not being sentimental to remark that insensitive or bungled improvements affect not just the attractiveness of a building, but ultimately its market value, too.

The happiest unions are those where a place with a marked style of its own, neglected perhaps, or fallen from favour, comes into the possession of a person who loves that particular period, or style, and who sets themselves the task of restoring it to its former perfection. Interest in restoration is growing with countless new owners of old homes. In Britain a name has been coined for these eager couples who can never pass a skip without inspecting the contents for a pair of wooden shutters, or maybe, for a sash window with the original rippling crown glass almost complete, and who spend their weekends visiting demolition yards and

INTRODUCTION

museums; they are 'The New Georgians,' as opposed to neo-Georgians of 'repro' terrace house fame. While the obsessive zeal and pedantry of such dedicated conservationists can seem excessive, there is no doubt that they have helped to encourage a much more enlightened attitude to period architecture of all times and styles, and a much more intelligent approach to restoring it. More and more people are waking up to an awareness that they are fortunate to own things like Victorian stained glass and encaustic tiling, or Art Déco sunburst front doors and fumed oak panelling. The problem confronting the keen restorer is how to find enough time and money and how to be sure of doing things right. The best advice anyone can give is to find out as much as one possibly can about the buildings of the period, and adjacent periods, since there is often an overlap between the first introduction of a stylish new feature in the metropolis and its eventual appearance, much modified, on a cottage in a country town or in what were once colonial villas and bungalows. In which context it is interesting to note that it was the Yankee thoroughness and enthusiasm in the restoration of Williamsburg which got scientifically-minded restoration going, and that some of the most gorgeously polychromatic examples of High Victorian taste (and the best restored), are to be found in the chief cities of Australia. Correct information is invaluable to anyone embarking on a restoration project; the notion that stripping everything back to bare wood or plaster was a step in the right direction is now frowned upon in New Georgian circles, especially when the next step is to wax over the stripped wood (stripped pine, however mellow, is incorrect) or worse still, to paint them in an unsympathetic modern paint in an unsuitable fashion colour. These are admittedly purist quibbles, and obviously people are allowed to paint their own homes their own way, but it is always an intelligent policy, if you plan to break the rules, to know as much as you can about the rules you are breaking. Not only does this make sense, aesthetically and architecturally, but it also means you will most certainly make a better job of restoration.

So many shoddy conversions look wrong, and cost no less because they have been done by people with no awareness of the style they are chopping about. Knocking down interior walls and running in huge RSJs (steel girders) may see progressive at first glance, if it creates a large space lit by many windows, but the gain often turns out to be illusory; the new space might prove to lack a proper focus around which to group furniture, and to be draughty and expensive to heat. Most distressingly of all, it may feel makeshift and

unconvincing because its true style has been ripped out without providing for a coordinating principle to replace it. The worst, most crass example of this that I can remember was on the ground floor of an outwardly attractive Regency rectory. The inner walls had been removed to create a meaninglessly large but shapeless space littered with windows which had lost their proper relationship to each other, and dominated by an immense freestone ranch-style fireplace instead of the decorous marble surround it once featured. You would not have to be an architectural historian to sense the incongruity of macho ranch-style features in a space still governed by the sprightly, refined spirit of the Regency, where delicately detailed windows gave on to tidy lawns enclosed by clipped hedges and shrubberies. In stylistic terms this is tantamount to rapine.

The period in most peoples' lives when their physical environment becomes enormously important, is in the first years of marriage, when so much of the delight and excitement in the new partnership overflows into building and 'feathering the nest'. Suddenly it matters that the home base should represent the couples' ideas about 'the good life' and provide a welcoming home to which friends can be invited, and in which they can be entertained. This means considering such things as comfortable seating, a table large enough to seat several people, lighting, music, pictures, a spare bed – there may never be enough cash to spare, but what with wedding presents, and sales, and fleamarket finds the place begins to fill out and get an identity of its own. Astute couples have already worked out that the style of furnishings to go for, undervalued and still cheap, are the ones just the wrong side of the moving frontier of fashion, when yesterday's rubbish becomes today's collectables. When the Thirties are the rage, you rummage in the debris of the Forties, and even, if your style sense is very acute, in the still despised muddle of the Fifties. This can be a clever investment when fashion catches up, but most people are not so clued up and are more concerned to make a home that looks friendly and feels comfortable. This is the stage when homely vernacular styles have great appeal.

By the time this imaginary pair have reached the state of affluence when they can afford 'good' things instead of stop-gaps, they will have run through a succession of looks, and having probably become bored with the more immediately appealing effects, are beginning to re-appraise the merits of classic shapes, craftsmanship, fabrics that grow old gracefully, materials that acquire patina when 'consummated by use', elegance and restraint. They may go for an ultra modern look or a classic one, with country house overtones, but their minds are clear and their judgement informed. Achieving a personal style while putting a home together is dependent on experience and self awareness, and for many people the journey lasts a lifetime.

Money certainly helps to flesh out one's ideas about decorating once one is clear about the style and how to achieve it, but at the start, it is actually a help to be hard up: cash restraints can put backbone into an enterprise, while stimulating inventiveness.

Where someone is attempting to create a harmonious look out of a jumble of possession, on very little cash, details are critical because they pinpoint the small but important changes which can often be made for next to nothing. Hanging pictures differently, for example, or mounting them all identically, changing the lighting system, painting a stencilled border to replace a missing cornice, bleaching floorboards to a silvery grey instead of carpeting them, creating much needed bedside tables by heaping blockboard circles on crude timber frames and covering the result with old fabrics and lace.

Training in ingenuity and resourcefulness is woven into the lively and practical texts that accompany the representative styles illustrated in this book. The more-dash-than-cash aspect of style is one which always needs emphasizing. It is only too easy to flip through magazine features about enviably delicious interiors, where a genuine Matisse hangs casually above a rose marble chimneypiece against walls covered with watered silk or sheathed in stainless steel or antique stamped leather, concluding glumly that only the fabulously rich can afford style and the rest of us might as well give up.

It would be absurd to deny that wealth can command style; it always has, since the time of the Pharoahs, and our own repertoire of effects would be much poorer had there not been extravagant patrons who could commission a Michaelangelo, a Tiepolo, a Robert Adam or a John Fowler. But as some of the looks in this book eloquently demonstrate, modest means working within ancient local tradition, often arrives at an effect which touches a much deeper chord than a silver gilt rococo boudoir dreamed up for some dead princess. Peasant interiors in the vernacular, where sturdy materials and honest workmanship are allied to traditional colours derived from local clays, or natural dyes, are simple, robust, and beautiful in an uncontrived way which speaks more directly to people than fanciful effects.

Amateur decorators, which means the majority of people, who generally only get to practise on their own homes at their own expense (an exercise that cannot be repeated too often), are usually more successful in working within real constraints. A limited budget is the most common one, but there are often others like restricted space, hand-me-down furnishings or carpets, and rooms without character, or bonuses like shapely windows or, a handsome fireplace. At first sight the situation can seem irredeemable but it is quite extraordinary how often one's imagination fretting away at a problem, can arrive at an unexpected or elegant solution. A friend of mine, moving from a small but roomy suburban house into a tiny central London two-room maisonette, has worked miracles of compression and neat contrivance. She has made a small flat feel not large but comfortable, and as neatly packed with necessities as possible. A large hatch connects kitchen with livingroom, making both feel roomier and cooking much more sociable. A futon-sofa doubles as a spare bed. Unused space below the stairs has been made into a storage cupboard. The tiny hall and kitchen are paved with white ceramic tiles, a deliberate extravagance which makes sense in a small space because it gives a look of quality as well as reflects back lots of light. Though she had to begin by discarding rooms full of junk, there really is a place for everything, and it is no trouble at all to keep everything in its place. It would not be easy for two people to live in all the time, but it is just right for a single working woman with a job that involves frequent travel. It might not make the pages of the glossy magazines but in the truest sense of the word, in triumphing over circumstances, 'not drowning but waving', with commonsense and brisk elegance, it seems to me to be a vivid and successful expression of personality which is always the most convincing *style*.

Jocasta Innes

NEO-CLASSICAL

If you are interested in a style that has the hallmarks of formality, grandeur and elegance there are no other periods in history to compare with the Neo-classical.

A traditional, restrained interpretation can be seen in this music room where imposing, classically-proportioned windows flanked by decorative Ionic pilasters dominate the setting. Here, the strong vertical lines, broken only by the low, uninterupted row of furniture, appear to make the room look even taller. Light is allowed to pour in through simply-draped, round-topped windows on to bare, limed boards — in sharp contrast to the magnificent crystal chandelier.

The effect is pleasingly formal — and in keeping with its setting — grand and spirited.

Around 1750 the Neo-classical style had begun to influence painters and sculptors in Rome, in 1760 architects and designers were enthusiastically establishing the style, and by the early 1800s its influence had spread to all major European countries. Many well-known architects and designers are associated with the style, including Robert Adam, whose predilection for fine carving brought much elegance to the style, and Josiah Wedgwood, whose classical Etruscan ware and Jasperware are famous. One of the leaders of the movement was the eighteenth-century patron of arts, Thomas Hope, who stressed a more archaeological approach. Hope was brought up in considerable luxury in Haarlem, Holland, and was steeped in the classical tradition. He travelled widely in Europe and the Near East, where he developed a passion for Egyptian antiquities.

Hope then set himself up in London as an arbiter of taste and leader of society. He published several books, and his *Household Furniture and Interior Decoration* (1807) was to influence decoration, and furniture design for the following half century.

The classical components of ancient Greek and Roman architecture were adapted to contemporary purposes, and in some cases, motifs would be mixed together, combining Grecian with Etruscan, Egyptian with Roman.

During this period, it was usual for the upper classes to make the Grand Tour, visiting Europe to complete their classical education. On their return, they were frequently inspired to rebuild, redecorate and refurbish their town houses and country estates. And many of them turned to the works of Adam and Hope for guidance. They built and decorated their mansions on a grand scale, and filled them with the formal style of furniture, pictures, sculpture and *objets d'art* according to the Neo-classical ideal. The look has become synonymous with the grandeur and elegance of British, great town and country house style. A style that is well documented and can easily be recreated from the wealth of reference available.

Classical colours

So often the Neo-classical style is seen simply in terms of the classical orders – the Greek Doric, Ionic or Corinthian columns supporting the portico or in main reception rooms of a stately home. Colouring is also associated with the natural hues of stone, the cool white of marble, or the elegant, slightly faded pastel interiors as designed by the Adam brothers. But, in fact, the colours used in the earlier Classical period were much stronger and brighter, such as deep terracotta combined with black, saturated yellows, blues and greens embellished with gold. Thomas Hope, for example, was especially fond of mid-toned yellow furniture, decorated with black and trimmed with masses of gold. The effect was rich, colourful and vibrant.

Although existing original treatments are likely to be considerably faded, you can get a good idea of the authentic colours from prints and paintings of the period, and several museums keep many of the original designs.

Meanwhile, in establishing your colour scheme, aim to combine the original, brighter hues for the backgrounds of walls, ceiling and panelling with lighter, neutral tones, such as white or ivory, for the relief decoration. Alternatively, you could create a stunning effect using a black backgound with rich terracotta, or vice versa.

Neo-classicists much admired the 'black' and 'red' painting on ancient Greek vases. It was these painted vases, along with other ancient urns and amphoras that inspired Josiah Wedgwood to perfect his world-famous pottery.

Relief decoration

Most wall and ceiling surfaces were first plastered and painted, and then either embellished with decorative mouldings and beadings in wood or plaster, or painted in some other decorative way. The overall effect was individual, elegant and highly decorative. This was further emphasized by the use of contrasting background colours where, for example, a rich, saturated colour would be used for the inner panel with lighter-toned mouldings, and a mid-tone used for the surrounding area. It was common practice to give a panel a more dramatic effect by adding a black painted motif to the centre. Walls and ceilings often incorporated painted murals, which would be framed with beading or plasterwork to create a cameo effect: a most imitable idea you could easily achieve with the help of an artist. Similar types of design were used for carpets and also for bedcovers and hangings.

Several manufacturers working in fibrous plaster make classical columns, pediments, pilasters (half

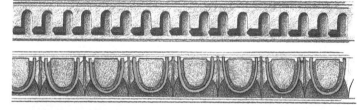

Top left: *Wedgwood Jasperware vase with white figures in relief.*
Top: *Detail of an Adam ceiling.*
Above: *Architectural details in fibrous plaster.*

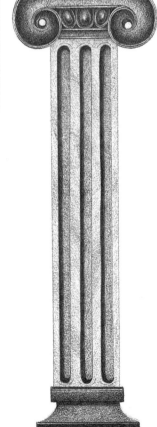

columns), niches and arches, cornices and ceiling centre pieces. On a smaller scale, you might try converting the recesses at each side of a fireplace into arched niches, or installing one on a hall or landing wall complete with a piece of statuary.

Craftsmen still working in plaster will supply and fix authentic classical relief

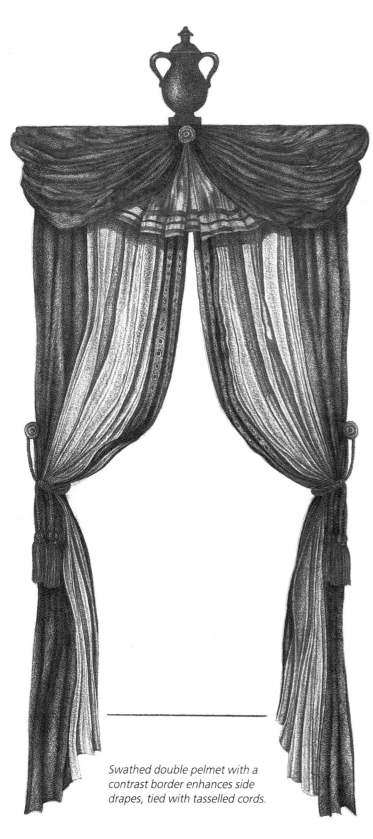

Swathed double pelmet with a contrast border enhances side drapes, tied with tasselled cords.

or pointed (in Gothic style), rounded or (see page 38) with a fanlight at the top; oval or circular with decorative glazing bars.

Before installing new windows, consider the architectural period of the house, and look for the correct style or have them specially made by a reputable firm. In general, windows should be left uncluttered, and if possible, fitted with shutters decorated or detailed to match the walls and ceiling, as previously described.

In recent years it has been the fashion to install 'picture' windows and double glazing, often at the cost of loosing beautiful, original glazing bars in the misguided belief that the new window allowed in more light, was easier to double-glaze, and that it looked more 'modern'. If you are replacing such a window, an important point to look out for is to make sure that the glazing bars are the correct width. Most original bars are considerably narrower and more elegant than contemporary equivalents.

Window treatments

In the most elaborate interiors, windows were frequently left undressed, relying on shutters for warmth and privacy. Shutters have long been designed as integral parts of the architectural style and interior design, and were decorated in a similar way, and with as much care, as walls and ceilings. They would also be carved and embellished with motifs and mouldings, gilded or hand-painted with colourful vignettes, in keeping with the classical style.

On south or west facing walls, where it might be important to regulate sunlight, you could combine shutters with very simple roller blinds in plain cream holland.

If your windows are not of classical proportions and cannot be changed, then consider disguising them with an opulent curtain treatment. The choice is dazzling. You can drape side curtains with decorative headings from ornate cornice poles, or choose from a variety of sophisticated designs using swags and tails. Remember that heavier fabrics hang better than flimsy types, so choose from cut velvets, richly coloured brocades or watered silks, for example (môiré imitation would be acceptable); lined, glazed chintzes could be used for bedrooms (including bed drapes) provided the designs are suitably Neo-classical. You might also look for ecclesiastical fabrics with vine or trefoil motifs, in velvet or silk damask, or fabrics with heraldic devices, such as, fleur-de-lis, Tudor roses, lions or griffins.

Alternatively, you may prefer plain fabric draw curtains and pelmet swag, both edged with a contrasting border or fringing, and finished with twisted silk rope and matching tiebacks, as shown on this page.

For sheer delicacy, you could try draping a semi-transparent fabric like muslin over gently gathered side curtains, as in the music room, overleaf. Notice the fabric rosettes covering the projecting roundels over which the fabric is draped, and in particular, the proportion of the length of curtain fall.

decorations, such as the Ionic pilasters and the egg-and-tongue cornice, as in the music room shown overleaf. For the appropriate paint finish, follow the instructions supplied.

Windows

The Neo-classical window relies greatly on elegant shaping and correct formal proportions. Visually tall and imposing, windows may vary from a simple sash – arched

Going for grandeur

The Neo-classical interior owes its rich textural contrasts to the great wealth of natural materials used, such as marble, stone, highly-coloured and inlaid woods, gilt, brass and silver, glass and sumptuous silks and brocades. The fact that most surfaces, including walls and ceilings, were highly decorated in relief gave more textural interest than had hitherto been seen.

Interiors, planned on a grand scale, were built and furnished by specialist craftsmen to the highest standards, and at relatively vast expense. However, where budgets would not allow the real thing, wood and plaster were painted in the trompe l'oeil style.

In the bedroom, the walls have been given a mock frieze and Corinthean pilasters, picked out in cool grey paint on pale duck-egg blue. Medallions, painted with cameo heads, are placed formally between the pilasters.

The four-poster bed is canopied and draped at all four corners in heavy, ivory silk, fringed and elegantly corded and held secure with hand-made tasselled tiebacks.

An Egyptian-style cane-seated chair and chest of drawers in dark wood with brass inlay, make strong visual contrasts. The gilt mirror, with its columns-and-frieze design, marble obelisks and busts completes the look.

The effect is one of calm, cool order reflecting elegance and charm.

Neo-classicists were greatly inspired by classical mythology and often incorporated various heroic scenes in their friezes and wall decoration.

There was also a certain

Bedroom in Neo-classical style with trompe l'oeil wall dècor.

nostalgia for this idealistic life, which it was believed was lead by the Gods on Mount Olympus and enjoyed by nymphs, shepherds and satyrs in sylvan glades. For the keen follower, enjoying picnics while drifting about in Grecian draperies became part of the summer social scene, and very wealthy enthusiasts even built large 'picnic houses' (Chiswick House, London, is a good example), as much glorified summer houses.

Fake it

The dining room shows that on a more humble level, even plain plaster walls can be painted to give the illusion of marble panels and cornices. This is the work of an artist whose enthusiasm for the technique does not stop there. Lunch is set on a table with a fake marble top, and the fire surround displays hand-painted 'Delft' tiles.

As a painting technique, trompe l'oeil (meaning literally, to deceive the eye) was originally used in the Classical era, appearing as Roman wall-paintings from about 100 BC, and was avidly

copied at the time of the Neo-classical revival.

Instead of hanging framed pictures within the marbleized panels, as here, you might use the technique to create, for example, the impression of an

Left: *This style translates easily into all areas of the home. Here dining room mock wall panels are painted and bordered with marbelized effects, as is the table top.* **Above:** *Satyr's-head mixer taps sum up classical elegance.*

Softer tread

To give rooms and corridors a softer effect, use rugs, carpet squares and library runners respectively. Look for formal designs in restrained classical colours to suit the period. Antique oriental (Persian) rugs in traditional glowing colours would be suitable.

If you must close-carpet, go for a plain colour and incorporate a period border design — perhaps garlands and swags, laurel leaves entwined with ribbons or the egg-and-tongue motifs. You may be lucky enough to own French, eighteenth-century Savonnerie or Aubusson carpets with their classical and Arcadian scenes. Designs include formal wreaths and cornucopias juxtaposed with helmets and Roman ruins — motifs made popular with the excavations at Pompeii and Herculaneum and at the Roman Forum, which began in the 1750s and were important factors in the development of Neo-classicism. Reproductions of these or similar eighteenth-century carpets would be suitable for surroundings of harmony and elegance.

seemingly turns it into a gargoyle.

This is probably the work of an individual craftsman specializing in wood carving who has designed the kitchen fixtures, from cupboards and work surfaces to drawers and accessories. Notice the chunky drawers and their impecable fit, and how they suggest huge slabs of carved stone.

This style of fixture would be ideal in large, stone-built houses, for example, where it would reflect the appropriate scale and architectural material, and yet have all the benefits of contemporary conveniences.

In keeping with the style, you could add a series of mythological heads to the tops of the cupboards, or above the windows or doors to relieve the severity of the design.

idyllic, secluded garden, or a classical vista including in the background several grand ruins. For a more formal effect, add either oval or round painted medallions, to echo the one above the fireplace.

On tap

Straight from Greek mythology to the kitchen sink! This rather amusing accessory in the shape of a satyr's head, disguises an ordinary mixer tap, and

Flooring

Ideally, the foundation of all floors should be firm underfoot. Springy floorboards on ground level or first floors would not give the true classical effect. However, many houses have this type of floor, and if they are in good condition, they could be stripped, sealed and polished and left in their natural colour.

On ground floors, marble slabs or terrazzo tiles would be most suitable. But on upper floors it would be perfectly acceptable to simulate marble in the form of sheet or tile material. You should, of course, have the joists checked for strength before installing tiles of any weight. Remember that large floor areas will need border interest, or use several colours to form an all-over geometric pattern. Keep to fairly neutral colours – black, grey, off-white, or the softer pastels of real marble.

Alternatively, you could use one of the painted techniques like marbling, either with a suitably antiqued finish, or painted to look like newly laid marble slabs. You could also use paint to simulate the black and white inlaid marble tiles of traditional Dutch interiors (this effect can also be created with lino, vinyl or ceramic tiles).

Using either paint or tiles, you could design a sophisticated border around the edges of a room to echo a classical theme, such as trailing acanthus leaves, vines, or the formalized Greek key and Egyptian lotus leaf patterns.

Furniture

Many leading exponents of the style would design every detail of a building and its interior decoration, this included the furniture, which was designed in proportion to the room, and to team with any *en suite* pieces. Everything was carefully positioned, and a formal floor plan provided to make sure the grand scheme was followed through, and to ensure that items could be correctly re-positioned after cleaning.

Furniture in general, and chairs in particular, showed a strong emphasis on horizontal lines, and prominent features were curved or sabre-shaped front legs, the arms set high on the back uprights giving a 'high-shouldered' appearance; the top rail swept backwards and forming a continuous curve with the rear legs.

Parlour chairs and dining room chairs tended towards standardization, being made of hardwoods; mahogany or rosewood inlaid with classical motifs in brass. It was into the

Left: Black and white floor details can be copied in paint or tiles. **Above:** *Look for similar Victorian reproduction furniture.*

An Adam-style gilt-framed mirror is an ideal accessory. You may be able to convert a picture frame by adding bevelled mirror glass.

arms and legs of drawing room furniture that Thomas Hope recommended that antique heads of helmeted warriors and winged figures should be added, while archaic lions, griffins, sphinxes, owls and winged female terminals were also introduced. This period saw a mania for symbolism, which was translated into a vast range of animal forms.

If you own genuine pieces of Neo-classical furniture then you have a wonderful starting point. If not, look out for antiques and good reproductions. These can often be bought at auction houses, and antique shops.

There are also some delightful pieces of Neo-classical-style cane and wrought-iron furniture that would add a flavour of the period, and the occasional item will add interest to a rather severe scheme. Some pieces have a distinct 'Chinese Chippendale' feel about them, and although, strictly speaking, they are not Neo-classical this look was also very popular at the time.

Mirrors

Mirrors make a wonderful focal point in any room, and can be used to enliven large areas of wall space and to reflect light and space. Neo-classical architects were particularly fond of large mirrors, decoratively carved and gilded. Place them over a fireplace, above a console table or comode, in your drawing room or hall (see also the bedroom on page 16).

Upholstery

Upholstered drawing room sofas and chairs are generally straight-backed with wooden frames, and are rather uncomfortable, since line was more important than either springs or paddings. The upholstery (usually confined to the seat but sometimes extended to the back) was covered with sumptuous cut velvets, silk or satin damasks or specially woven Gobelin tapestry (to match wall hangings). Look for couches in the style of Egyptian or Greek day beds. Furniture designer, Caroline

Quartermaine, produces modern painted versions which would lend a spirited feel to a contemporary Neo-classical interior.

However, in a modern drawing room, where comfort is paramount, you may prefer simply shaped sofas and chairs but covered in a fabric richly patterned with formal motifs. Look out for the splendid Victorian or Edwardian Neo-classical reproductions of couches, chaises longues and chairs. If the shapes are right, then they can easily be re-upholstered in a stylish fabric.

The Knowle sofa (a day bed with hinged sides, tied decoratively to the back with tasselled cords) is another acceptable piece of furniture, and copies are still made.

Even fitted furniture can be given something of the flavour by adding mouldings or beadings and trimming it with brass handles and escutcheons.

Adapting the style

In adapting the style it helps enormously if you are starting with fairly large rooms and high ceilings. Height and the illusion of height is a key element of classical Greek proportion based on the ancient classical orders.

The overall scheme should be carefully planned and special attention paid to the divisions of the wall (cornice, frieze, wall panels, dado) and the ceiling design so that the proportions are pleasing and fit the classical ideal.

In order to judge the overall effect, try out your plan first using templates cut from brown paper and taped in place, or chalk lines drawn on the plaster. Adjust them if necessary before continuing to the next stage. Seek professional advice if you are planning to use plaster mouldings, and follow the manufacturer's instructions for applying reproductions.

Both wall and ceiling panels can be finished with flat paint, marbleized or ragged effects – but you may prefer simply to use simulated marble (or other textured) wallpaper.

Use either wood or plaster beading to outline panels, and to suggest the frieze and dado rails. These should be painted and gilded according to your scheme, before pinning them in place.

Specially designed mural panels printed on easy-to-apply paper or vinyl make acceptable alternatives, as would photomurals made from prints of the ancient world, or photographs of original wall paintings or classical buildings.

Nevertheless, rooms of smaller dimensions can successfully be decorated in this style providing you keep to the correct scale. For instance, do not make wall panels too big nor the dado too deep. Use only a narrow cornice and discard the frieze if necessary, and make sure the ceiling is not overly decorated. Vertical lines should be emphasized with uninterrupted low levels of furniture and dado rails (see page 12).

In this period, furniture was formally arranged around the edges of a room thus affording greater opportunity for the full effect of this truly magnificent decoration to be seen and enjoyed.

GEORGIAN

Prettily proportioned, restrained and graceful, this early Georgian panelled parlour is an example of eighteenth-century style as it might have been enjoyed by a country squire or a middle-class merchant, an unpretentious and delightfully simple distillation of high Georgian fashion.

Often referred to as either 'The Age of Reason' or 'The Age of Wit', the eighteenth century could equally be dubbed 'The Age of Taste'. A cultured stylishness was much admired and of itself could elevate a man into the very best society. Despite his ordinary background, Beau Nash could get away with publicly rebuking a Duchess at the Assembly Room, Bath, because he was a recognized leader of fashion.

Fashion in the home was no less important and many books were published advising on colours, materials and proportions. In the *Complete Body of Architecture* (1756) Isaac Ware recommends that wainscoting, meaning wooden panelling, was most suitable for a parlour, stucco for noble rooms such as great halls, and wallpaper, silk or tapestry hangings for a lady's apartments. Batty Langley's *Builder's Jewel* (1754) sets out precise 'Rules . . . to find the breadth of the dado of the Tuscan order', and for 'Doric', 'Ionic', 'Corinthian' and 'Composite'.

Classical precedents reigned supreme, from the robust Palladian style of the beginning of the century to the refined Neo-classicism of the Adam brothers, all the rage from the 1760s. But the characteristic eighteenth-century urge to experiment also led to some notable deviations from ancient Greek and Roman models, in Rococo fantasy, chinoiserie whimsy, and the nostalgic romance of Gothick.

Only the very rich were able to indulge their tastes to the full by commissioning the greatest artists, architects and cabinet makers to build and furnish their homes. Those unable to afford such extravagance had to be content with less refined interpretations of the current trends. Even the more humble products of the eighteenth century, the terraced town house, the cottages and country furniture, seem to have an almost infallible grace. Neo-Georgian, too often an unfortunate pastiche, has remained a popular style to this day.

Panelling

Simple wooden panelling from floor to ceiling, often incorporating fitted cupboards, alcoves and a fire surround, was a common and inexpensive means of decorating a room in the eighteenth century. Grander versions used exotic hardwoods such as cedar and olive, which were left unpainted, or featured intricate carving, but panelling of cheap deal or pine was, as here, invariably painted. As well as providing added insulation when used to line a room, wooden panelling often divided rooms within a house.

The most popular method of construction was known as 'fielded panelling', in which bevelled panels were slotted into surrounding frames of wooden moulding. Panels were not nailed in place, allowing for slight movement in the wood to avoid splits and cracks. Designs for panelling varied from the elegance of the understated to an inappropriate grandeur, according to how skilful the local joiner was in adapting classical proportions to a scale suitable for his client.

Above: *Floor-to-ceiling wood panelling incorporating the fire surround.* **Right:** *Detail of a stencilled wooden floor.*

Sadly, genuine eighteenth-century panelled rooms have usually been ripped out by succeeding generations, keen to modernize. Panelling is again fashionable and there are firms that specialize in recreating eighteenth-century style panelled rooms to dignify anything from a city boardroom to a private study. Any good joiner can master the techniques of panelling but not necessarily the design, which will have to be worked out according to the individual proportions of a room. The purist may want to resort to original eighteenth-century instructions.

An alternative is to use paint to create an impression of panelling, sectioning the walls in subtle shades of one colour, as in the parlour shown on the previous page. The addition of wooden mouldings, pinned to the walls and mitred to frame the painted panels will give a more three-dimensional effect.

Paint

It is a twentieth-century misconception that stripped pine is old-fashioned. If found anywhere in a Georgian interior it would be the scrubbed surface of the kitchen table, not the panelling.

Up until about 1750 the only paints widely available for interior use were mixed by tinting a white lead base with earth pigments to get a range of greys, browns, off-whites and dull olive greens. These were often applied uniformly over panelling, mouldings and cornice. Later in the century more variety was introduced using paint to high-light mouldings as in the parlour overleaf. White joinery became fashionable, contrasted with panels of paint, or, for the wealthy, wallpaper or fabric, in vibrant colours like sky blue and strawberry red.

Robert Adam favoured an almost gaudy spectrum of colours on white to embellish his delicate plasterwork. Equally smart were mouldings picked out in gold against an ivory background. These more lavish paint effects are, on the whole, only suitable for the more opulent Georgian interior.

Paint was also used on floorboards, and might imitate the geometric designs of expensive marble flooring.

Stencilled designs, similarly, were a cheap substitute for wallpaper and were particularly popular in eighteenth-century America where they were also used to decorate plain furniture. Baskets of flowers, stencilled in muted colours, can give the most uninspiring pieces a rustic Georgian look.

Furniture

Good eighteenth-century furniture is beyond most people's financial means and pieces by Sheraton, Chippendale and Hepplewhite fetch extremely high prices. However, Georgian designs were copied by the Victorians and Edwardians alike and these old reproductions are more accessible.

Only a few pieces are necessary as Georgian rooms were generally sparsely furnished. Chairs were placed around the edges of a room and tables folded against the walls to leave space in the middle. Only towards the end of the century did arrangements become less formal with conversational groups of chairs and small tables.

Upholstery was padded rather than sprung, and rush and cane were commonly used for chairs. Look for wing chairs with curved cabriole legs. Upholstered stools and chairs without arms were also favoured because they could accommodate the very wide, hooped skirts that were fashionable for women.

Alcoves

Alcoves, imitations of ancient Greek and Roman niches for statues, were a favourite means of displaying ornaments. As in this parlour, one of the most popular Georgian designs was an arch, surmounted by a stylized shell and lined with curved shelves. The shelves, having a prominent central curve with shallower curves at either side, suggest a similarly

Left: The plain, broad, yet elegant proportions of this early Georgian chair are offset by damask upholstery. **Above**: *Reproduction wooden niches can be fitted into wall recesses.*

curved display. Plates and dishes, placed at each side, can be turned towards the middle in a very pretty way. These attractive wooden structures were often built into a panelled interior to fill the recesses on either side of the chimney breast, and have panelled cupboards beneath. Fibrous plaster versions are cheaper than wooden reproductions and can be fitted into a wooden surround.

Draped and swagged

An eighteenth-century bedroom should, like this handsome panelled room, be somewhere for living and not just sleeping in. In the middle and upper class Georgian household, rooms for entertaining tended to be on the first floor. Often the main bedroom, also on this floor, served as the venue for daytime guests, business callers and the instruction of staff, and would have been furnished with chairs and possibly a small writing desk. The muslin that curtained a lady's dressing-table mirror could be lifted by a maid to veil her face if visitors called during her toilette, so serving a practical as well as a decorative purpose. For purely decorative reasons, gather spotted muslin into a fat rosette and tie it with a large silk bow over an oval toilet mirror.

Except in the poorest homes, the four-poster bed was universal. The prettiest are tall, elegant affairs, with slender carved posts. Tent beds, lighter in construction and far cheaper, were a common substitute. Curtains were draped over an iron framework trimmed at the top with small brass finials of the sort that are still made to trim brass curtain rods. A light metal frame of this sort can be added to an ordinary divan bed and looks most effective when swagged with looped drapes.

Fabrics were an expensive luxury and only the wealthy draped their beds with heavy velvets or silk damasks. Block printed cottons cost less but, until the 1750s, were limited to the blacks, reds, purples and browns obtainable from madder. Later in the century the palette was expanded, and favoured designs were adaptations of lush Indian floral patterns, like the drapes on this bed, or naturalistic European flowers.

Monochrome *toile de jouy*, first made in the 1770s and still widely produced, must be one of the most stylish fabrics with which to create an eighteenth century feel in a bedroom. Printed in rich purple, red, sepia or indigo blue on a creamy ground, the traditional *toile de jouy* often portrays pastoral scenes in the style of Boucher, chinoiserie vignettes, or birds and foliage.

A splendidly draped four-poster bed dominates this handsome bedroom. The wainscot and ample fireplace give a sober effect.

Drawing-room

Festoons of nuts have been looped against the dark painted panelling in this Georgian drawing-room to look uncannily like carved classical swags. The sweeping curves could be imitated with fabric, or possibly dried flowers and used over oval pictures, doors or windows.

The splendid wing chairs are upholstered in the kind sumptuous fabrics, in bold patterns, that a prosperous Georgian might have used to enrich his home. Close nails, upholstery tacks with domed brass heads, were a frequent form of added decoration, serving the practical purpose of attaching fabric to the wooden frame of a chair or stool and sometimes curving into complementary patterns. They are still made and make an attractive alternative to the braid which covers modern upholstery tacks.

The dado rail, appearing just above the tea table, was originally introduced to protect expensive wall hangings from the furniture which was pushed back against the wall. It remained a common feature of decorating schemes well into the nineteenth century.

Above and **below**: *A small table with chairs placed prominently in a room is a Georgian way of taking tea – often by candlelight.*

Parlour

The increase of clutter and the delicate elegance of the furniture give this comfortable room a look of the late eighteenth century. Tea, that favourite Georgian infusion, is on the table and a canary chirps in a Georgian bird cage.

The plain fireplace has been painted to look like marble, a trick widely used in the eighteenth century to ennoble plaster or wood. Once you have learned how to marble, and there are some excellent books available on the subject, you will find that it can also work well on table tops, skirting boards, door surrounds and even cornices.

Against the fireplace wall are a pair of pole screens, used to protect a lady's fair complexion from the heat of the fire. Smaller, hand-held face-screens are also typically Georgian. Both are highly collectable. The prettily turned boxwood or ivory handles of face-screens have often lost their flimsy screens and can be bought for very little. You can add your own screens by cutting shield-shapes from thin sheets of wood or thick cardboard and decorating them with urns and swags.

Candles, or the less costly rush lights, were the only forms of lighting available and much thought was given to ways of maximizing their effectiveness. Mirrors, sometimes incorporating candle holders, were used to reflect light by those who could afford them, and graceful silver candelabra, like that on this tea table, were placed in pairs on dining tables. Chandeliers made of brass, silver or wood at the beginning of the century were hung just above head height. Crystal chandeliers, so extensively copied today, were a later luxury.

Windows

The typical Georgian window is a tall, sash-window, extending down to a few feet above floor level and divided into small oblong panes with glazing bars, which became finer as the century progressed. Indoor shutters, folding back into the window casements, provided extra warmth and security. Sometimes Georgian windows have had their glazing bars removed to make way for the larger panes of glass of the late nineteenth century and original shutters will often be found clogged and rendered useless by layers of paint. Restoring both is worthwhile.

Again, the cost of fabrics effected the design of window coverings. Waxed and printed linens were used for economical blinds, of the Roman rather than roller type. A more lavish appearance could be achieved with festoon or drapery curtains, both quite frugal with fabric. Festoon curtains are made by attaching lines of brass rings to vertical strips of tape, sewn to the reverse of the fabric. Cords passed through the rings are used to raise the curtain in looped swags. Drapery curtains work on the same principle but the rings are lined up diagonally to pull the curtains up and aside.

Above: Festoon blinds and pelmet dress a shuttered window. **Right:** *Silhouettes prettily displayed on ribbon.*

Pictures

Pictures were hung noticeably higher in Georgian homes than is the custom today and sometimes tilted forward so they could more easily be appreciated. Picture chain was used to support the large oils with heavy and ornate gilded frames, which were found in the great houses.

Lesser weights were hung with wire or cord which was sometimes covered by silk ribbon, topped with a large bow or rosette. Use two wide, watered silk ribbons, and hang vertically from picture rail to the top corners of a larger painting, or hang small pictures, oval portrait miniatures or silhouettes in vertical lines on a single strip of ribbon, adding a bow to the top of each frame.

Prints of works by popular contemporary artists such as Hogarth were an alternative to originals and the so-called 'Hogarth-frame' is still much in demand. Flower and bird prints look charming grouped in a drawing-room or bedroom. The superb and ornately framed overmantels that we may think of as typically Georgian, were confined to the grandest homes. Look instead for an oval portrait print in a simple gilded frame to place above the fireplace.

Flooring

Carpets, whether imported Persian rugs or specially woven patterned carpeting made at Wilton or Axminster, were such a luxury that, even in palatial houses, they were made to fit around, rather than under, large pieces of furniture. Floorboards were often scattered with sand to absorb the dust and rubbed with dried herbs. If you cannot bear to strip back to plain boards, sisal matting is a warmer and less noisy alternative.

To enrich your boards or matting, look for faded, second-hand oriental rugs. The Georgian who could not afford a rug would make do with painted or printed oiled floor cloths. Make your own from canvas and paint it with the geometric patternings of marble paving or a suitably classical design. These are more decorative than practical so do not place your floor cloth where it will suffer heavy wear.

Fanlights

In order to give daylight to the hall and staircase, especially of terraced houses, glazed fanlights were often installed beneath the portico over a front door. They were so called because their design was often based on the radiating ribs of a fan. Many fanlights, whether semi-circular or rectangular, have sadly lost their glazing bars of wood or lead which formed a delicate tracery of pattern on the glass. An original Georgian fanlight looks blank without its glazing bars but, fortunately, there are expert restorers who can replace them. Do not make the mistake of buying a modern door that incorporates a fanlight in its top panels. The proportions of these mock Georgian doors are wrong.

Wallcoverings

Britain was one of the foremost producers of wallpaper in the eighteenth century, not necessarily patterned, but also in plain colours. Like carpets, wallpapers were expensive and designed for large rooms. Those papers that were patterned were in bold, opulent designs. Flocked paper, referred to by Samuel Pepys as 'comfortable damask' was made by scattering wool clippings over a design painted on in glue. Many modern flock papers follow patterns that have hardly changed for over two hundred years and can look tremendous in a grand Palladian interior. For an altogether lighter effect, find a reproduction of one of the eighteenth-century Chinese wallpapers. These were once imported as hand-painted panels and were greatly prized (see Gustavian style page 77). Fabrics, such as damasks, and tapestries, were also used as wall coverings and hangings.

In these days of cheap manufactured goods, it is hard to imagine a time when wallpaper was so heavily taxed that it was out of most people's reach, or when a pair of curtains was a luxury. Nowadays, however, the labour and materials for panelling a room make what was a Georgian commonplace into a modern indulgence.

Left: *Contrasting examples of painted floor cloths.* **Above:** *Typical wallpaper patterns.*

REGENCY

If you are looking for a style which combines a sense of space, elegance and a gracious past there is surely no historic period as suitable as the Regency. The term, strictly used, describes the years in which George, Prince of Wales, was Regent until becoming George IV. Actually as a style the term, as generally used, has been stretched to cover the late Georgian period, starting around 1790, up to the early years of Queen Victoria's reign, the 1840s. Before it came various forms of the Neo-classical, either very strict as with the Palladians or very frivolous as with the Adam style. The Regency was a gentle reaction against both these extremes, better suited to a domestic setting of no great pretentiousness.

Regency is an elegant word, and the style follows. The essential ingredients of Regency furnishings and architecture are a light Neo-classical style, but often given a lift with oriental or, at least, exotic touches. The early Regency saw everything getting finer; staircases had finely made banisters and hand rails while windows had ever thinner glazing bars. Plaster mouldings, especially for the cornices of the rooms, replaced the chunkier wooden versions of the mid eighteenth century and often followed classical ideas, with delicate foliage and plants winding around the rooms.

In this room, a basically simple rectangular plan has been enlivened by a few details which have been cleverly accented. The slightly Gothic round-headed window, with its slender glazing bars, is neatly echoed with a simple diamond-patterned wallpaper, and a tiny cornice of simple moulding provides a neat detail where walls and ceiling meet.

In fact, look carefully, and you will see that the apparently ornamental details are simpler than they appear at first glance. The window is, in fact, a basic sash design, with the shutters and shutter box grained to give greater emphasis to the window area. The graining continues around as a wainscot, again a way of defining the form and shape of the room.

Lightly furnished, with much of the papered walls left bare, a strong contrast is then made with a vertical display of porcelain plates. The restraint with which the few items of furniture have been placed encourages a restful atmosphere, a sitting room in which quiet conversation takes place. A Biedermeier day bed compensates for being heavy by the elegance of its curves while the chair beneath the window has elegant tapered legs, a far cry from the hefty claws or paws of mid Georgian furniture feet. If there were to be animal feet, then Regency style would dictate dainty hoofs. The furniture, though relatively sparce, is more than adequate both to make the room comfortable and to give a well lived-in atmosphere. Lighting from a central Venetian glass chandelier is here provided entirely by candles.

Applied decoration

The Regency period was much taken with the oriental. The Prince Regent's own choice of Indian style for the Brighton Pavilion, with its chinoiserie interiors, ensured that this became a fashionable look. So the use of bamboo, either real or simulated, was one popular way to make things look slightly exotic and one effect that is easy and economical to introduce. Other favourite patterns are based on the neo-classical repertoire; for example the Greek key or fret, which can be found in frieze papers and wallpaper borders. The idea was to copy the architectural moulding that had been used, in wood or plaster, in eighteenth-century interiors. Alternatively strips of wallpaper border can be applied to items such as lampshades. As ribbons or in a woven or embroidered band these repeating patterns can be used as edgings to plain curtains or cushions.

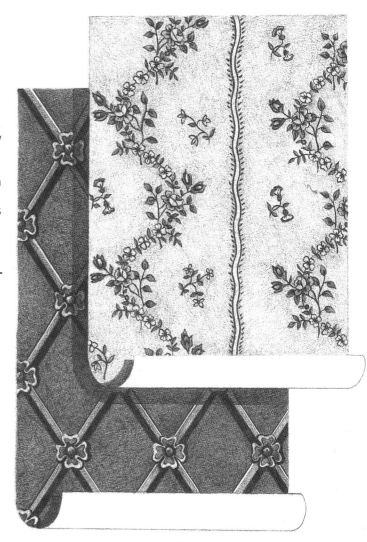

Paint imitation bamboo using matt varnish tinted with artist's oil paint. Apply broad bands to suggest joints, darker spines, eyes and freckles for a pretty effect.

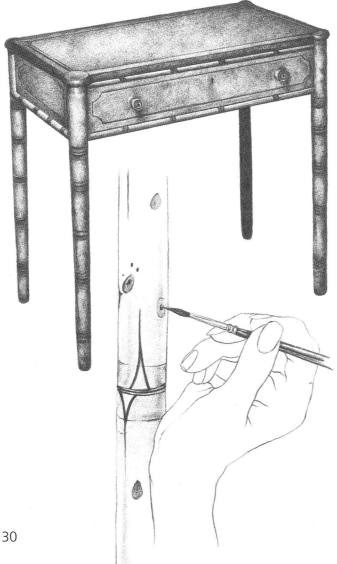

Fabrics and wallpaper

Wallpaper and border patterns of delicate flowers contrasting with formal fret and trellis motifs.

Although the best known Regency pattern is the so-called 'Regency stripe' there were lots of much more flowery patterns in both wallpaper and fabrics. Sometimes the flowers are woven in and around ribbons, sometimes sprigs of tiny flowers are scattered on a pale ground. The flowers chosen were usually unassuming little blossoms; the wild rose as opposed to the great Victorian favourite, the cabbage rose. Heavily detailed chintzes were not used in the Regency period. Another popular pattern was the elegant trellis, which combined the geometric with the naturalism of plants entwined in it.

Materials

Chairs and benches often had inset cane panels, as an alternative to painted panels (the latter especially popular in American furniture of this period, there known as Federal style). Although perfect examples of this technique would be highly expensive to buy, it is possible to pick up the occasional chair or sofa in need of repair. If you cannot do the repairs yourself, there are specialist craftsmen who can bring them back to their former splendour at a much lower cost. As previously mentioned, bamboo, true or false was very popular to suggest one of the more exotic elements of the style. The favourite woods of the time were ornamental, such as rosewood or maple, and suitable for veneer.

Lighting

At this period lighting was provided by candles and oil lamps. The centrally hung chandelier or lantern was the usual main source of light, with additional side light from either table lamps (the modern column shaped lamp bases are very suitable) or from wall mounted fixtures. Because these sources of light were generally soft, make sure your lighting arrangements are muted, golden rather than white light being suited to the style.

Floors

To capture the style, choose large loose carpets or oriental rugs in faded colours or, if you are in the creative mood, why not make a painted oilcloth? Floor boards were sometimes exposed, but were usually left unpolished or, in modern practice, unvarnished, so that a matte, light shade results.

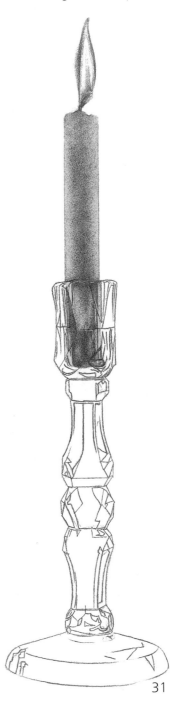

A gilt edged, black-painted chair with a delightful cane back topped by a hand-painted vignette of musical instruments. Note the turned legs in imitation of bamboo.

Repeat

Repeat patterns of scenes and events, particularly on the French cotton known as *toile de jouy* (which is reproduced today) were used, often as vignettes. These textiles were usually printed in strong colours on a white ground and often show scenes of ruins or eighteenth century picnics. They are usually festive and add a touch of gaiety to the quiet good taste of the Regency room.

Paint finishes

Furniture was often painted, black or white with gilding, for example. Japanning (an imitation lacquer finish) with a base colour of dark green, black or dark red and was a widely used technique. The addition of a laquer tray, boxes or other small ornamental objects will give a flavour of the style: or, if you are clever, you could paint or japan simple pieces of furniture yourself.

Candlelight gives the softest, almost romantic, glow to a room, and nothing would be more suitable on a dressing-table or mantelpiece than tall, cut-glass candlesticks. Their faceted surfaces adding twinkling reflections in true period style.

Left, above, right: *Classical draperies,* bateau *beds, polished, mahogany and carefully placed prints against chastely patterned walls add up to the sophisticated allure of Regency style.*

Dining in style

In the dining room of the same house, the diamond-patterned wallpaper has been repeated but this time the height of the wall has been broken by a grained dado. The window, although probably still with shutters intact, is here softened by curtains of fine muslin, caught low down and bordered with a ball fringe. Above it a pelmet of draped muslin has been added, although sometimes at this period the pelmet would have been a contrasting fabric, probably heavier and more colourful than the main drop.

In the eighteenth and nineteenth centuries it was always obvious which room was meant to be the dining room, because the patterns of the decoration told you so; for example a fine plaster cornice moulding of grapes and vine leaves might run around the room. The vine was, for obvious reasons, regarded as particularly suitable in a room used for entertaining and this kept to the classical idea, since Bacchus, god of wine, was a favourite figure of the classical interior. Here, the Wedgwood dinner service, with additional plates mounted on the walls, ensures that we are reminded of the connection.

Chimneypieces in the Regency period had become much simpler. Sometimes there might be a simple motif, such as a patera (a circular ornament) on each corner, but here there is a grey marble surround with a slab for the mantelpiece. The mirror over the fire is almost full height and performs its double

function of enlarging the impression of the size of the room and helping to intensify the available light. An embroidered fire screen and, just visible, a brass edged fireguard complete the effect.

The dado is made from simple matchboarding rather than the panelling that would have been usual a couple of decades earlier. The glass fronted cupboard in the corner displays china of a suitable period but not necessarily expensive antiques. Like many things in this house it has been given a period touch by a little imaginative persuasion; in this case cardboard ogee details have been applied to the glazing.

Obviously the charm of this room is mostly dependent on the well chosen and charming objects in it, but lighting and a restrained palette help to evoke a period feel which would still hold, even if the furniture, such as the octagonal dining table with its inlaid border of contrasting veneers, were not of such high quality. Candles are used both in the Venetian glass chandelier and in the sconces, but if you want a more dependable light source, then low wattage electricity, in the right fittings, can produce a very acceptable effect.

Young Regency

A room for a well-behaved child, still keeping the Regency flavour. The simple day bed with two-colour striped cover is echoed by a simple striped paper with a frieze paper or possibly stencilled decoration of stylized swags and ribbons. Stencilling was popular in the early nineteenth century (as it had been since at least the sixteenth century) but with a specifically Regency air, usually following the light and linear patterns that appear in wallpapers. In this case, the frieze serves an extra purpose: to neatly disguise a cupboard at the top left.

Mature Regency

An adult bed would have, if you are being closely faithful to the style, canopied or tented drapery. This was a particularly French, or Continental touch. The equivalent style in France was known as Empire, whilst in America the term Federal described a mixture of Adam and Regency styles. There was much exchange between the countries, however, and a furniture designer such as Sheraton, who used this kind of drapery, was willing to acknowledge that he had borrowed the idea from the French. Since the major pattern books of both architects and furniture designers were known throughout Europe and North America, there was bound to be a lot of exchange of ideas.

Drapery and upholstery

Curtains are hung quite simply, without much gathering, and often with a separate draped pelmet. Sometimes they were not meant to be used, since there were shutters beneath. The more elaborate attention in drapery was given to the tent-like curtains which hung over beds, even over day beds (which were really a kind of chaise longue). Furniture was tightly and smoothly upholstered, with additional bolsters and neat piping. Buttoning, though only very shallowly applied, came in at the end of the Regency whilst the more extreme flounces and rouching were not seen until the 1850s.

Wallpaper

Friezes and dado papers in complementary patterns, or contrasting between plain and patterned, were used in the Regency period and can be found increasingly easily today from those manufacturers who are concentrating on reproductions or even printing from the original old blocks. After the eighteenth-century use of wooden panelling, a simple plaster wall required a bit of extra visual interest and these papers introduce a welcome note of variety. Frieze papers are sometimes little more than a narrow strip, but they can be very attractive if there is no cornice moulding, and make a decorative bridge between walls and ceiling. The main thing is to ensure that the different patterns do not add up to a 'busy' effect, otherwise the room will look rather more High Victorian than Regency.

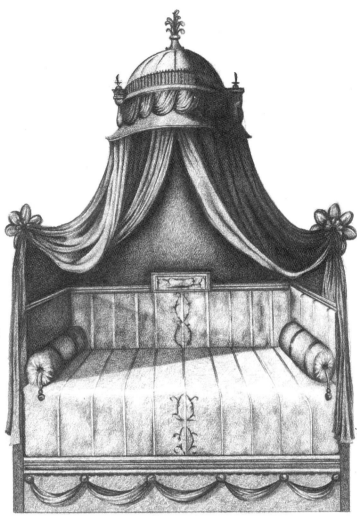

Ironwork and garden ornaments

Good quality cast iron was a notable feature of Regency architecture, both inside and out. Within the house it might be made up as banisters or used for cast-iron grates, which were tending to become more ornamental than the chimneypiece itself. The basket-shaped grate, complemented by a nice set of fire utensils, can be found without too much trouble and if you have a chimney in working condition, then a live fire will add enormous charm to any room. Remember that the fireplace was also an important source of light before gas or electricity and so it was given great

This Sheraton-designed sofa bed shows a strong French influence with its elegant drapery, held back by rosettes of silk cord, and festoons on the base valance.

prominence.

Outside, the ironwork was used for balconies, verandahs and porches. If your house is of the right period, then reinstating or repairing existing iron detail will do much to emphasize the sense of a Regency style. Equally, even if you have the smallest town garden, a formal layout with classically shaped urns or pots will continue the style of the interior to the outside and give an even better feel of the Regency period.

Colour

The sense of colour changed quite considerably through the period of the Regency. Earlier schemes tended to have pale grounds and stronger shades in the patterns; later, moving towards the Victorian love of darker shades, the overall colour scheme became richer.

Picture hanging

In Regency houses pictures, at least in humbler homes, tended to be displayed in a cluster. Heavily gilded and ornate frames look quite out of place, although they were usually mounted or else set into a narrow gilt inner frame. Sometimes small paintings or even ceramics may be suspended on ribbons, possibly one above the other.

Mirrors, space

Mirrors are an invaluable aid to gaining space, in rooms of any style. However the Regency period was especially fond of generous sized mirrors, often hung above the mantelpiece. The glass is usually bevilled, with relatively slender frames, either gilded or of painted or japanned wood. Alternatively, if you want to reduce space, then try using screens to gain intimacy and warmth; after all, you can always move them out of the way if you want to regain the full extent of the room, for instance once winter is behind you.

Right: *Such a magnificently arched mirror might have been installed above the drawing room chimneypiece in a well-to-do home.* **Far right:** *Simple wallcovering stencil designs.*

Faking it

If you are handy with the paintbrush, needle or fretsaw all kinds of shortcuts to a Regency look are available. Trompe l'oeil graining, painted or japanned furniture, the addition of fake glazing bars on glass-fronted cupboards or bookcases, imaginative cutting and pasting with bits and strips of fabric or paper, will save you a fortune and gain you a period look.

Stencilling was a popular wall decoration often used in secondary bedrooms and attic rooms instead of wallpaper. Delicate motifs, such as those shown below, can be repeated as allover patterns, or used simply as borders around windows, doors, and cornices.

GOTHICK

A modern interpretation of the Gothick style can be grand or cosy, frilly or simple, ravishingly pretty or refreshingly ascetic. In this elegant room the strong architecture of the large windows and plain vaulting takes priority over added ornament. Light pours on expanses of bare board and, free of clutter, the room has an almost monastic austerity.

Gothic style takes its inspiration from the religious architecture of the middle ages, the pointed arches, vaulting and delicate stone tracery, the airy spires and pinnacles of Gothic churches and cathedrals. Distinguised from the earnest Victorian Gothic Revival which strained to be historically accurate, Gothick with a 'k' first appeared in the eighteenth century, a fanciful and romantic digression from the main design movement of Classicism. Horace Walpole, dilettante and politician, is often credited with inventing the Gothick style with his fairy-tale conversion of a small farmhouse, Strawberry Hill, London, in between 1750 and 1770. This is Gothick at its most exuberant, vaulted, arched, and iced with a crazy confection of stolen decoration; an archbishop's tomb has become the pattern for a chimney-piece, a chapter house has shrunk to make a parlour.

Unlike the Victorian version, eighteenth-century Gothick delighted in taking liberties, using the ecclesiastical masterpieces of the past as a glorious pattern book of designs and motifs. On a more humble scale a pointed arch might be copied for the back of a country chair, a cottage window, or an iron railing.

Gothick is a game of adopting and adapting, transposing and transforming. Europe is rich with Gothic sources and in England you may not have to search further than a local parish church in your hunt for ideas. The play of light on the stone floors and white-washed walls of the plainest medieval church may become your starting point or perhaps you will decide to paint a dado or a door panelling in imitation of an intricate rood screen. You can play with Gothick and, like Horace Walpole, make your own castle on whatever scale you please.

Windows

Gothick is a style that relies largely on architectural effects, domestic versions of the arches and vaulting that typify Gothic churches. Whether original or mocked, windows are particularly important. If you are lucky enough to live in a house that already has arched windows then you have a head start. If not, you can always improvize.

A typical Gothic arch is tall and pointed but you may choose a variation such as an ogee or trefoil arch. Square sash windows could be screened to form arches by attaching cut out plywood arches to the top of the window frame. You should first experiment with cardboard patterns for the best proportions. Alternatively, curved glazing bars can be added over the glass to form arches.

Most church windows have leaded lights. These too can be added to an existing window and look particularly pretty when forming a combination of diamond and rectangular panes as in the windows shown on the previous page. The design can be enhanced with small panes of coloured glass. Used sparingly these will not darken a room as would a full-blown stained glass window.

Curtaining a pretty arched window so as not to obscure its shape and proportion can be problematical. Unless privacy is important, you may choose to leave your windows unadorned.

Colour

Gothick, as opposed to Victorian Gothic, requires a lightness of touch that can be spoiled by dark and heavy colours. At its most frilly, crocketed and pinnacled,

Above: *Arched windows from medieval church architecture greatly inspired Gothick style.*

Below: *Decorative plasterwork delicately picked out in white against a deep pastel ground.*

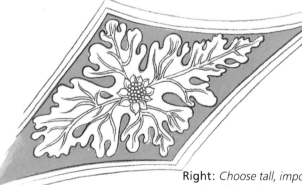

Right: *Choose tall, imposing candlesticks and creamy church candles for the true effect.*

Gothick is a lacy froth of decoration. Intricate Gothick designs such as white plasterwork tracery are delicious contrasted against a sharp pastel colour. Think of icing on a cake, for immediate inspiration. A plainer Gothick look such as the room

featured overleaf, with its combination of white walls, bare boards and exposed stone-work is redolent of white-washed convent simplicity. The paie colours of wood and stone make an ideal foil for furniture and fabrics.

Flooring

Most Gothic churches had stone or tiled floors. The cold effect of flags or plain tiles may be ideal for a kitchen or hall but, for a slightly warmer feel, scrubbed boards either lightly stained or sealed or sisal matting also have the right ecclesiastical flavour. Rugs can always be decoratively arranged on top. The subtle colours and patterns of oriental knot-pile carpets are particularly well suited to a quasi-medieval look and even the most faded, second-hand examples can bring richness to an otherwise puritanical decor.

Lighting

For instant Gothick romance you cannot beat the warm flickering glow of candle light. Rather than sacrificing the convenience and

practicality of electricity altogether, use candles to supplement other lighting. Avoid a central ceiling light and move table lamps around a room to find the most dramatic shadows, remembering that it is better to have several weak sources of light rather than one that is too harsh. Use wall mounted candle sconces or set candelabra or single candlesticks on window sills (only of course if your windows do not have curtains) for a theatrical glow that will remind you of all those Gothick horror stories!

Furniture

Gothick furniture translates into wood the carved stone-work of Gothic architecture and shrinks it to size. The result is often both charming and amusing as an arched window, perfectly proportioned but only four feet high, serves as a cupboard door, or the intricate tracery of a rood screen becomes the back of a wooden settle. Eighteenth century Gothick furniture, such as that made by Chippendale and Hepplewhite, is rare and expensive. So too is the Gothic-style furniture, that continued to be made throughout the nineteenth century. Victorian Gothic furniture, however, is relatively common and, although more heavy-handed than the earlier pieces, is highly decorative. In contrast, there are available some very simple Gothic-style stacking chairs made by contemporary craftsmen. Their sturdy tubular and sheet metal construction makes them ideal dining or occasional chairs.

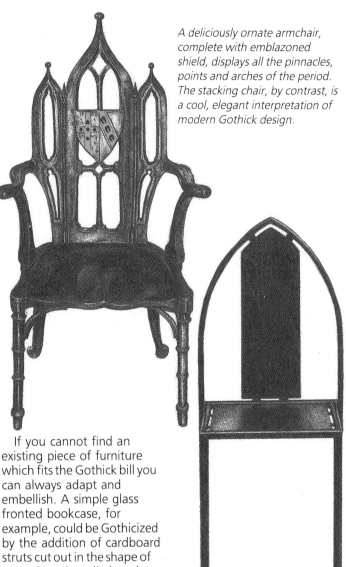

If you cannot find an existing piece of furniture which fits the Gothick bill you can always adapt and embellish. A simple glass fronted bookcase, for example, could be Gothicized by the addition of cardboard struts cut out in the shape of an arch and applied to the glass. Fretwork tracery can be laid over plain wooden panelling and cupboards topped with castellated pediments. Alternatively you can add painted decoration in the Gothick manner.

You need only a few 'Gothicky' pieces to furnish a room and the effect should never be too cluttered. In the room shown on the previous page, the two country chairs with their elegantly arched backs are enough to reinforce the Gothick architecture, reflecting as they do the curved lines of the windows on the left.

A deliciously ornate armchair, complete with emblazoned shield, displays all the pinnacles, points and arches of the period. The stacking chair, by contrast, is a cool, elegant interpretation of modern Gothick design.

Niches

Simple arched wall niches, echoing shapes found elsewhere in a room, are the perfect way to display ornaments. In the room shown overleaf you will see that two hold candlesticks while others are left empty. A group of small niches could become a showcase for a collection of candlesticks or they could equally well hold small statues, gothic-style glass or prized pieces of period china.

Cool dining

Cool, calm and stunningly
simple, this is the kind of
dining-room where you
would expect the scent of
freshly baked bread to mingle
with that of beeswax furniture
polish. The components are
straightforward; a smoothly
flagged floor, thick walls and
a deep window embrasure,
white paint, polished wood,
and a long table covered with
a snowy white damask cloth.
The effect is to evoke a
timeless rural idyll.

Again it is a pointed, arched
window, without curtaining,
that provides the decorative
motif. A version of its curves
sweeps up the back of the
carver at the end of the table
and another fills the square
backs of the remaining
Gothick chairs. These
repeated arches are the only
pattern in the room, and
flowers, including the suitably
ecclesiastical arum lilies, the
only ornament. The room
could almost be a medieval
refectory.

Some things are easy to
imitate. The table has an
altar-like quality, draped in
white and topped by two tall
wooden candlesticks.
Second-hand damask table-
cloths and napkins are
relatively easy to find and any
long table, regardless of age
or style can be effectively
camouflaged. Use tall
candles, preferably the
creamy, beeswax church
candles that both look and
smell authentic.

On the wall on either side
of the door are two candle
sconces with glass reflectors.

---

*Arched chair backs and window
frames in a country dining room,
whose stone flags and austere
décor reflect perfectly the
Gothick love of church design.*

These provide a surprising amount of light as well as looking pretty. Add the light of a blazing log fire and the table candles and you can have a candle-lit dinner without having to grope for your cutlery.

The success of this room lies in its perfect restraint. To achieve it you have to be strict: no upholstery, no chintzy curtains, no fitted carpet.

Bedroom corner
Cottage Gothick can be as fresh and pretty as it can be austere. This corner of a bedroom with its elfin fireplace is like something from a children's story book.

With so much squeezed into such a small space, fireplace, hearth, door, window, mantelpiece and shelf, it could easily look messy. This has been avoided by the liberal use of white paint on walls, woodwork and even the grate.

Above the fireplace is another example of a shaped wall niche, in this instance mirroring the proportions of the adjacent arched window. Slightly wobbly and sitting a trifle askew, quirks which endow it with an added rustic charm, the shallow recess has been built up from the mantelpiece and incorporates a second shelf for extra display space. This is an idea that could be repeated with equal success, and on a larger scale, over a drawing-room or dining-room fireplace. A deeper recess with further shelving could also prove a neat way of storing books.

In front of the window the painted chair has cut out quatrefoils decorating the top rail. For those who are skilled with a fretsaw this is the kind

of embellishment that can transform an ordinary chair to fit a Gothick setting. Otherwise, the design could be painted or stencilled on.

Rush seating is a country craft still widely practised and makes a softer alternative to plain wooden chair seats.

Unless you are one to rise

Top: Quirkiness is both Gothick and pleasantly rustic, as in this cottage bedroom, with its tiny corner fireplace and plethora of arched points. Note the Gothick quatrefoils on the rush-seated chair – ideal motifs for 'picking out' in paint. **Above:** *Cool and simple. Curtains on swing-back rods cover dormer windows.*

with the dawn you will probably want curtains in your bedroom. The effect of these curtains cleverly emphasizes rather than detracts from the shape of the window. The elegantly scalloped pelmet curves to form a Gothick ogee arch in the centre, following and complementing the pointed window arch. As long as there is enough space above a window and wall space at the sides for the curtains to be drawn right back, this is an idea that could be used to enhance any shape of arched window, whether the pelmet is cut from hardboard and painted to suit the overall decorative scheme or, as here, made from matching curtain fabric. Alternatively, an arched pelmet could be used over a plain window to suggest the Gothick style. Plain white walls are an excellent backdrop for a wide choice of fabric designs.

Bedroom
Pretty pieces of small furniture have been used in this cottage bedroom which could so easily look crowded and heavy-handed. The symmetry of the matching painted chairs on either side of the neat little dressing table and mirror adds to the sense of order and harmony.

The original Gothick windows show how an arched effect can be achieved within a square window embrasure and the curtains on hinged rods are a clever way to maximize light and avoid obscuring the charm of the four white arches.

The pastel colours of the antique bedspread and Georgian stripe of curtains and valance add gentle pattern.

41

Fabrics

When looking for 'Gothicky' patterned fabrics you could choose a design that echoes Gothick shapes, a large paisley or formal, symbolical motif for example. Fabrics that have an ecclesiastical feel or strongly architectural patterning are often suitable. If you cannot find the right thing you might consider block printing or stencilling a design yourself. Simple heraldic motifs like the fleur-de-lis, or architectural shapes such as the quatrefoil, can be very striking printed in a single colour on a plain calico or linen.

The type of fabric depends entirely on your chosen style of Gothick. Cottons and linens are cottagey while, for a more flamboyant Gothick look you might decide on something rich and rare like a damask or figured velvet. Cheap butter muslin, cunningly draped, can soften a window but, being transparent, will not obscure its shape. Avoid synthetic fabrics. They invariably look out of place.

Lighting

Keep electric lighting simple and traditional, no spot-lights, strip-lights or high-tech desk lamps. However concerned you are with authenticity you almost certainly will not want to rely solely on candlelight. Instead, use it to highlight, illuminating a niche or a mantelpiece. Remember that there are many more ways of holding candles than table candlesticks. Lanterns look good even when not in use and will stay alight outside and in draughts. Make your own and add a spired top or a Gothick finial. Candle sconces can also be tailored, cut from thin sheet metal for an arched shape. Torcheres, tall, free standing candle holders, can look very medieval. You might find an example to copy in a church and commission a local blacksmith. Grandest of all would be a chandelier, glistening with a cluster of candles. You might be lucky and find a suitable Victorian chandelier, perhaps made for a church in the Gothic style, or a reproduction that you could unwire. Look for something in brass, iron or wood, not crystal although some of the less flowery Murano glass chandeliers have a definite air of Gothick fantasy and these are still made in large quantities.

Effects with paint and paper

When the Georgians went flamboyantly Gothick they achieved their interior effects of vaulting and intricate tracery in carved wood and plasterwork. These are still feasible, if expensive, ways of Gothicizing a room.

The delicate patterning of

Above: *A selection of furnishing fabrics showing formal, heraldic and ecclesiastical patterns which will happily blend with Gothick interior schemes.* **Below:** *A handsome wrought-iron torchère, which you might have made by local craftsmen, would add an appropriate medieval touch to a hall or dining room. Choose slow-burning candles for maximum life, and a warm, glow.*

Gothic stonework with its repeated forms and friezes of frilly arches, also lends itself very readily to being reproduced in two dimensions. Use a moulded wooden or plaster dado rail at waist height and a picture rail about eighteen inches or so below ceiling level to mark out your walls. You now have two areas, one just below the ceiling, one above the skirting board, ready to be filled with lacy Gothick designs. Paint in white over a fresh pastel, apple green or duck egg blue,

for example. If you want to go further, fill the wall space in between with a large design of slim pointed arches, possibly against a paler shade of your chosen pastel.

You might decide that vaulting is best left to an expert stonemason or

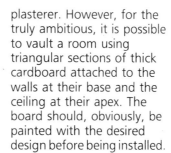

Walls can be stunningly Gothecized by painting a cornice, dado or, as here, all three divisions in white on a pastel ground.

plasterer. However, for the truly ambitious, it is possible to vault a room using triangular sections of thick cardboard attached to the walls at their base and the ceiling at their apex. The board should, obviously, be painted with the desired design before being installed.

Thick cardboard, cut with a sharp knife into fine Gothic tracery, can also be used, stuck flat on to walls or ceiling for a more two dimensional appearance than paint alone.

Display

Gothic churches and cathedrals often support their carved stone statues on corbels, horizontally projecting brackets. Set within a slim, arched niche, a single corbel, or one set above another, would make attractive mini platforms for a candlestick, a figurine or a vase. You can buy fibrous plaster corbels and, if you can't find any that look suitably Gothick, paint them with fluted rib vaults or arches.

Themes

Once you have arched your windows or painted your dado rail or built your ecclesiastical niche, you will have chosen a Gothic form which you may wish to repeat throughout your house. There are endless possibilities; arched door panelling which can also be applied throughout a wooden kitchen; frets added between straight stair banisters to transform them into a series of long, thin arches; a wooden fire surround carved to match the panelling; bookcases which arch to a point with scalloped paper edging overhanging the

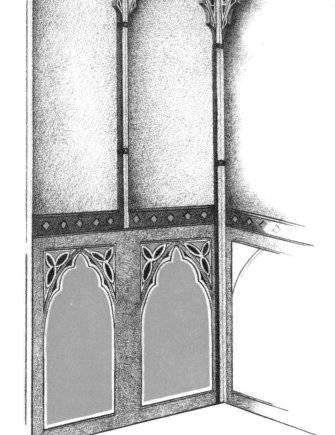

Fibrous plaster niches and corbels for displaying Gothicky statues and collectables can easily be installed, and their plain surfaces painted with mock fluted ribs.

shelves. You could even make a Gothick bathroom with a white canopied bath and an ogee arched basin mirror.

Gothick is an irreverent style, light-hearted and, at its best, both pretty and amusing in its clever mimicry of medieval sources.

VICTORIAN

If you are a magpie collector and you thrive on cosiness, clutter and comfort, then there can be no better excuse for interior self-indulgence than adopting the high Victorian style. This fantasy bower of a bedroom, adrift with lace, is Victorian in spirit if not in every detail. Forget Georgian elegance or Regency restraint and treat yourself to Victorian abundance.

Under the rule of Queen Victoria the British population boomed, the British empire expanded, and the growth of manufacturing industries, sustained by huge overseas markets, meant that more people had more money to spend on more goods. The newly prosperous mid-Victorian middle-classes crammed their homes with an elaborate concatenation of worldly goods, displaying their wealth and success through acquisition.

Styles of furnishings were various and curious, corpulent Victorian versions of Gothic, Rococo or Elizabethan. Drawing-room upholstery swelled into deeply-buttoned mounds, fattened out by the increasing use of springs. Every available surface was shrouded, covered by table-cloths, runners and mats dripping with heavy fringing. On top were ornaments and mementoes, jostling for space; wax flowers under glass domes, patterned china, ornate silver, cut and coloured glass, cases of stuffed birds, decorated boxes. The more the merrier. The same principle was applied to floorspace, often an impenetrable jungle of easy chairs, fat sofas and occasional tables.

Despite increasing mechanization, the standard of Victorian craftsmanship remained very high. Even the cheapest Staffordshire flatback figures were finished off with hand-painted decoration. The products of Queen Victoria's reign, from the solid, good quality furniture to the irresistibly pretty ephemera of frilly valentine cards, fill antique shops today.

There is an ample supply of Victoriana for creating your own interpretation of nineteenth century style. Only remember that, when the comfortable Victorian wife furnished her parlour fit to bust and took tea by gas light in front of a blazing coal fire, it wasn't she who would have to clean out the grate, polish the brass fittings, dust the innumerable ornaments or brush down the upholstery. The ready availability of servants meant that Victorian interiors were far from labour-saving.

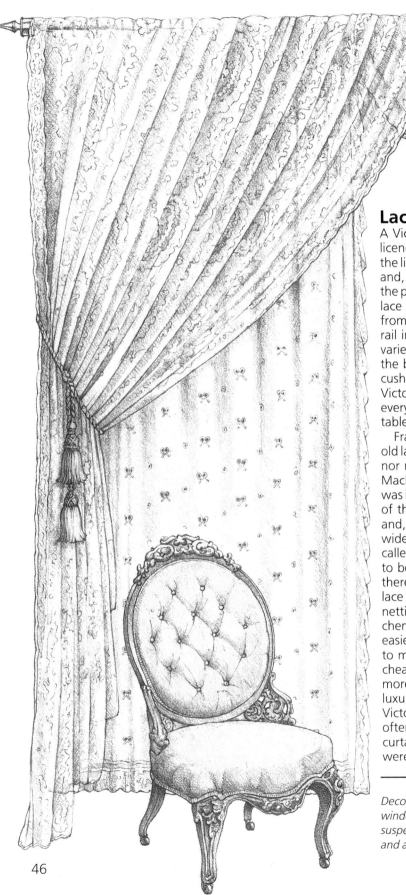

Lace

A Victorian bedroom is a licence for frilly femininity and the liberal use of silks, muslins and, as in the room shown on the previous page, lace. Here lace has taken over, hanging from the cornice to the picture rail in a transparent frieze of varied designs, wafting over the bed canopy, edging the cushions and, in the best Victorian tradition, dressing every surface from bedside table to mantelpiece.

Fragile though it appears, old lace is neither hard to find nor necessarily expensive. Machinery for making lace was invented at the beginning of the nineteenth century and, by the 1840s, was widespread. Pillow lace, also called bobbin lace, continued to be made by hand, but there are many other types of lace including filet, crochet, netting, ribbon lace and chemical lace; which were easier to produce and quicker to make. Because it was cheaper, lace became much more common, no longer a luxury for the rich alone. Victorian windows were often clothed with heavy lace curtaining and yards of it were used to trim clothing

from evening dresses to underwear. Table and bedlinen might also have lacy edgings.

Hunt for old lace in antique markets and antique shops. Often the most unprepossessing pieces can be revived. As long as an old piece of lace is still reasonably strong you can bleach it for snowy whiteness and starch and iron it for freshness. Alternatively, if you want your lace to look 'antiqued' you can dye it yourself by soaking it in a weak solution of tea.

Use narrow strips of lace to edge sheets, pillowcases and cushions. Bigger pieces could be used to make cushion covers and a large lacy tablecloth might be turned into a bedspread. In sufficient quantity, old netting, ruched or artfully draped over a brass curtain pole would make pretty curtains.

Cushions

Cushions always create a sense of luxury, especially when piled in inviting mounds. In this bedroom they are heaped on the bed and overflow on to the floor in a froth of white lace.

Pretty bedroom cushions, made from old and new lace, are easy to buy but more fun to make yourself. Cushion covers are the perfect way of using up small oddments of fabric; dressing table mats, scraps of embroidery, fragments of painted silk, a mixed bundle of old lace.

Buy a variety of cushion pads, square or round, and experiment with different combinations, using old and new fabrics and decorative trims. Stretch spotted muslin over a pastel silk so that a hint of colour shows through and edge it with a deep lace ruffle.

Decoratively edged, heavy cotton window nets, with drapes suspended from a cornice pole, and a ladies' button-back chair.

Use cotton broderie anglaise with crisp lawn, starched linen with fine crochet, a faded, flowery chintz with ivory lace and satin bows. Every cushion in your collection can be different until they drown the bed and chairs and start to spread over the floor.

Wallpaper

Printed wallpapers were very popular in Victorian interiors, especially repeated patterns of flowers, sombre for the drawing-room, paler and prettier for the bedroom. Small, sprigged designs, like that used in this bedroom, always look Victorian and will not fight with other patterns. If you want something a little bolder, many companies are now reproducing original Victorian wallpapers with larger designs of flowers, bows, trellises and birds, often with matching fabrics.

Above: *Striped or all-over patterned wallpapers in bold floral designs.* **Right:** *Antique oil lamps complete the effect.*

Lighting

By the 1840s many Victorian houses were equipped with gas lighting but most would still have had a chamber candlestick by the bed as an immediate source of light. A modern table lamp with conical shade is no substitute. Look instead for converted gas lights or oil lamps. If you cannot find an antique there are many reproductions available. Look for a genuine copy of a Victorian original rather than a twee interpretation. Small, bell-shaped china shades or beaded shades are pretty for a bedroom.

The bed

Victorian brass beds are some of the most attractive products of the industrial revolution, sturdy, unpretentious and decorative. They were made in their thousands and are by far the most common type of Victorian bed to be found in antique shops and to be reproduced.

In this bedroom the plain brass bedstead has been transformed into an airy four-poster by wiring brass curtain rods to the four corners and linking them with slim rods which could be either metal or painted wooden dowel. A flurry of lace tossed over the canopy and the fanciful addition of ribbons and posies of tiny artificial rose buds make it a bed worthy of the most whimsical Victorian heroine.

Some wooden bedsteads could equally be converted into four-posters, remembering that the framework of the canopy, whether wooden or metal, need not be elaborately finished as, when cleverly draped, it will not necessarily be visible.

Four-posters are still the epitome of romance but, after the 1860s, the Victorians favoured the half-tester which had two posts, a canopy and side curtains screening the upper end of the bed. A half-tester effect can be achieved, even with a modern divan, by fixing a wooden canopy to the wall behind the head of a bed, anything between four and six feet above pillow level. This can be hung with fabric gathered under a pelmet to fall behind the bed-head and at either side.

Victorian beds, usually raised to avoid draughts, always had a valance or bedspread, as much to conceal the inevitable china chamber pot as for decorative purposes.

The half-tester (two-poster), much favoured by Victorians, can easily be copied or a divan bed adapted, to give a period flavour to your bedroom.

Bathroom

Although plumbing, with all its refinements of water closets, baths and hot and cold running water, was available at the beginning of Victoria's reign, it was not until 1910 that it became standard practice to build houses with bathrooms. Most Victorian lavatories were still relegated to the garden. For washing, every bedroom would have had its washstand with bowl and jug and baths were also taken in the bedroom in a hip bath filled by hand.

Few would want to take their Victorian interior to this level of authenticity and a bathroom with the advantages of modern sanitation can still, like this bathroom, have a decidedly nineteenth century flavour.

A cast iron, free-standing bath, sitting on decorated feet, is the first essential. Copies are made by some manufacturers and originals can be found and, if necessary, enamelled. If you have the space, this kind of bath always looks splendid placed centrally rather than pushed against a wall. Generous porcelain washbasins, often supported on cast iron brackets, and elaborately moulded lavatories, with the essential wooden seat, can be bought as antiques or reproductions, and were sometimes further embellished with a monochrome design of flowers, as pretty as that on any dinner service.

Tiles were also patterned, or moulded with fruit and flowers. For a large expanse of tiling, as here, you would need to find a good copy of a Victorian design but for smaller areas, above a washbasin for example, a

patchwork of antique tiles can be very attractive.

Small pieces of furniture such as this bedroom chair and the wooden towel horse are added extras, while the bare boards, open fireplace and curtain pole with wooden rings make a suitably old-fashioned background. Finish off with accessories; huckaback linen towels with crocheted edgings, brass taps and soap rack, a cork bathmat, a porcelain lavatory chain handle, a real sponge.

Comfortable clutter

Rich colours, over-stuffed armchairs and sofas, and an accumulation of objects and pictures characterized the Victorian drawing room. Dark red and bottle green, as here, were particularly popular, complemented by woodwork grained a deep brown.

Above: *Victorian plumbing was proudly conspicuous. Their generous baths, palatial washbasins and inspired water closets have the monumentality of sculpture.* **Right:** *A wonderfully crammed drawing room complete with draped piano and crinoline lampshade.*

Wallpaper and carpet, often fitted, were strongly patterned, and favourite fabrics were heavy velvets and also horsehair and needlepoint for upholstery.

No Victorian drawing room would be complete without its fireplace, the focal point of the room in an age before television. Depending on its grandeur, a Victorian fire surround will usually be cast iron, carved wood or marble, the bigger and more imposing the better. Any Victorian decorating scheme for a drawing room will centre on

Victorian clutter, which now seems so cosy, began at the front door. Hunting trophies were displayed and, as here, give authenticity to the hall, as do the dado and sepia photographs.

the fireplace. Install a fire surround even if you have no chimney flue. For high Victorian style add polished brass fire irons, fire dogs and fender, an overmantel with ornate gilded frame, and a clock softly ticking in the centre of the mantelpiece.

In this drawing room the general effect of comfortable clutter is accentuated by the patchwork of pictures covering the wall from picture rail to dado, frames almost touching. You need a large choice of pictures to achieve this successfully but they need not be high quality originals and, if you do not have enough to cover a wall, group them closely, leaving gaps between groups of pictures rather than spacing them out.

Look for sepia photographs, evocative and quintessentially Victorian, combining as they do a captured memory and a favourite pastime of the Victorian amateur scientist. Mix them with prints, especially reproductions of popular contemporary artists such as Millais, or Holman Hunt which told a story or pointed out a moral; or choose watercolours of the day, the amateur work of house-bound ladies of leisure. All are inexpensive.

Above the serried pictures, the picture rail has been extended to form a narrow shelf for the display of oriental porcelain. This could work equally well for any selection of pretty plates. Also note the

fringed foot-stools, the antimacassar on the left-hand armchair, originally used to protect upholstery from men's hair oil, and the writing box in the foreground; letter writing was another universal Victorian occupation.

If you have any space left you might consider that centre of home entertainment and hallmark of Victorian respectability, a piano.

Hall

Embossed lincrusta paper, a Victorian invention, often also used on ceilings to imitate shallow plasterwork, extends to the dado rail in this narrow Victorian hall. Versions of lincrusta are still made and can look thoroughly authentic, especially when painted a dark colour.

Above the door is a stained glass panel. The influence of the Gothic Revival made the quasi-medieval look of stained glass very appealing, and it was often used instead of frosted glass. If you can find even a fragment of Victorian stained glass you may be able to incorporate it into a door or window.

The decapitated deer peering down at new arrivals are entirely in period. The Victorians were fascinated by 'curiosities', many of which would now seem quite grisly, and Queen Victoria's fondness for Balmoral, her Scottish home, elevated all things Scottish and baronial to the height of fashion.

The cast iron and marble hall stand, incorporating hooks, mirror, shelf and umbrella stand, is an all-purpose piece of furniture in the spirit of the combined dressing-table and fire escape displayed at the influential Great Exhibition of 1851.

Plants

The Victorians had a passion for indoor plants, especially exotica from the furthest reaches of the empire. The larger and glossier a pot plant the more attractive it was considered, and capacious and ornate jardinières were made to hold them. Palms were great favourites but the most popular of all was the aspidistra from the Far East, a well-nigh indestructible plant with heavy, shiny leaves. Aspidistras are still sold in some florists.

Encasing nature was a Victorian preoccupation, whether in the form of stuffed animals or plants in a conservatory. Advances in glass and iron techniques enabled The Great Exhibition to be housed in the cavernous Crystal Palace and also meant that glass houses on a much smaller scale became more common and their designs more spectacular. Often a conservatory would connect with a living room, providing a romantic, leafy retreat, and filling a room with the scent of flowers throughout the winter. A conservatory is still a delightful way of extending a house and it is possible to find companies who make very good copies of Victorian designs. If you have no garden space, it is possible to build a conservatory even over an existing flat roof.

Create it yourself

Industry was one of the great Victorian virtues but it was considered a sad reflection on a husband's means for a woman to have to earn a living and only the poorest women went out to work. The remainder were confined to the home, their household chores taken care of by servants, and a limited range of amusements at their disposal. As a result, lady-like crafts and hobbies flourished, with an emphasis on the meticulous and time-consuming.

Little girls sewed samplers with salutary biblical quotations while their mothers pored over petit point to make slippers, bell-pulls, pincushions, pictures, cushion or chair covers. They made the finest patchwork, they cut out tiny silhouettes, they pressed flowers, they covered boxes with tiny shells or straw marquetry, and covered footstools with patterns of minute beads, embroidered with fish scales or beetle wings. Their ingenuity was remorseless, the results of their labours some of the most charming survivors of the nineteenth century.

A Victorian-style conservatory will not only extend your home but will enable you to bring inside all the beauty of a period garden.

Take a leaf from their book and create some of your own Victorian-style handiwork. Many needlework kits, for example, are based on Victorian originals for cushion covers or pictures. Cover a screen with reproduction paper scraps or your own choice cut from old magazines and Victorian prints. Use small diamonds or hexagons of silk and velvet to make patchwork, or make a rag rug for your kitchen floor. The best sources of inspiration are the antiques themselves. It is hard to beat the Victorians for their inventiveness, sheer skill and patience with all things home-made.

Berlin woolwork cushion worked in bright coloured yarns on linen canvas from a design printed on point paper.

A Victorian-style screen covered in a random selection of reproduction prints and mottoes.

Scotland

In 1852 Prince Albert bought the estate of Balmoral Castle on the Dee in Scotland. During the next two years he rebuilt it in the Scottish baronial style. Albert's death in 1861 plunged Victoria into mourning (rendering all things funereal rather chic), and increased her sentimental attachment to Balmoral. Victoria's example set a taste for Scottish style from plaid dresses to little 'tartanware' boxes and needlework tools.

You could well take this as a decorative theme for a Victorian room, using tartan carpet, tartan upholstery fabrics and adorning your walls with antlers and prints of romanticized Scottish landscapes. Scottish Paisley shawls, made in imitation of the fine prints imported from Cashmere, were an important fashion accessory and were also used to cover chairs. A Victorian Paisley shawl, voluminous enough to cover a huge crinoline, can be flung over a sofa or draped as a tablecloth.

Covering up

Even a writer as sensible as Thackeray felt it necessary to apologize for the mention of ankles. Perhaps it was this exaggerated prudery which led the Victorians to cover and drape. This penchant for concealment is a great advantage when it comes to recreating a Victorian look.

In addition to lacy cloths, curtains and bedspreads, muslin was another favoured form of camouflage in the bedroom. A Victorian lady would often drape her dressing-table and dressing-table mirror with muslin, drawing it aside from the mirror glass and looping it up with large satin bows. Butter muslin by the yard is a cheap way of disguising the most ordinary piece of bedroom furniture.

Downstairs, fabrics were heavier and darker, although white damask would invariably have been used for the dining table. For the drawing room, chenille, a type of imitation velvet sometimes patterned with blowsy flowers, was a popular table covering. If you cannot find an antique cloth, choose a heavy cotton velvet and cut it to size so that it falls to the floor. In this way any table, even a make-shift pedestal with a cut-out plywood top, can be convincingly transformed.

Trimmings

No Victorian interior would be quite complete without its heavy drop of fringe, trailing on the floor at the bottom of a thick tablecloth or dripping from a curtain pelmet. Look for something in a chunky design, perhaps a thick wool bullion fringe or a coarse trellis with onion drops. Use it also to edge swagged curtains, to trim upholstered chairs and sofas, or let it droop over shelves and mantelpiece.

In keeping with the Victorian craze for covering and draping, one of the prettiest ideas for the dressing-table mirror is the draped and beribboned muslin swag.

NINETIES

The Victorian age left everyone exhausted. Cluttered rooms, confusing patterns, dark colours and scarcely a shaft of light, it was hardly surprising that a reaction would follow. That reaction, which we call here the Nineties style, was preceded by the Arts and Crafts movement. This move, spearheaded by a group of artists, designers and craftsmen laid great emphasis on the return to high standards of skill, in which the use of good materials and simple motifs were essential in the production of carefully made artifacts, often hand-crafted. Patterns were taken from nature but applied with discipline. In general it was a much airier style, with light and clear colours, space and attractive objects all freeing the house of the cobwebby look that had become usual in the middle decades of Victoria's reign.

The names associated with these beginnings of a more modern approach to the decoration of houses were amongst others, William Morris, Walter Crane, William de Morgan, and C. F. A. Voysey. The Nineties style has also a little of the continental Art Nouveau look about it, with plenty of curves and hardly a right angle to be seen. In fact the Arts and Crafts movement was much admired, both in northern Europe and America, and versions of this style can be found much further afield than merely Britain.

This sitting room is most clearly an Arts and Crafts interior, from its irregular floor plan, to the leaded lights on the upper compartments of the generous window, which appears to incorporate a door into a greenhouse or conservatory. Arts and Crafts architecture made much of the way in which rooms were interlinked, and aimed at overall informality. In this room the recesses of the fireplace and the garden window are at different angles from the other sections of wall. They help to make the room feel countrified and informal and very much in the spirit of the Nineties style.

Where the decoration is concerned, the same idea is followed through. The strongly patterned Morris wallpaper is confined to the upper part of the walls, and the white-painted wainscot is papered with textured wallpaper, or lincrusta, as it was known. There is much pattern here, but the colours are light and bright so that the room does not shrink with the weight of its decoration.

The matching set of comfortable armchairs is upholstered in a moquette or velvet woven with an oriental-type pattern, picking up the intricate colouring of the oriental carpets and rugs which are part of the Nineties look. The chairs around the table, with upholstered backs, have slightly ornamental carved details.

The chimneypiece is topped by double shelves and the Persian inspired de Morgan tiles around the fireplace complete the picture of comfort which this style conjures up so well. A low brass fireguard and tongs, with an open fire burning, sets a welcoming domestic scene.

Applied pattern

After wasting much effort on being 'realistic' the later Victorians put a great deal of effort into designing patterns which were rather formal, or alternatively were modelled on the kind of naturalistic patterns of flowers, birds and animals that had been popular in the medieval period. So someone like William Morris, whose company, Morris and Co. designed the famous wallpapers and textiles that are still being produced, looked at the little wild flowers that you find in the background of tapestries and reproduced them in beautiful, fresh colours on furnishing fabrics and wallpaper. A Nineties look could equally be gained by using some of the bolder designs available, with giant honeysuckle and peony heads or even just great swirling acanthus leaves, always tied together by a symmetrical framework in the design. Carpet designs took a combination of these forms with the traditions of the oriental rug (based on formal pattern), while hand embroidery was popular and covered with floral designs.

Room dividers

The Victorian room was always divided up into many little compartments; the Nineties look still favoured the use of screens but now as an ornamental accessory which might also usefully keep down the draughts around a passage door, or provide shelter to chairs grouped around the fireplace. This is one of the easiest ways to set about getting an Arts and Crafts look for, after all, you can easily cover a screen, bought cheaply second-hand from a shop, with appropriately patterned fabrics to make it look in style.

Top: *A selection of furnishing fabrics showing lively, all-over patterns of peonies, carnations and other wild flowers, made popular by William Morris.*
Below: *A simple, easy-to-make, three-panel room divider showing illustrations in the colourful style of the Pre-Raphaelite painters.*

Electric light fitting with silk shade designed for a dining room (1897), and a gasolier (right).

Press moulded Art Nouveau ceramic tiles, showing a panel for a fireplace surround (right).

Lighting

The 1890s were the beginnings of the era of electricity (the first house to be lit in this way was Cragside, in Northumberland), and the heyday of the gas light. So light fittings are extremely important; people who had the sophisticated new system were proud of it, and tended to show off their newly acquired fixtures and fittings. For the authentic look, you can go either for antiques or choose from the vast range of good reproductions available. Look for standard lamps, table lamps and centrally hung chandeliers and gasoliers, often with fringed or pleated shades and quite ornamental stands, or fittings.

Upholstery and hangings

A charming idea from the 1890s is that of hanging lengths of fabric along the walls, instead of wallpaper, and often with a contrasting fabric, or high-backed piece of furniture, to suggest the dado and wainscot division of the wall. The cloth has to hang fairly straight, so that it is scarcely gathered, and, of course it would need to be taken down and cleaned from time to time, unlike wallpaper. Tables were generally covered with an attractively patterned cloth, and comfortable chairs had upholstered backs, seats and arm rests, but without the bulgy buttoning of earlier Victorian furniture. Again, by choosing the right kind of fabric, for the upholstery or cushions, even a very simple settle can give the right sense of period. In keeping with this liking for heavy fabrics, with bold patterns, curtains were hung simply — from bold rings on a curtain pole or lightly gathered so that the textiles are shown to best effect.

Picture hanging

Pictures displayed in style often hung from exposed wires, suspended from a picture rail. The comfortable Nineties room had a very layered look, and the picture rail might separate the patterned wall covering from a white-painted upper area. Often the pictures were set into wide mounts with quite narrow, plain frames.

Chimneypieces

The fireplace and its setting had great importance in the design of the late Victorian house. Sometimes it was based on traditional architecture, so that you might find a great stone fireplace with inglenooks, taken from a seventeenth century manor house, but in town houses it would consist of a small iron grate, set with William de Morgan tiles (or those which followed) and with a generous mantelshelf, with space for several well-chosen ceramics. The overmantel, a piece of furniture, specifically to hang above the fireplace, was invented during the 1890s. Genuine pieces are not too difficult to find today and if, in this way, you can display a suitable collection of ornaments it would give the room an immediate sense of period. If you cannot find a real overmantel, then a horizontal shaped picture, possibly semicircular in shape, will give a sense of style and completion to that section of the room.

Studied style

In this well-lit study or sitting room there is a blend of Arts and Crafts furniture with French Art Noveau. The Thonet bentwood rocking chair faces a William Morris chair and, in the foreground, a chair designed by William Godwin, who virtually single-handed introduced a style which became known as the Anglo-Japanese.

Although fairly crowded by modern standards, this room sums up the attitude to space of the 1890s and early 1900s. The walls are hung with all kinds of pictures, porcelain and pottery, and over the door runs a shelf which is also well filled with more pots and decorative plates. Extra detail is provided by panels of contemporary stained glass, set in squared leading, an inspired way of achieving the effect of decorative glass and leadwork, even if you do not have windows which actually include either.

Around the room are various shelves for displaying collectables, and side tables (including two polygonal ones which have an oriental flavour about them) and the major pieces of furniture, of which there are relatively few, are light in their construction and form. The Nineties style has come a long way from the ponderous pieces, all flounced and buttoned, which would have been normal from the 1860s onwards. These are probably no less comfortable but are far less dominant in the room with their light woodwork and, in the case of the Thonet chair, a cane back and seat.

Bedroom pattern

In this rather spartan bedroom, the strong patterns of the William Morris wallpaper, the de Morgan tiles around the grate, and the semi-oriental look of the fine rug are given full rein. The dark ebony, or ebonized, wood of the chimneypiece has given it the look of a Flemish picture frame - it would not be improved by

Left: *This room is the fruit of a lifetime's discerning collecting. It displays many original pieces of furniture and fittings, such as the lamps with their original everlasting bulbs.* **Top**: *A bedroom, austerely furnished but alive with the magnificent flowing patterns of Morris and de Morgan.* **Below**: *Choice objects of the period.*

white paint, however tempting. Similarly, the flimsy Morris armchair, and the matching half settle (at the foot of the bed) and the more robust single bed are good examples of the furniture design of the period. It was a time when it was considered more important to treat the turned wood with loving care than to turn every detail into some fantastic beast or mermaid, as would have been the case earlier in the century.

Pictures are hung from the picture rail which runs all the way around the room and one (half out of shot, to the left) has a characteristic rosette pattern laid on to the gold mount, whilst otherwise remaining quite plain.

Above the picture rail the ceiling and upper wall are painted white and there is an inscription with appropriate lettering above the fireplace. The skirting is also painted white so that despite plenty of heavy pattern the effect is neatly compartmented and not in the least overpowering.

Finishing touches

On this desk are various objects, absolutely typical of the period; pewter candlesticks from Liberty, lustre vases of art nouveau style (notice how all the ornament is plant-like, or at least, takes the form of branches) and some stoneware in an eighteenth-century style from Doulton. The desk itself has typical art nouveau inlay, mother of pearl and different woods, with an elaborate metalwork interior. The bentwood chair by the desk also emphasizes this interest in elaborate line, always curving. Even the metal handles to the desk drawer reflect the same idea: this kind of detail is important to keeping the general sense of a Nineties style. A fine piece of furniture renovated with the wrong handles or hinges will just undermine your efforts to convey the period. Try to collect objects that convey the right spirit, even if they are not by well-known contemporary artists or craftsmen (prices for these would be extremely high anyway). In fact Art Nouveau, in particular, became very commercial and so all kinds of things were made in the style long after its heyday.

Shelves

Shelves turn up all over the place in the Nineties interior. You find them over the fireplace (see p 56), incorporated into an overmantel, but most typically, they sometimes run around the room high up, at the level where you would normally expect to find the picture rail. On it you can then display decorative plates, tiles and dishes, and build up a colourful collection, in Nineties style. If you are planning to follow this type of shelving, it is useful to remember that you will often find yourself dusting the shelf from the top of a step ladder!

Stained and leaded glass

The late nineteenth century was the moment when the art of stained glass design and manufacture came back into its own. By the 1890s, it was widely used in domestic circumstances (it had originally been made mostly for churches and grand civic buildings) and helped to pick up the clear, jewel colours that were used in the fabrics and ceramics of the time. Since the Arts and Crafts house often had large, but

quite elaborately divided windows, sometimes oriel or bow shaped, the glazing was mostly broken up by leaded panes, usually just in the upper section so that it was not 'busy' in the way of Tudor-style lattice windows. If your house does not have any window details of that sort, you can get the effect by merely hanging or standing a panel of stained glass or leaded panes against the window, see Studied style, page 56.

Ceramics

In ceramics, the use of metallic and lustre glazes was a hallmark of the period. The tiles that you can still buy, though at mounting prices, reflect the vivid colours — turquoise, garnet red, lapis lazuli blue – of the potters of the east and sometimes their subjects too; peacocks, carnations and gazelles for example. The ceramicists took great interest in the authentic processes and materials of the work they admired, and William de Morgan was in fact responsible for reintroducing the technique of applying lustre to the glazes. The shapes of the pots were

rounded, often with a bulb-shaped base and narrow opening. Some pieces combined ceramics with metalwork, so that the neck or the body of the pot might have a detail superimposed over it. Similarly, metalwork was quite often combined with glass; the use of such

materials meant that the design was left relatively simple, allowing the contrast to make its own point.

Above: *A wooden picture rail-high shelf filled with ceramic plates and dishes, is essential to the style.* **Below**: *Bulbous-based pots, displaying vivid coloured glazes, make a strong period look.*

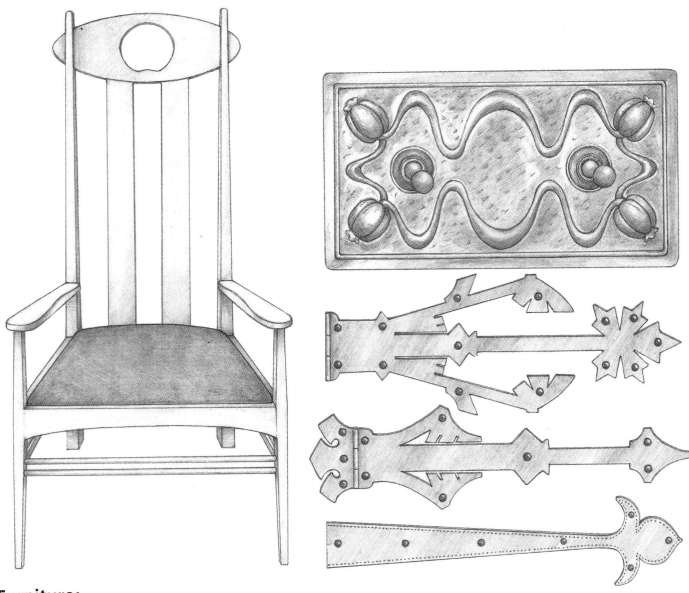

Furniture; materials and techniques

Much of the furniture of the Arts and Crafts was simple, based on traditional forms. However a Nineties look also takes in the first stirrings of the Art Nouveau in which more complicated techniques and designs were adopted. You see the use of inlaid materials, which set up an idea and was taken much further by the avant garde designers who were known as the Glasgow School (Charles Rennie Mackintosh being the best known of the group) or their Vienna Secession contemporaries,

people such as Josef Hoffman. William Morris and the designers of the period loved dark wood, often with spindly sections and cane seats. They were similar to examples from old country cottages or manor houses, but made more sophisticated; no one could fling themselves down after a hard day's work in one of these armchairs or settles! They also borrowed the simple ornament of country furniture; little chips were cut out along sharp edges or they were softened by chamfering, which did not detract from the functional design, but gave the piece a certain distinct quality.

Door and window furniture

Great wrought iron hinges, locks and handles were a feature of the Arts and Crafts movement; another area in which they took their ideas from country crafts and skills and displayed them with great panache. If you are creating a Nineties look, then items such as door handles, window catches and fittings, lock pieces or even keyhole plates need to be in keeping with the style. Many enthusiasts go as far as fitting period finger-plates on doors and electric light switches — even sets of decorative door

Top left: *This superbly designed dining chair by C. R. Mackintosh displays his predilection for geometrical lines.*
Above: *Copper light-switch plate with Art Nouveau decoration (top), and a selection of brass cupboard-door hinges in the Art and Craft style.*

and cupboard hinges. If you are not able to find or afford authentic metalwork of the period, there is available a wide range of good reproduction pieces. Details such as this can make or mar the whole effect, however minor they may seem in relation to an interior.

AMERICAN COUNTRY

American Country style has its roots firmly fixed in Europe, and crossed the Atlantic along with the first settlers, to be developed in New England and Pennsylvania before being taken further afield on the wagon trains of those tough pioneering people. It has recently re-crossed the Atlantic and is enjoying a European revival.

In the main, the settings are basically simple, and fairly spartan by today's living standards. They rely on the furniture, rather than the decoration, to give a room its atmosphere and style. Accessories, such as rag rugs, furnishings and bedding were more practical than pretty, and frequently started life as something else; the famous 'Mayflower' patchwork for example, was made from precious scraps of dress fabric combined with hessian from old feed sacks, and rag and pegged rugs were made from scraps of discarded clothing and dress fabrics, again combined with a hessian backing. The 'make do and mend' philosophy was essential to survival, and often gave birth to some decorative improvisations.

Much of the furniture was attractively decorated with original painting or stencilled repeating patterns, achieving its unique style as a result of the need to compromise between backwoods necessity and old world sophistication. The early settlers wanted similar furniture to that which they had left at home in Europe. Carpenters and cabinet makers were inspired by the multitude of different timbers available, but were hampered by lack of tools. The shape, type and function of these early pieces owe their origins mainly to the Dutch and English provincial farmhouse, although some of the decoration (particularly the cheerful stencilled patterns) are reminiscent of Alpine and Austrian painted furniture. Pieces include dressers (combining practical storage facilities with the opportunity for decorative display), corner cupboards, ladder-, rail-backed and rush-seated dining, and 'wainscot' chairs, refectory-style or drop-leaf tables, settles, and huge storage chests. The traditional wooden rocking chair evolved from the Windsor chair and became as ubiquitous as were large, but simple chests-of-drawers and truckle, metal and wooden framed beds. In the bedroom, featured overleaf, the footboard is carved with traditional, bold curves, and displays typically turned corner posts. The furniture frequently had to be dual-purpose – suitable for use in a kitchen-living room, or designed for a parlour that doubled as a bedroom.

Many items were simply designed – a look summed up in the Shaker Furniture of the early nineteenth century. Like the Pennsylvanian Dutch the Shakers (a strict religious sect) believed in functional furniture, and for religious reasons no decoration was allowed.

The American country style emphasizes the rustic handcrafted look, and the feeling is that nothing was ever wasted, including time!

Colour

Walls, ceilings, floors and many basic furnishings were of 'natural' colours – richly figured woods, jute-coloured hessians and paler linens, creamy fleece-coloured wool, un-dyed cottons, calico and crash, whitewashed or limewashed walls and ceilings, the rich terracotta of earthenware, natural stone, slate and cedar wood, combined with the rich hues of vegetable dyes – deep green, navy and mid-blue, ochre, red and terracotta. All subtle but highly saturated colours. Some of the colours used could be called 'earth tones'; the tones tints and shades found in nature and more specifically the rich, glowing colours of the North American Fall. These neutral backgrounds were enlivened by splashes of brilliance in the form of colourful quilts, rugs and paintings as shown in the bedroom overleaf.

Family portraits

Later, when naïve painting became popular (representational pictures, with a rather two-dimensional flat look, and lacking in perspective) richer colours were introduced – the clear blue of Delft china, sunshine yellows, oranges and golds, like the girl's dress in the opening picture, strong, bright, deep, 'plummy' red, grass green, blueberry-purple, and bold aquamarine and turquoise. These colours 'spilled' over into embroidery and patchwork, and were also used for stencilling and wallpainting.

Family portraits were painted in this bold style, and hung, generally unframed, in a prominent position, often above the fireplace. Anyone wishing to copy this feature could try enlarging a photograph, tracing it off and painting it freestyle, using artist's oil or acrylic paints and a stretcher-mounted canvas.

Pattern

Most patterns were applied to surfaces after finishing, being painted or stencilled on walls, floors and furniture as well as on other domestic paraphernalia. Even fabric was patterned in this way, since printing and complicated weaving were impossible for the early settlers to achieve. They tried to re-create in paint the impression of the printed, patterned or woven fabrics such as carpets and luxurious wallhangings and papers, which they had left behind in Europe. However, they adapted the motifs of fruit (sometimes pouring out of a cornucopia), flowers, birds and animals, baskets, and plants – endowing them with an immensely decorative quality. The pineapple – a symbol of hospitality – became a particularly popular motif (see the wallpaper on page 60). This type of almost childlike design has become synonymous with American folk-art.

Do it yourself

Many home decorating and specialist craft suppliers sell stencil kits of various 'country-style' designs. However, you could easily trace off or draw a motif freehand and cut your own stencil from cartridge paper, acetate film or parchment, providing you design it correctly making sure that the background remains intact when the motifs are cut away.

Above: *Family portraits in naïve painting can be simply framed or left mounted on the stretcher.*
Below: *Stencil designs are an inexpensive way of adding a flavour of the style. To make your own stencil, trace off the motif. Cut out with a scalpel, making sure that connecting bars hold the design intact.*

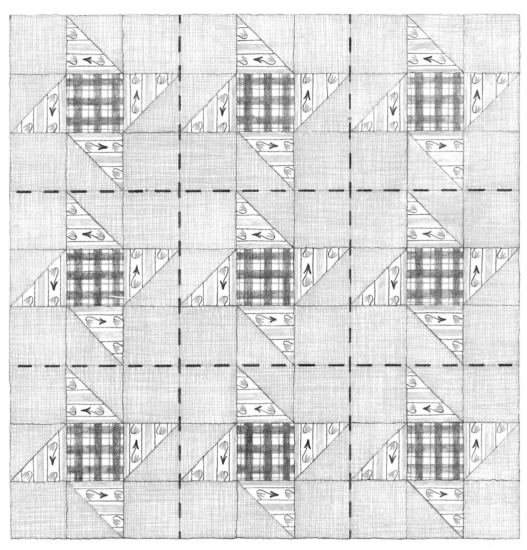

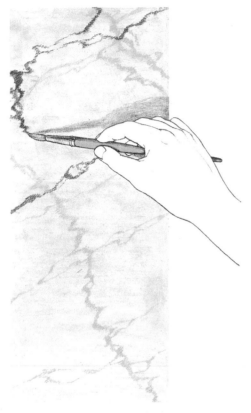

Left: *Pieceblock patchwork using a nine-patch block. Here each block is made up from nine squares, which can be further subdivided into triangles (or squares), thus creating wide scope for a variety of patterns. To make up, first join triangles to make squares, then join three squares together to form rows across, and three rows together to form one nine-patch block. Repeat, joining the blocks together to finish the patchwork.*
Above: *For a fake marble finish, use a fine brush, with colours to simulate real marble, and apply the veins in sequence.*

Patchwork

Pattern was used to offset the neutral background of plain walls and austere furniture by embroidered samplers, pictures, wall-hangings, chair backs and seats, appliqué work on curtains and upholstery fabric, and patchwork quilts, which were used , not only in the bedroom as a covering for warmth and decorative effects, but as throw-overs on settles and other wooden seating to soften them. English patchwork techniques such as hexagonal and shell patterns requiring backing papers, as used by the early settlers, were fairly rapidly

superceded by the American pieceblock method. This was a quicker technique, since much larger units and straight seams were involved, and the separate blocks could easily be repeated and assembled into large overall patterns. The essential need at this time was to create warm bedcovers, quickly; and in order to eek out precious coloured fabrics, simple designs evolved like the nine-patch block shown above – and thus began the great American patchwork tradition.

The early printed designs on cotton used for curtains, bedlinens and covers, and

fabrics of a heavier weight used for loose covers and upholstery, often simulated the original stencil designs. For a more 'neutral' type of design, the crisp look of checked and striped gingham became popular, and is still very much associated with American-style casement curtains, sometimes made up café-style, and used in rooms with wood-clad walls.

Focal point

The fireplace, or stove, was very much the focal point in the room, and some rooms had the typical Dutch ceramic stove, later replaced by cast

iron. The fireplace, overleaf, has been paint finished and given a mock marble finish to enliven the dark metal surface. This is fairly easy to repeat and would cheer up an existing un-used fireplace, or alternatively you can pick up a motif from the wallpaper.

Form

Early architecture and furniture was simply constructed – homes began in a very basic way, but when the 'Old Colonial' type of houses began to be built, they followed classical lines, here called Federal. Most of the furniture (see opposite) was clean-lined and relied on craftsmanship and good hard-wood for its style and elegance, while cheaper woods were paint-finished and hand-decorated with stencilled, or painted designs, see page 62.

Decorative borders

Stencilled patterns were also used on walls as border designs, to outline any interesting features or to simulate a cornice or frieze to give elegance to a very plain wall structure. They might also be used to suggest a picture rail, although most walls would have a wooden beading to form a chair rail or dado, with the lower section treated differently from the

Above: This cosy corner with its hardwood chair, display cupboard and stencilled designs evokes the Old Colonial style. Printed café curtains coordinate with the stencilled frieze. This is a pre-printed border from a range of wallcoverings. Needlepoint cushions and a framed sampler complete the look. Right: A recreation of an early American living room features the guest bed hidden behind stencilled curtains.

upper part (sometimes clad with tongue-and-groove boarding), as in the corner detail opposite. Border interest was also added in several ways to curtains, bedcovers, cloths and cushions using fabric appliqué, embroidery or

stencilling, and adding a luxurious or individual touch to a plain, ground fabric. Sometimes these border designs were worked in patchwork – it was all very much part of the 'waste not, want not' philosophy of the early, settlers.

Walls

Walls were originally made of natural materials (including wood), and were sometimes roughly plastered and then white- or lime-washed; floors were either stone, slate (after the initial beaten earth) or made of wide wooden boards, scrubbed clean.

An attic-style bedroom with sloping ceiling and neatly patterned walls. The original fireplace and stout wooden bed (complete with cotton cover) and the quilt chest sum up the style. Note the poker-work design inside the lid, the portrait and the gilt dressing-table mirror.

Texture

This relied a great deal on the natural quality of the materials used, such as the many different types of indigenous wood, stone, brick, slate, worsted and hessian, and tended to be homespun and hand-crafted.

And because of this, texture appeared to be haphazard rather than designed. The fabrics, in particular, were rather coarse and rough, and even when finer fibres such as cotton were woven into cloth, they still retained this type of rough texture.

Furniture

The wooden furniture, lovingly polished, added a warm touch – so did the woven strip and colourful hand-pegged rag rugs. Harsher textures appeared in metal, as used for ranges and stoves, lamps, light fittings and candlesticks, in door 'furniture' (latches, hinges and handles), and curtain poles and rings (wood was also used). Some of the early plates and tankards were made of pewter, taken from Europe. Gloss was provided by glazed earthenware and some ceramic tiles – but mirrors were rarely seen in the original settlers' houses (vanity was considered sinful).

Windows

Windows were generally very simply constructed with a deep recess. Roller blinds were popular and were often combined with shutters, which could be internal, or external as seen in the European houses of the same, and earlier, periods. These were necessary because of the severe winter weather, and not necessarily for privacy. These eventually developed into storm or porch windows or doors, which were fixed to the outside. Curtains were unpretentious affairs, usually functional and short, and used primarily to retain heat during the winter months.

Adapting the style

Start with the basic structure – the room should be as simple and unadorned as possible. The ceiling may be beamed, woodclad (tongue-and-groove boarding) or plainly-plastered and painted. Walls can be similarly treated, and then individually painted with simple designs, or decorated with stencils. You can use paper or vinyl wallcoverings which simulate this style, and 'trim' them with the companion borders (or use these to add interest to a plainly papered or painted wall). Many of the original designs are now available in co-ordinated collections, and come in authentic colourings and colour combinations. Add a dado, chair- or wainscot-rail, and treat the lower part of the wall differently – painted boarding or a heavily-textured paper/wall-covering. In some situations (hallway, bathroom, kitchen) ceramic tiles can be used instead.

Doors

Look for the right type of door – planked timber – and add heavy metal hinges, latches and handles – some doors might be the stable type. Alternatively give a plain door a woodgrain finish, using the technique known as *scumbling* – in some cases dragged paintwork could be used on woodwork and furniture. The finished effect should not be too dark.

Flooring

The floor should also be as basic as possible – stripped wooden boards, stone flags, slate, or very simple ceramic tiles (you can look for

Plain wood varnished and combed to look like woodgrain.

simulated effects in vinyl or vinyl tile) – black and white tiles could be laid chequerboard fashion. Wooden floors (or those covered with hardboard or chipboard) can then be decorated with stencilled designs, trompe l'oeil carpets or 'floorcloths'. If a carpet is essential, keep to a natural-coloured, tweedy-textured variety. Add a hand-pegged wool, or rag rug (even the woven 'strip' type) to soften the harsher type of flooring, and to add an authentic touch to an otherwise plain carpet.

Furniture finds

For the furniture, search for pieces with a country farmhouse look (since much of the original furniture was modelled on this style) in a light, or warm-coloured wood particularly pine (no heavy dark oak or mahogany). A fairly rough piece could be painted and decorated. Items might include cope and storage chests, dressers and corner cupboards, half-tester and four-poster beds, metal (not brass) and wooden bedsteads, generously sized chests-of-drawers, wooden clothes presses and wardrobes, washstands, Windsor and rocking chairs, and ladder- or rail-backed, rush-seated dining chairs, settles (even an old church pew), drop-leaf and refectory-style tables, or large scrubbed pine farmhouse styles.

Upholstered furniture can be almost Victorian in flavour – a horsehair-stuffed leather sofa for example, or a roll-backed chaise longue. Items should be individual (not a suite in sight) and easy chairs might be the 'tub' type with a spoon back. The upholstery fabric should not be too opulent – a simple tapestry or coarsely-textured hessian, canvas, wool tweed, flannel, even denim! The rough texture can be softened with a throw-over shawl, or tartan travelling rug.

In the bedroom, the bed should be a proper bedstead (not a divan) and a patchwork quilt is an absolute essential! If you cannot buy one, then perhaps with guidance from a library book, you could try your hand at one of the pieceblock patterns or the traditional 'Mayflower'

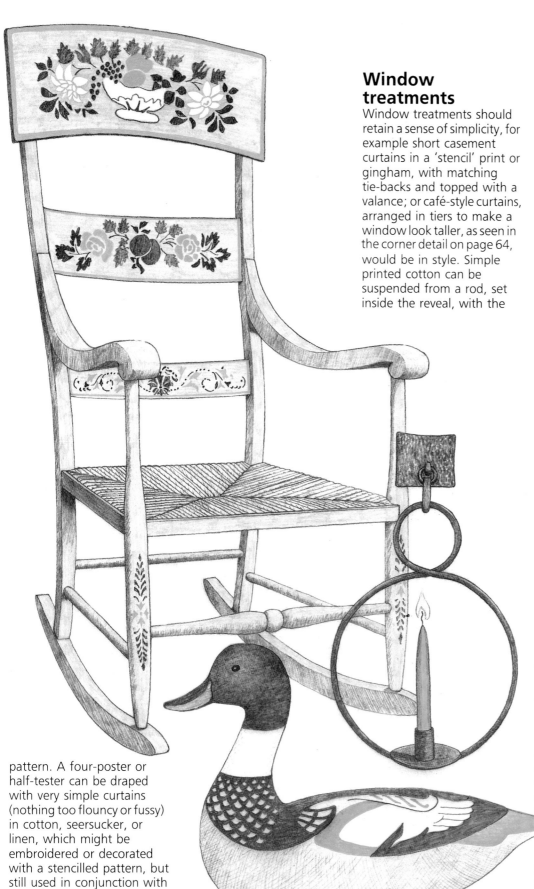

Window treatments

Window treatments should retain a sense of simplicity, for example short casement curtains in a 'stencil' print or gingham, with matching tie-backs and topped with a valance; or café-style curtains, arranged in tiers to make a window look taller, as seen in the corner detail on page 64, would be in style. Simple printed cotton can be suspended from a rod, set inside the reveal, with the window outlined in a border design to co-ordinate with the fabric. Alternatively, try full-length curtains, suspended from poles with rings, or with scalloped or castellated tops formed in the material. Plain holland blinds, with a stencilled pattern on them, can be combined with internal shutters. If the room is overlooked, and privacy is required, rattan blinds or louvred shutters could be used – or perhaps you might install a delicately pierced metal, wood or hardboard screen.

Accessories

Accessories will help to set the style – framed, hand-embroidered samplers with a suitable religious text; Berlin woolwork showing animals, alphabets, flowers and fruit; unframed naive paintings, as previously described; cast-iron woodburning stoves (or oil equivalents), which can be lit in winter (suitably protected with a traditional fender) or baskets filled with fruit and/or flowers. To complete the effect, add cushions in appliqué, patchwork and needlepoint, cast-iron cooking pots, candlesticks, tin light fittings, irons and trivets, butter churns, wooden decoy ducks, pewter plates and tankards.

Far left: *A traditional rag rug, with its genuinely hand-prodded look, combines traditional symbols with wild flowers in an intricate design.* **Left:** *Rocking chairs that have a broad back rail can be decoratively painted.*

pattern. A four-poster or half-tester can be draped with very simple curtains (nothing too flouncy or fussy) in cotton, seersucker, or linen, which might be embroidered or decorated with a stencilled pattern, but still used in conjunction with a patchwork quilt.

Left: *Add a touch of authenticity with a reproduction tin light fitting and decoy ducks.*

BIEDERMEIER

Biedermeier encapsulates all the classical simplicity that many of today's interior designers, collectors and antique dealers search for. Whether it is a single sofa, an armoire, or a pair of upright chairs, Biedermeier fits as comfortably in the most minimal of contemporary interiors as it does in more traditional settings surrounded by cherished antiques.

The term Biedermeier is a combination of the German adjective *bieder* meaning honest, unpretentious, reliable or plain, and *Meier*, which means farmer, and is also a common German surname. Biedermeier simultaneously describes both the lifestyle and the literature of German-speaking countries between the Congress of Vienna in 1815 and the Prussian Revolution of 1848, and in an art historical sense, the sober, simple style prevalent in Austria, Bavaria, Prussia and neighbouring countries from 1815 to 1830.

Most evident in furniture, the Biedermeier style was a local variant of the late Empire style without the pomposity, and a reaction against the elaborate ornament of Rococo. Moreover, Biedermeier was embraced by Germany, Austria, Scandinavia, and much of central Europe because craftsmen could not afford to do otherwise; during the Napoleonic Wars and the Continental Blockade expensive materials and money had become scarce — as a result austerity and simplicity became the order of the day.

The rising bourgeoisie had a strong desire for a peaceful, productive domestic life in a comfortable environment, and out of this grew Biedermeier: practical, calm, solid, reassuring, and above all cosy.

By 1853 the style had become unfashionable — Gottlieb Biedermeier, a ludicrous imaginary poet personifying solid, philistine bourgeois qualities, appeared in the Austrian satirical magazine *Fliegende Blätter* from 1855 onwards. However, at the end of the nineteenth century Biedermeier re-emerged with a major exhibition in Vienna, and prior to and after the Great War Neo-Biedermeier and Biedermeier-inspired interiors were still common in Germany. In the 1920s the simplicity of Biedermeier influenced the Bauhaus and was seen to preempt Modern taste and style, eventually spreading to Holland, Italy, France, England, America and Russia.

While the style of Biedermeier had its origins in the Classical tradition and the Empire style, particularly the Grecian element, and was influenced by both late eighteenth-century Neo-classicism and the formality of English Regency, it was German austerity exemplified; basic, utilitarian, peaceful, inexpensive, sturdy, plain, and of pleasing proportions, with the main consideration being comfort.

Recognizing the style

Early Biedermeier furniture was often made of dark wood – mahogany veneer or other wood stained to resemble ebony, inlaid with symmetrical classical motifs in a paler wood. The decoration, traditionally in shapes such as scallops, stars, vases, sun-rays and lyres, was kept to a rigid minimum. The work was deliberately not expensively worked over or gilded.

The fashion for *bois clair* came later, with the use of light woods such as birch, walnut, grained ash, and fruit-woods including pear, cherry, and maple.

While the earlier furniture was characterized by straight lines and angular shapes, the lines of later Biedermeier gradually became more fluid, with more curves and serpentine shapes, as shown by the lyre motif, with its centrally-placed straight lines encompassed by harmonious curves. Chairs had curved legs, and sofas had rolled arms and generous upholstery.

Below: *Detail of ebonized motifs in birchwood.* Bottom: *Superb upholstery and highly grained wood epitomize the sofa.*

Sofa, so good

As comfort was one of the main tenets of the style, great importance was placed on upholstery and fitted coverings. In fact, it was in Vienna in 1822 that Georg Junigl first patented sprung upholstery. Cylindrical cushions or bolsters were very popular and were usually placed at either end of the sofa (see Good Morning on page 72). Later Biedermeier came to be characterized by the sofa. In the bourgeois living room, the sofa itself took on a much greater importance. For the first time it became more than a chaise longue – chairs would be grouped around it, with a small round table in the centre, thus making the sofa the place for intimate conversations, as seen in Sitting around on page 72. On a more aesthetic level, and with reference to classical times, individual upright chairs would sometimes be draped with folded fabric.

Upholstery fabrics

Typical Biedermeier upholstery fabrics were almost always utterly plain in both colour and texture. With the invention of sprung upholstery, the fabrics used had to be that much more durable to withstand the increased movement and stress. Fabrics used should be strong and hard-wearing, but the essential ingredient is that they are woven from natural fibres, such as good quality worsteds and silks with a fine rib or satin weave.

For a visually pleasing contrast, choose mid- to dark-toned fabrics for light wood furniture and mid- to light tones for darker wood.

Broadway Biedermeier

The morning room, featured overleaf, shows a Russian birchwood sofa beneath a North German birchwood mirror. The two unframed portraits, contemporary with

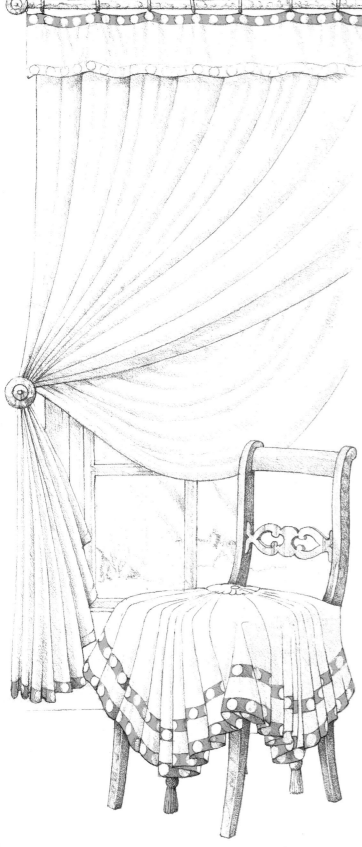

the period, are dated 1811 and 1825. The morning room is in Allen Klein's apartment in the Ansonia, a turn of the century apartment building on Broadway, New York. Allen Klein, an internationally famous designer of opera sets and an inveterate collector of Biedermeier, became fascinated by it twenty years ago, shortly after moving into the apartment, when 'Biedermeier was firewood' in Berlin. He grew 'not to love the style but to need it . . . I don't think I chose Biedermeier, I think Biedermeier chose me.' 'Some people hunt for people; I hunt for furniture, paintings and objects of the Biedermeier period. Biedermeier isn't just a style of furniture, it's a political period, a way of living.'

Allen Klein has furnished his apartment in the Biedermeier style, and what is not Biedermeier is 'pure design', with the simplicity of line and form entirely dominating the sense of decoration. One thing he has been unable to do is prevent water occasionally leaking down the walls. Consequently there is no wallpaper, although this was frequently used in Biedermeier homes.

Wall coverings

Obviously, wallpaper is not essential for the Biedermeier-style of interior. The walls and floors should be as plain as possible, in keeping with the element of austerity and simplicity. Should you prefer wallpaper, you can, of course, choose from an enormous range of Regency or Gustavian stripes (see pages 30, 32, 78) or other subtle geometric patterns. Allen Klein's bathroom walls are covered in striped ticking,

with small watercolours, drawings, and miniatures of the period.

Deliberately understating the wall covering serves to place emphasis on paintings, engravings and mirrors hung on the wall, and to throw into relief the classical Austrian flouncing of the draperies and curtains. Pale walls also give an illusion of greater space. On the other hand Paul Dyson, of Harvey Nichols, London, who has decorated his London home as far as possible in Russian Biedermeier, upholstered the walls of the drawing room himself in velvet, with matching velvet curtains edged in a beautiful gold fringing.

Floor coverings

Like the walls, the floors should be simply adorned, and in many cases this means plain wood, either bare floorboards or herringbone parquetry, lightly varnished or stained, perhaps in a pastel colour. Simple, plain tiles can be used in the bathroom and kitchen.

Naturally, personal taste dictates the use of carpets or rugs, and their type, size, and colour. Allen Klein has a Persian rug in his bedroom and a hand-knotted V'Soske rug on his sitting room floor (overleaf). The latter was chosen for the 'elegance and naivety' of its tulip pattern, and being dark it also serves to highlight the *bois clair* of the furniture.

Most Biedermeier aficionados prefer a floor of plain wood, with the rigid straight lines of the boards giving order, direction, and perspective. It is also aesthetically pleasing to have both furniture and floor made of the same material.

Comfort was provided by chair drapery, which was all the rage before the invention of sprung seating. But this style (remnants of Neo-classicism) like the more refined window drapery, (above) was replaced by the more austere look of true Biedermeier.

Sitting around

In Allen Klein's circular sitting room (above), the round North German birchwood table in the centre is surrounded by a pair of Austro-Hungarian walnut chairs and a sofa of pear-wood inlaid with mulberry-wood. The lyre-shaped sides to the sofa and the scroll-like curves on the chair arms indicate later Biedermeier.

The table is often used as a dinner table for four; in the Biedermeier period only very grand homes had a specific dining room – for ordinary households the sitting room table was a combination of

Formally grouped fruitwood furniture encapsulates the style.

work bench, tea table, games board and dining table.

On the matt ox-blood walls hang numerous paintings and prints, most of which are contemporary with the first half of the nineteenth century. The small Doric temple on the right is a medal display cabinet in the style of Karl Friedrich Schinkel, interior designer and architect to the Prussian royal family, and the French chandelier was installed before anything else in the apartment.

Good morning

One corner of the morning room is shown on the facing page (top). In front of a window draped with gathered muslin, and on a herringbone parquet floor stand a Swedish birchwood chair, a birchwood needlework basket and a lyre-based work table, also in birch. The lyre type clock on top of it offers a pleasant miniature echo of the larger lyre shape below, while the arms and the back of the Biedermeier chair have a similarly fluid curve to them. albeit in a different direction.

The double portrait is

believed to be of Samuel Morse (left) and the future court painter to Queen Victoria, Charles Leslie (right). While at university the two friends apparently painted each other's portrait on the same canvas.

The painting is hung unframed, in keeping with the simple ungilded austerity of Biedermeier, as well as being characteristic of the way in which early American settlers hung their family portraits.

Lullaby of Biedermeier

The bed with its elegant lyre-shaped sides is known variously as a sleigh-bed or *lit en bateau*, and this one is made from cherry-wood. It is upholstered in corduroy (hard-wearing and utilitarian) so that what is a study by day, at night, with the addition of two linen-covered duvets, becomes a bedroom.

The practical nature of Biedermeier, as seen also in the multi-purpose circular table in the sitting room, is particularly useful in helping to create extra space in a small apartment.

An American tole lamp stands on the Viennese walnut bedside table, and the large painting on the wall above the bed is a portrait by René Cadeau from about 1833.

Persian rugs and carpets have a timeless quality and beauty, and they may be used successfully in virtually any type of interior. Here the bedroom rug is an antique Heraz. Traditional rugs of such classic simplicity can always be used to offset fairly severe furniture. Of course, the choice of colour and pattern is important – in order to complement Biedermeier the design needs to be as uncomplicated as possible.

Left and below: *Stylishly displayed furniture gives these rooms great distinction and charm.*

In contrast to Alan Klein's collectors' style, this interior shows the bare necessities of Biedermeier style. The lack of curtains is a throwback to the farmer who rose with the sun and slept with the moon.

Minimal chic, maximum joy

The emphasis on stark frugality tends to appeal to collectors and admirers of Biedermeier. Quite often the layout and design of the room consists of little more than a few carefully chosen pieces or objects (a bed, a table and a chair, for example) on bare floorboards, with perhaps an eighteenth or nineteenth century painting to grace the plain wall.

Biedermeier is very much a collector's style, and not everyone can afford the very high prices that original pieces now fetch at auction. Buying authentic art from the exact period is also beyond most people's means, but there are some excellent prints available from all the main art galleries and specialist fine art dealers that would give the right effect.

However, the sparse, minimalist, uncluttered look is certainly not difficult to achieve, and the overall effect is light and airy with great freedom of space, punctuated with plain comfortable forms, clean lines, and sturdy craftsmanship.

If you are unfortunate enough to have accommodation that is already furnished, take everything detachable or movable out, strip the floor and walls, and the ceiling if it needs it. Any wiring of lights, switches or power points should be left exposed but safe. Areas of wood need to be emphasized; strip all layers of paint off, rub it down, and impregnate it with a little varnish or stain. If you must paint keep the walls and ceiling matt and the floor a muted gloss.

A chair is still a chair . . .

If late Biedermeier is symbolised by the sofa, then earlier Biedermeier is epitomized by the upright chair. Usually one of a pair or a larger set, it is neat, unpretentious and subtle with simple, straight lines or slight curves. In Allen Klein's apartment pairs of Biedermeier chairs stand in every room and hallway.

Like most collectors, he is very attached to his first ever Biedermeier acquisition – in this case the German birch circular table in the sitting room. Another prized possession is the Swedish Biedermeier 'grandfather' clock that stands in the hall, shown opposite. With the design stripped down to the bare essentials and basic shapes, this clock is at once purely functional and extremely beautiful, especially in the harmonious arrangement of circle, cylinder and cone.

A musical arrangement

Harmonious is a telling adjective for describing the effect of Biedermeier furniture, and accessories.

The pure rhythmic lines and shapes echo the grace and beauty of music, especially classical music. Curves are derived as much from the lyre and the harp as from the bass and treble clefs that begin a musical score.

Just as Biedermeier furniture and interiors should be augmented by Neo-classically-inspired eighteenth century paintings, aural enjoyment should be provided by a composer such as Schubert.

Let there be light

Windows in the Biedermeier home were fairly simply dressed with lightly gathered or swagged draperies.

The simplest style consists of a single length of fabric, such as muslin or voile, draped across the top of the window and suspended at each side over projecting roundels. The length of drapery would vary according to the height of the window, see also page 82.

Another variation was to hang a lightly-gathered full length curtain from a pole suspended across the top of the window, which could be held back at one side, again over a roundel or by a simple cord as shown on page 71. Windows in the more important rooms tended to have pairs of curtains held back at each side, with a further drape across the top, from roundels, as previously described. To drape a light fabric asymmetrically across the window is a most elegant and complementary accessory to the Biedermeier look. The effect, an exercise in studied nonchalance, is artistic and feminine, allowing light to flood in to illuminate the room.

These styles are most imitable and relatively easy to make at home, since linings

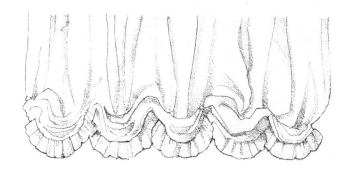

 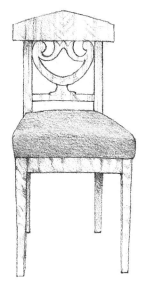

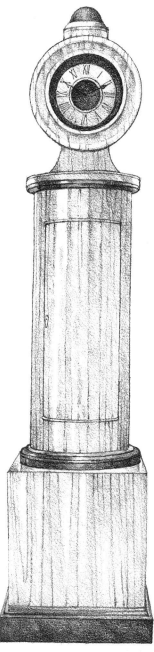

and seaming are not involved in the same way that they are with traditionally-made draw curtains.

You could also capture the look by installing Austrian or festoon blinds, with or without frills on the outer edges. These can be made at home using specially made looped tape, through which cords pass and can be pulled to raise or lower the blind.

Design fame

While a great part of Biedermeier furniture and artefacts were made by anonymous craftsmen all over Europe, a few designers achieved fame, and they (and others) are extensively represented in the Museum of Applied Arts in Vienna.

There one can see Franz Werner's *Practische Zimmer Mahlerei*, a three-volume work from about 1820 that contains over seventy Biedermeier designs, mainly classical schemes in clear colours but also including simulated landscapes and draperies. The Neo-classical/Classical influence was an accepted part of early Biedermeier. Trompe l'oeil classical vistas and walls painted to look like Greek or Roman draperies were not uncommon, but the increasing element of peace through austerity and the rejection of unnecessary decoration meant that they became obsolete.

Josef Danhauser, a Viennese furniture manufacturer from 1814 until his death in 1829, is represented in the Museum of Applied Arts by at least 2,500 designs, the most complete surviving record of the Biedermeier style. Danhauser was prolific,

designing everything from beds to pipe-racks, from spittoons to sofas.

Austrian austerity

It is said that necessity is the mother of invention, and this is certainly true of Biedermeier.

Up until the first few decades of the nineteenth century the type of furniture in vogue was elaborate, ornate, and gilded. Not only were the lines and shapes quite straight and hard, but chairs and seats were also very hard to sit on for any length of time. Biedermeier changed that.

Biedermeier marks the transition between the Neo-classical and Romantic styles, and it also forms a link between complicated, decorated eighteenth-century furniture and the smooth, flowing lines of Art Nouveau and the extreme simplicity of the Bauhaus.

Because of the volatile political situation in Europe in the early 1800s, furniture craftsmen and cabinet makers were forced to express their skills with the bare essentials and local wood. With typical

Above: *An Austrian blind is the perfect backdrop for Biedermeier furniture. Though similar in design, the chairs show basic differences. The earlier design (left), of dark wood and straighter lines, contrasts with the flowing lines of the later **bois clair** (right).*
Right: *A Swedish Biedermeier grandfather clock.*

German efficiency and practicality, an attractive and comfortable style of interior decoration was evolved out of hardship and adversity.

Inner city austerity

Nowadays many past styles are being rediscovered by young people – the Georgian style, for example, is *de rigeur* among dedicated London Conservationists – instead of nostalgia, an empathy with a previous generation. With the increasing number of young home-owners and first-time buyers, and the equally burgeoning groups of unemployed inner city youth being forced to squat in empty houses, bare floorboards, stripped walls, and austere living are already inescapable realities for

many. Biedermeier as a style, a period, a state of mind is being recreated and celebrated because it combines an antique style from a particular time in recent European history with the terribly fashionable minimalist look, the stark individuality of Punk (see Creative Salvage on page 180), well-crafted good wood, and simple, honest comfort.

As Gottlieb Biedermeier would say, 'God loves an honest farmer . . .'

GUSTAVIAN

For several decades Scandinavian style, has been synonymous with clean lines, oiled teak, pine panelling, saunas, Rya rugs with brightly-coloured abstract designs and hand-woven textiles. But of course, Sweden, like most other countries, has had many different architectural and decorative furnishing styles throughout the centuries.

One of the most attractive of all Swedish interior decorating styles, the Gustavian look, gets its name from the reigning monarch of the period, King Gustav III. This style began in 1770, and strictly speaking ended about 1810, although it was still being reproduced throughout the nineteenth century. It was definitely inspired by the Swedish love of the French Empire and Rococo, yet has its own very distinctive (less opulent and ornate) style.

It can perhaps be compared with the very best of late Georgian country interior decoration. Well-made and well-designed furniture, combined with a cool elegance. It was then decorated or embellished to look more expensive — but not overly so. Although much of the original Gustavian furniture and decoration was seen in country and seaside residences (the flat in the city for the winter, and the summer residence in the country, on lake or sea shore, has long been an accepted way of life for many people in Scandinavia — and not always for the wealthy) it looks as good in town houses and apartments as it does in country cottages and houses. It also translates very happily into properties built at the time of the Arts and Crafts movement — and later, during the 1920s, when Art Déco and the Omega Workshops were at the height of their popularity.

Many examples of this type of Nordic style have been encapsulated in paintings by the Swedish artist Carl Larsson, who had a country house called Little Hyttnas 'the hut on the point' at Dalarna. During the 1890s he painted his family in the setting of their home (one showed his small son, banished into the corner as a punishment, next to a very handsome Gustavian tiled stove — essential if you want to achieve the true Swedish look), and published them in an album in 1899. This helped to popularize the simple, but highly decorative style, at a time when houses in America and many European countries were full of flock wall-coverings, velvet, plush and chenille; upholstered furniture; overstuffed with horsehair, lace antimacassars and aspidistras, heavily-carved mahogany, and fussy-cane furniture.

The look and success in re-creating it does rely on having at least a few items of genuine or reproduction furniture in the style — however, it is possible to get both antique and copies from specialist shops.

Pattern and form

There is a distinct contrast between these two, yet they combine to give the Gustavian look its very essence and character. The shapes of the furniture and architectural features can be described as 'restrained Rococo', but not as highly-embellished as in Italy and France. For example, the upholstery fabric used on a curvaceous chair decorated with ornate beading may well be a simple striped, checked or floral cotton, a traditional striped brocade, tapestry or embroidered effect softened with lace antimacassars.

In the drawing room shown overleaf, notice the typical 'conversation' arrangement of sofa, table and dining chairs – and their loose covers. Here white silk upholstery is protected by tie-on covers made from a pretty blue and white printed cotton (see Furnishing fabrics).

Colour

Most genuine Gustavian interiors are pale and light – or they may look 'elegantly faded'. There is a particular Swedish blue frequently combined with white into striped or checked fabric, that is used on furniture, at windows, to drape or cover beds, to colour carpets and rugs. It helps to create the impression of high summer in even the darkest room. Bare floorboards (softened with typical hand-woven rag rugs or carpet) epitomize the Swedish blonde look – scrubbed, waxed and worn over the years to a mellow creamy pine. A greyed version of off-white is the colour most often used for walls, woodwork and furniture.

White, which has mellowed to a muted ivory over the years, is seen on fabric, furniture, ceilings and walls. While subtle reds and pinks, soft apricots and dusky golds combined with rich creams or beiges, may be chosen to warm up colder areas; in the main, cool colours are preferred to create a fresh atmosphere in rooms filled with summer sunshine.

Wallpaper and paint

Walls, ceilings and woodwork are usually interestingly but discreetly decorated. Subtle stripes often appear on wallcoverings, in a monochromatic effect or soft blue and white; others combine floral festoons with stripes (usually for a bedroom) – very much a lighter version of classical Regency striped patterns (see bedroom page 80). The drawing room in a wealthier home, such as the one overleaf, may have specially designed wall coverings. Here beautiful Chinese wallhangings, handpainted on rice paper and displaying peonies and exotic birds, were brought back from China in 1753 by the owner, Claes Grills, a partner in the East India Company.

Walls can also be plain-painted, but may be textured, using one of the painted techniques which is more likely to be colour- or lime-washed, or dragged, rather than stippled or marbled. Woodwork (and furniture) can be similarly painted, and always with a matt, lustre or eggshell finish – never gloss. Stencilled borders were also popular and might be used in conjunction with plain, colour-washed walls to suggest the frieze decoration. For making your own stencils, see **Do it yourself**, page 62.

Furnishing fabrics

Printed or woven in typically soft grey-blues, upholstery fabrics vary in design from narrow ticking stripes, through wider two-tone diagonals to delicate flowery stripes with lovers' knots and posies.

Choose plainer stripes for inset seating (of dining chairs) and floral stripes for curtaining or bedhangings, either for a more Rococo look, or for the bedroom.

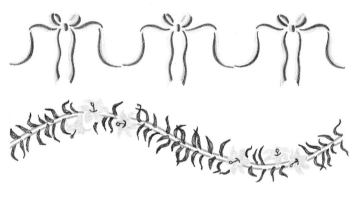

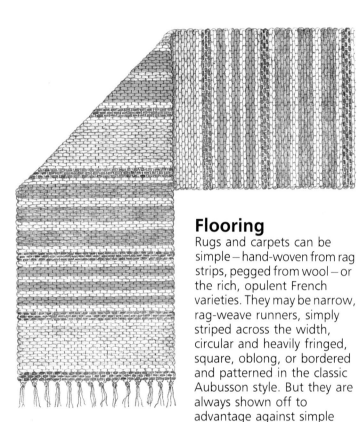

Flooring

Rugs and carpets can be simple – hand-woven from rag strips, pegged from wool – or the rich, opulent French varieties. They may be narrow, rag-weave runners, simply striped across the width, circular and heavily fringed, square, oblong, or bordered and patterned in the classic Aubusson style. But they are always shown off to advantage against simple wooden floorboards (narrow tongue-and-groove, never parquet), and in a few rare cases, on ceramic tiles in a hall or dining room setting. If you are using a rag-weave runner, arrange it to form a runway around the room, in the traditional Gustavian manner.

Drawing room furniture

This is an integral part of the Gustavian style, and has its own very individual and distinctive look. Shapes can be classically simple, or slightly more rotund and flamboyant, and will have either some delicate carving, or a trimming of finely-detailed beading. The majority of the furniture is matt finished – painted white, pastel, soft grey, or Swedish blue, giving it the look of slightly scuffed grandeur. In the wealthier home, furniture might also be gilded, like the mirrors and console tables on page 76. Some very simple pine pieces, like cupboards and dressers, may have decorative trimming painted on, as an alternative to being carved out of wood, and then pinned or glued in place.

Upholstered furniture often has a delicate looking wooden frame which is frequently painted and embellished, and the fabric used is unpretentious (see page 80), usually with a simple striped pattern or texture. Occasional chairs have padded seats (similarly upholstered) but with the wooden backs carved, or moulded in interesting shapes – spoon-shaped for example, with a fret-work inset, neatly railed or Gothic-arched. Legs on tables and chairs can be bowed, curved or classically straight. It was also traditional to include pieces of furniture made from hardwoods, such as figured walnut, mahogany, yew, or other unusual woods, which may be heavily carved and trimmed with ornate gilt or brass trim. Occasional tables are usually delicate, and may be in a lovely natural, perhaps unusual wood, or painted in the same way as other furniture.

Left: *Give the authentic touch to furniture and walls with a stencilled frieze of ribbon bows or garlanded swags.*
Bottom left: *Choose fabrics and wallcoverings with a 'restrained Regency' look of floral stripes, neatly repeating motifs or crisp checks. Colours should be romantic and subtly faded – or the traditional Swedish favourite of blue and white.*

Top left: *Striped ragweave runners will add an authentic touch to stripped and sealed, or painted floorboards.* **Below:** *If you can find a typical Gustavian sofa with wooden arms and rail back (the Edwardians made reproduction pieces like this) get the upholstery detail right – lightly stuffed and covered in a simple striped fabric.*

Boudoir style

A more frivolous approach to the Gustavian style is shown in this bedroom with its floral striped wallpaper, curvaceous furniture (painted and gilded), and the Empire-style daybed — used here as seating, and in addition to the main bed — upholstered to match in a gentle pink and white striped cotton.

To recreate this style, you may well be able to tone down a Louis XVI-style bedroom suite (still a bargain in the sale rooms), by removing some of the over-ornate trimming, or painting out the gilt highlights, or applying a glaze, or a final dragged coat of paint in a contrasting colour. If a dressing table is still too opulent, you could hide part of it under a 'skirt' in a suitable fabric. Basic bedhead and foot ends can be painted and/or decorated as

An Empire-style daybed adds elegance and style to a sitting room, or dual-purpose bedroom. The spartan look of bare wood floors and ceiling can be offset by delicately draped window treatments and lace tablecloth.

previously suggested, but they can also be fashioned into a four-poster, with a fabric valance and drapes and four simple posts.

Ceilings, as shown here, can be painted and corniced, or they can be covered with a tongue-and-groove boarding, coloured to match the walls (this wood cladding can also be used to make a dado). Walls can be papered in a soft shadow-stripe, or given a roses-and-ribbon look (see page 78). In some cases a really faded overblown rose pattern can set the right note, so long as the colours are not too aggressive.

The Hårleman bedroom

Various beadings and mouldings, in a restrained Rococo style, may be added to walls to form a dado, picture rail, or wall panel, and, sometimes, a frieze or cornice, as shown in the bedroom above. Similar decorations are often added to furniture, and to door panels, cupboards and shutters. Here, in the bedroom, the painted dado and wall panels are dragged to give an effect of 'faded elegance' and, at the same time, cleverly disguising the bedroom door.

The bed, made by Carl Hårleman, after 1740, for Svindersvik, the country mansion owned by Claes Grills (and where in 1780 King Gustav III regularly attended parties given by the new owner and famous

Above: *The elegantly draped Carl Hårleman bed complements perfectly the colour-dragged walls.* **Right:** *Typical sofa and dining table arrangements.*

society hostess, Catharina Charlotta Du Geer), is typically draped with heavy damask bed curtains. Bed posts are specially constructed to form the high curved frame over which the bedcurtains, valance and roof are attached.

Notice also the beautiful Italian quilted (Trapunto) bedcover, and the mahogany bedside bureau.

Many Gustavian beds — particularly the day- and dual-purpose beds of the period — were Empire style, with curved head and foot ends, designed to be placed parallel to the wall, and draped from above with a simple fall of fabric, either wall or ceiling-mounted.

Texture

This tends to be natural and to some extent homely, as seen in the living room above (lots of wood, rag-weave rugs and woven fabrics), but is contrasted by the lacy delicacy of fragile beadings, wrought metal-work, intricate carving, and net and lace drapes. Many surfaces have matt finishes, or are only slightly lustrous – and small touches of twinkling sheen are added by judiciously placed accessories. Furniture, like sofas, chests of drawers and chairs are often placed around the edges of a room in symmetrical arrangements. This includes mirrors with brass or gilt frames, brass curtain fittings, metal and glass used in light fittings, candle sconces and chandeliers, brass and glass combined for lamps and decorative glassware, such as candlesticks and vases.

Stencil decoration

Traditional bows, swags, floral festoons, cornucopias and other classical motifs can be used for stencil decoration, and in some cases these might be applied as a border to outline a feature, as in the cornice shown above, or to decorate an item of furniture, see the chest of drawers opposite, with its pretty bow motif. For making your own stencil, see page 62.

Notice here the Empire-style mirror which, in the absence of the real thing, might easily be painted on a wall (in matching colours) to cheer up the image.

Adapting the style

First of all, in any room, start with bare floorboards – strip, stain, paint, wax or colour them if necessary, to give the blond pine, or slightly 'limed', or worn look. Soften them with rag-weave rugs, or simple, monochromatic striped dhurries, but make sure the colours are right. Shades of blue, white and grey, or pastels with one rich earthy tone. For a grander setting, look for a patterned carpet 'square' in the traditional French Aubusson style – many carpet companies still include these in their reproduction ranges. Choose subtle colouring – avoid the brighter up-dates and look at the greys, blues, and pastels of original colourings.

Furniture finds

If possible obtain one or two original pieces, or several authentic modern copies. You can then add other items – shop around for a set of Victorian, spoon-backed chairs, which you may well be able to adapt by re-upholstering them in one of the suitable fabrics (see page 78). Or look for a simple occasional table of the period. Do not colour them, leave them natural and waxed. Consider one or two heavier pieces, perhaps with a 1930s reproduction Queen Anne style about them, but do so with discretion.

If you can get a dresser, a wall cupboard, head and foot ends of a bed, or a dressing table in the right style and shape, which are not in a good wood, you can always paint them with a suitable pale-coloured, matt finish. Alternatively, give them an 'antique' or dragged finish,

and add appropriate beading, treated to match. Add stencils or a touch of trompe l'oeil to create the Gustavian look.

Search for an Empire-style daybed, which you can convert into a sofa – leave the wood if it is good, but if not, then paint and embellish it as previously described. It might be possible to have a basic construction made on a slatted base, with curved ends, to which you can add well-upholstered cushions and a back rest. Choose the fabric carefully, to follow the theme, and to match the rest of the furniture (see page 80).

Some Edwardian drawing room furniture has the right shape and delicacy, and may just require new covers. Tie-on covers and squab cushions are sometimes more practical than complete reupholstery, particularly with smaller items like dining and occasional chairs.

Window treatments

Window treatments are usually simple, to let in and reflect the maximum amount of light. The traditional Gustavian house had tailored shutters to close against winter weather, and centrally-opening casement windows. The frame was usually softened by attractive white or light-coloured net drapes, with a matching swathed pelmet, mounted on white-painted poles or special brass fittings. Sometimes the curtains were dispensed with, and the top of the window had a decoratively-draped pelmet or valance only. In more humble Gustavian homes, the fabric might be muslin, calico, linen or a striped or hand-printed cotton.

If you can adapt simple net, or other gauzy fabric drapes, with valances or pelmets edged with delicate bobble-fringing, for example, this will give the correct look. If, however, you cannot combine them with shutters, as in the original style, and need night-time privacy, use a plain, pale-coloured roller blind, under the curtains,

close to the glass. Or choose country-style curtains in a suitable cotton print, or hand-woven fabric.

Simple window treatments in gossamer-fine fabrics showing swags and side drapes trimmed with bobble fringing, and below, cleverly shaped valances.

Lighting

Search for the authentic glass and brass oil lamps but do not convert them. Instead fill them with oil and use at night when they will bathe the room in a soft, warm glow. Light can also be provided from candles, preferably in crystal candlesticks, for the dining table, but for a dinner party, ornate silver candlesticks would be in style. For the walls, look for traditional brass or gilded candle sconces with a reflector or mirror behind. For more formal rooms, crystal chandeliers are essential, particularly over the centre of a dining table, but a smaller one can also be used to light the bedroom, and looks equally good combined with a canopy or other fabric bed drapes.

Bedhangings

In the bedroom, beds such as four-posters and half-testers can be draped in a similar way to windows. They may well have tented 'ceilings' with softly gathered valances and bed curtains. Dressing tables, small side or circular tables can be similarly treated, but the effect is always one of a fresh, crisp, country style — and usually combined with beautifully-textured woven bedcovers.

A very pretty idea for a single bed is to mount a fall of fabric from a coronet above an Empire-style bed (it is possible to transform a divan with suitable head and foot ends), held back at each side by gilt or brass curtain bosses.

Finishing touches

If you can obtain or copy one of the traditional Swedish heating stoves (tiled or decorated with traditional patterns — often reminiscent of Dutch Delft), to take up a large corner of the room, you will have one of the essential ingredients of the style; and if it is a working model, it will throw out considerable heat to warm the room in winter.

Choose other accessories to echo the Gustavian style. They should be decorative, but not fussy. Scatter cushions

Top: *Coronet and drapes above a daybed created a regal look.*
Left: *An authentic accessory of a dual-purpose mirror and candle holder prettily reflects light.*
Right: *The focal point and essential item in all Gustavian homes is the tiled stove.*

are rarely seen, but touches of lace and crochet are acceptable. Pictures should be sombre family portraits or landscapes, heavily framed. Mirrors, light fittings and candlesticks can all be in suitable Rococo style, and for grander settings, the careful addition of Neo-classical urns and covered vases.

Generally, flowers and plants should be simple — a crystal or silver bowl filled with pink or white roses; white china or glass vases can be used to hold a posy of wild flowers (dog daisies and buttercups), or a bunch of white marguerites or white lilac in season. Pale pink geraniums and pink, blue or white hydrangeas can be grouped on windowsills, but keep to pale colours and basic arrangements.

ENGLISH COUNTRY HOUSE

The English Country House style has evolved over many centuries to become the major style that inspires decoration in every Western country. Its history, which has given the English house a diversity hardly equalled elsewhere, has its roots in informal grandeur. Comfort and the cool co-ordination of colour and design are assembled in paints, papers and fabrics, reflecting the flora and fauna of a garden beyond.

The link with the natural elements is unmistakable. With the use of cotton and wool for upholstery, together with wooden furniture, the influence of the countryside pervades as one of the essential ingredients of this style. However, thanks for its formal preservation should go to the enthusiastic restorers who, from the beginning of the century to World War II, faithfully restored so many country houses to a state of remoteness in time; something which had been almost submerged in a wave of Edwardian philistinism.

Looking back, each era of history has been influenced by the current fashions and fads of Europe – and further abroad – resulting in this look which is uniquely English and which has given us a reputation as great arbiters of taste. Some of the influences are somewhat unexpected; the enthusiasm with which Americans have come over to England from the late nineteenth century onwards has stamped on the English Country House style new values of comfort which had hitherto been missing from the chilling interiors of some of our finest country seats.

The elegance and romance of this style are achieved by the casual but orderly placing of good-quality furniture and fabrics, especially chintz, which have a smart but homely and relaxed feel. Yet the look is vibrant, hospitable and grand. It has become very popular today, so much so that many of us almost unconsciously decorate and arrange our homes in a typically 'English country house' way – and now this type of decoration is found as much in cities as in the countryside.

The indoor garden

Chintz and the flower theme are unmistakably English. The first known use of the flower in wallpaper goes back to the sixteenth century – a Tudor rose emblem printed from woodcuts. Later it was the ornamental composition of Chinese wallpaper which transformed the English sense of space, reinterpreting the blooming peonies and opulent waterlilies and adapting them to European taste.

Chintz followed fast on the heels of the boldly designed brocade and flock papers of the early eighteenth century. It derives its name from the Hindu word for Indian calico cloth painted over with a design, 'chint', and was originally the result of healthy eighteenth-century bucolica, which entailed a burgeoning of botanical themes in all the arts. Garlands, festoons, bouquets – every kind of floral ornament is very much the staple theme of this look.

By the beginning of the nineteenth century English manufacturers in many branches of industry were conferring with fine craftsmen. These developments led to both the roller printing of calico as chintz in the North of England and Wedgwood's pottery works in Stafford. By the time the Prince Regent had succeeded George III, wallpaper was in the height of fashion and pretty patterned papers were made to match chintz curtains and chair covers, often in conjunction with imitation stucco borders. As Lady Rupert Neville of Victorian country house, Horsted Place, wrote: 'Victorian architecture [1837-1901] is rather coarse, so it is not easy to find the right furniture to place against it. It is the same with the patterns one chooses for the wallpapers – they have to be bold.'

But not everyone approved – Oscar Wilde is said to have commented (as he lay dying in 1900): 'My wallpaper is killing me . . . One of the two of us will have to go.'

In the drawing room at Horsted Place, shown on

The English Country House look is a style to which half the world aspires. Grand and feminine, but never pretentious, chintz and floral designs rub shoulders with elegant needlepoint bell pulls.

pages 84-85, chintz is used for the wallcovering, curtains and dividing drapes. The design is clearer than some – with large background spaces of cream between groups of pink cabbage roses. Nevertheless, a room of huge dimensions is clearly needed to avoid being over-powered by the pattern. For a lighter, more tranquil background you could alternate the chintz with wide Regency stripes in cool shades of cream.

Thread rare

Needlepoint, the art of working with wool or silk on canvas, has been a very popular form of domestic recreation for centuries. As the eighteenth century advanced, the influence of both Chinese and Indian art was reflected especially in textiles – out of which arose the vogue for chinoiserie as it was termed here or 'rachinage' by the French. These colourful designs were interpreted in all kinds of embroidery, including patchwork, appliqúe, crewel work and needlepoint.

Petitpoint and gros point, both variations of needlepoint, are common to the English country house. Here two beautifully embroidered bell-pulls, over-hung with paintings, match abundant cushions fashioned in the same way, along with ones that are hand painted. Other popular forms of embroidered objects include rugs, fire-screens and samplers, of which there are many superb kits and designs available.

As much a part of the style as the handsewn accessories are the gigantic family portraits – the superb examples in this drawing room are by Sir Joshua Reynolds from the Burlington Collection and Sir Edward Hughes who painted the portrait of Lady Abergavenny.

Fine furniture

These nobly spacious rooms with their high ceilings and ornate detail hold much furniture in fine wood that dates back to the eighteenth century. It was during this period that chairs started to be properly upholstered and began to be more comfortable. But it was not until the nineteenth century that furniture arrangement became more relaxed, with the informal arrangements that we associate with the present-day English country home. Familiar, dumpy sofas with loose covers and fringes, and armchairs in rich fabrics, plain and chintzy, were added to provide the comfort that was not offered by the grand but austere furniture of the previous century.

Unfortunately, as availability diminishes the price of antique furniture soars (a mid-eighteenth century writing cabinet fetched a record £400,000 in 1985) and reproduction pieces become more sought after. But in fact, you can pay almost as much for an expensive reproduction as you would for the real thing!

In this drawing room, deep sofas covered with silk or velvet, chosen for comfort rather than the date stamp, face each other across a pair of low level dark wood tables. Matching hand painted and embroidered cushions in pansy and rose designs are plentiful – providing both comfort and decoration. Furniture grouping depends on two objects being symetrically placed – two sofa tables; two porcelain lamps with matching pleated silk shades; two Chinese ginger jars; two bell pulls at each side of an oil painting. The sense of balance and proportion maintains the formal style.

If you are a rich perfectionist you could perhaps invest in a grandfather clock by Justinian Morse Barnet or a George III circular table, cross-banded in satinwood; or Empire chairs. Even chinoiserie furniture, which was popular in English country houses of the mid-eighteenth century, dying out in the 1760s, has for the greater part survived to grace many morning rooms.

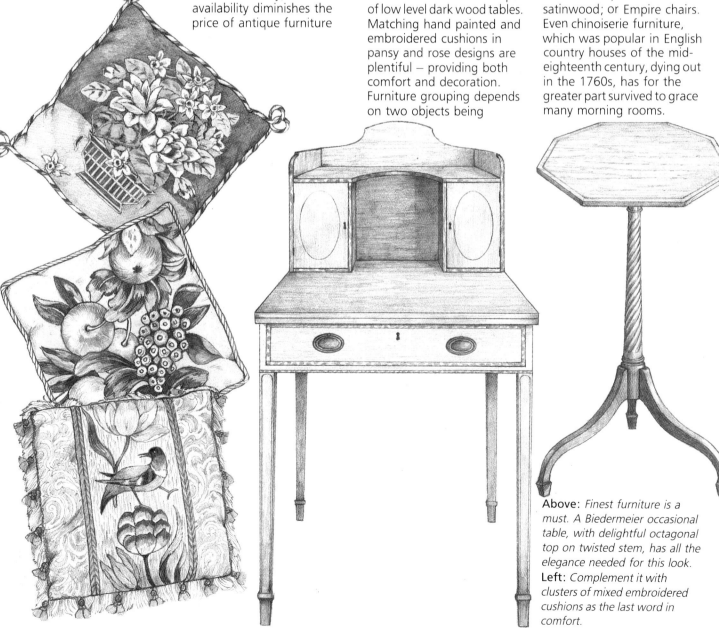

Above: *Finest furniture is a must. A Biedermeier occasional table, with delightful octagonal top on twisted stem, has all the elegance needed for this look.*
Left: *Complement it with clusters of mixed embroidered cushions as the last word in comfort.*

Gloriously dishevelled

The late nineteenth century in the English country home was the era of the accessory – bursting with flowers, precious collections, pictures and rugs as shown below.

Here several occasional tables hold a variety of lamps, photographs and a beautiful collection of Battersea enamel boxes, tiny enamel pill boxes and hand-painted Limoges china amongst other equally special ornaments and prints. The effect is gloriously eclectic.

The large floor space, of mellowed floorboards, is covered with softly faded oriental rugs, and runners placed for added comfort beneath the sofas and chairs.

Day into night

The English country house bedroom is both pretty and grand. The chintz fabric in a happy combination of pink and green garlands of giant cabbages roses would suit any large rural bedroom. Matching fabric for the window drapes, padded bedhead and stool give the room a warm, welcoming feel.

The eye cannot help but be drawn to the massive bed as the centre piece. Its size and height are of great

Cascades of pale silk transform the solid bed into a frivolous lit a la Polonaise.

importance to the style of the country bedroom. Undeniable luxury is exhibited in the beautiful, ruched silver-grey silk that makes an elaborate canopy over the bed, placed unusually in a central position – rather than over the headboard, and tied in glamorous bows. The more rustic brass bedsteads did not appear in Victorian bedrooms until around 1850.

Textiles were expensive right up to the time of the mechanized spinning of the eighteenth century, so beds and their hangings became, and remained, a major status symbol in the English country house. It was common around the mid-nineteenth century to have matching bed and window furnishings, but later this went out of favour. You can make your own choice; an all-over coordinated look may be too much for a smaller room.

The bedlinen here comprises square, French pillows with frills and counterpane in white linen with *broderie anglaise* of the finest detail. The plain cottons and linen of the bedclothes and pillowcases form a quiet contrast to the grand chinz patterns of the walls and fabrics, and were considered by the Edwardians more healthy than the stuffy drapes of the nineteenth century.

The bedside table is an unusual oval shape with two shelves and drawer. Interestingly, bedside furniture was very rare in English bedrooms before about 1760; prior to this time it was more usual to have a chair in this position. Commonly, English country bedrooms contained commodes (a low chest of drawers) often bearing exquisite marquetry with *bombé* front and the top of marble or scagliola or ormulu.

A corner of the dining room is devoted to enamelled treasures.

Country house kitchen

The deep armchair, upholstered in contrasting glazed blue stripes, has a frilled valance and white *broiderie anglaise* cushion. You could also use embroidered silks, muslins and cottons as brought to England from China in the Regency period. These became increasingly Europeanized with the adaptation of the floral designs and motifs of the nineteenth century; the English country look becoming clearer and lighter from this period onwards. The elegant Regency stool at the foot of the bed is a typical aesthetic feature of bedroom furniture of this style, and also provides a useful function.

The English country house theme is nothing if not layered and in the kitchen this includes books, utensils and dishes. There will be plants and herbs on the windowsill; ranks of storage jars and an eclectic array of stacked china. Catch the spirit of the room with a sheer profusion of utensils and crockery; you could add even more by hanging ancient copper kettles and heavy iron pots from hooks in the ceiling. My real favourite is a large mounted salmon trophy to hang above the Aga cooker for that look of unmistakable rural charm.

Bigger, more ordered and more gadget-conscious than its cottage equivalent, the country house kitchen still strives to keep its working face hidden and disseminate the feeling of 'nursery teas'. But the green expanded dresser is a triumph of functional design.

The kitchen must be a congenial room – it is the heart of the English country home and an essential part of day-to-day family life. It should exhibit the best of both worlds – the hidden efficiency of modern appliances with the outward warmth and atmosphere of country nostalgia. The first gas stove, shown at the Great Exhibition in London in 1851, did not come into its own for almost a decade. While in 1893, the first electric cooker, being a clumsy, almost unrecognizable object, was exhibited in the Chicago Columbia Exhibition. It filtered through to Europe with surprising speed, but failed to reach the remote country houses for well over half a century. The real bastion of English country cooking is, of course, the Aga. The first models were fired with anthracite but now you have the options of oil or gas to provide as many as four ovens at differing temperatures – so practical for country house entertaining, and very cosy.

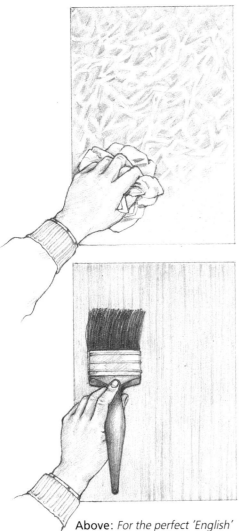

Above: *For the perfect 'English' backdrop choose rag-rolling or dragging in soft, muted paint colours. Dragging with transparent oil glaze you can cleverly modify the base colour to your exact taste.*
Right: *Pride of place on the mantelpiece goes to family porcelain and heirlooms.*

Collecting in style

One of the advantages of a large country house is having sufficient space to display personal collections. For the collector the style includes anything from china birds, samplers, silver filigree, prints, small botanical watercolours, glass boxes, engravings, oleographs and *étuis*, photographs, blue and white porcelain and enamel ware to painted figurines. A mixture of soft colours sifted together like pot pourri will produce the right atmosphere. You could also add a mirror close to your collection which will sprinkle light over the enamels and mother-of-pearl.

Period paints

To keep with tradition paint can be either marbled or rubbed on with rags and varnished with matt finish. The Victorians were particularly fond of drag washing. Panelling is another feature of this style but it need not be dark and sombre; you could rag-roll it for a softer, lighter look. Try pale yellow, accented with a putty eggshell dado rail or, as in the drawing room on page 84, with the palest peppermint green and gilt framing. Traditionally, wall finishes also included cool, marbled panels, varnished with a matt finish for a tranquil background.

On show

For the connoisseur of porcelain, why not indulge your flights of fancy and put together a selection of Staffordshire printed William Penn treaty soup plates from the mid-nineteenth century with a pink lustre cake plate *circa* 1840; baby blue dragon dinner plates *circa* 1920 with pink Chinese floral decorated teapot (c.1770) and Victorian pink-and-white gilded porcelain candlesticks for the perfect display of pretty pink and blue on a stone-mullioned Elizabethan fireplace.

Although the provision of a library only became increasingly important after about 1660, it certainly seems that no English country house is complete without one. Library furniture always tended to be more sober and conservative than that in other rooms, as befitting the solemnities of such apartments, where Chippendale-style furniture in mahogany is a favourite. Correspondingly the style for this room would have the traditional rich, warm colouring, extensive bookshelves, very comfortable seating and once again occasional tables groaning under the weight of fascinating memorabilia. This is the room to which one can retire to relax in peace and absorb the atmosphere of past centuries. For the elegance of the nineteenth-century look add needlepoint rugs, bureau bookcases, light chintzes and comfortable armchairs upholstered in pastel shaded tapestry or needlepoint.

It was not really until around the 1660s that books became 'popular' and at that time they were protected on shelves behind fringed

curtains. Now we are lucky that they are so available and, as Anthony Powell said: 'Books do furnish a room' — so place rows and rows of books from floor to ceiling, perhaps set in grand, arched rosewood shelving, to enhance the fine fine leather bindings. Paintings and sketches set amongst the volumes add interest and can even become a focal point if large and inspiring enough. Sporting scenes and animals make good subjects for the library.

The best dresser
In contrast to the more familiar stripped pine dresser, the one shown has received an unusual paint treatment in British racing green. This enormous three-arched dresser, laden with a vast array of tureens, blue and white plates, cups and larger-than-life jugs, is the centrepiece of the kitchen. It is fitted with a traditional wooden plate rack above the sink which will hold almost thirty plates.

Alternatively, made-to-measure glass fronted dressers are very accommodating as well as decorative and can be used to display fine old English china — for example a fish design set — without the fear of getting them covered with cooking fat and dust. A cheap alternative to the 'dresser' is an open trellis in attractive wood, on which to hang your *batterie de cuisine*.

Kitchen comforts
No self-respecting rural kitchen lacks a couple of sturdy, country chairs. Here, a homely wooden rocking chair adds a comforting touch with a spotted, green cushion to

complement the furniture, while a tapestry cushion and heavy fabric drape decorate the cook's armchair. The scrubbed pine refectory table, synonymous with the country house kitchen, looks handsome and welcoming spread with kilner jars of pickled fruit, dried flowers, huge earthenware bowl of oranges, bottled herb vinegar and pestle and mortar. There is ample room for cookery books beneath the second sink, set into a fine oak work-surface.

The juxtaposition of sunshine yellow walls with deep green furniture works well to add great colour to the room. Yellow and green are favourite culinary colours and vary in shades from deep olive

Country kitchens are no longer the cold, uncomfortable places they once were. A blazing Aga, soft lighting, Windsor-style chairs and cushions turn this room into somewhere the whole family will want to gather.

green to pale peppermint and ochre to pale cream. The sturdy wooden floor also contributes to the colour and character of the room. Choose flooring that is hardy enough to withstand the worst onslaught of Wellington boots and dogs; quarry tiles, flagstones (somewhat difficult to install), ordinary concrete slabs cleverly disguised with boot polish, square terracotta tiles or even bricks.

ENGLISH COUNTRY COTTAGE

The English Country Cottage style is based on practicality. Traditionally, country cottages were the homes of villagers and farm workers with simple, unsophisticated tastes. Materials and furniture were basic and functional, and often locally made – and these elements form the spirit of the look. Windsor chairs (spindle back), oak chests and Welsh dressers, for example, combine with stone or slate floors and plain walls to create a simple, practical environment.

Over the years the interiors of country cottages continued to reflect their exteriors, and the structural materials used. For instance, bricks were first discovered and made in the fourteenth century, but because they were too expensive to use for smaller dwellings, early cottages were made either from stone or timber filled in with mud and wattle. Walls were usually thick, windows and doorways small, and roof thatching was commonplace. Inside, rooms were small and basic and the central focal point became the open fire or kitchen range.

Generally, any decorative colour and pattern associated with the English Country Cottage style reflects traditional and fairly humble origins – sophisticated embellishments having little or no place in this style. In the past, any wall hangings or points of interest came from working connections, such as pottery, brass or wood, while the softening effects came from nature. Wild flowers were displayed in summer and clustered dried arrangements in winter. However, in many cottage homes, thrift was essential for survival, and long summer evenings would be spent making colourful rag rugs and warm patchwork quilts from discarded clothes.

Nostalgia plays a major part in the present revival of interest in the English Country Cottage style.

Cottage lifestyle

Town dwellers look to the romance of the country and imagine it as peaceful, home-loving and contented in comparison with the frenetic pace of town or city life. By redesigning their homes in this style they hope to capture the spirit of the past and, with it, acquire a less hectic lifestyle.

Country-born people, however, know that this is a lifestyle and not a look. For them, it entails home cooking, home decorating and home maintenance; it is not something to be played at by weekend visitors and the style of the English Country Cottage continues to reflect this. Prettiness, practicality and persistance are the keynotes to the success of the style. It is relatively inexpensive to achieve since it relies, to a great extent, on making use of what you already have and adapting when necessary in much the same way as the inhabitants of country cottages have been doing for centuries.

The English Country Cottage style is designed primarily around practicality and informal comfort. For many people, nostalgia for a bygone era is reflected in the cosiness of the cottage hearth, and consider it essential to the style.

Interior furnishings are often passed down from generation to generation with the result that nothing looks modern or contrived. Any additions would be picked up from local second-hand shops and, as the owners are proud to point out, at bargain prices. But though the look is traditional, it is also individual. You will never see two country cottages looking the same and this offers great scope for imaginative interpretation.

The style also adapts well to town life. Workers' cottages in town often have similarly small-proportioned rooms and the country look can make a refreshing change from the sophistication of town living.

Background colour schemes

Background colours are, instinctively taken directly from nature. Autumnal colours are best; pale and rich chestnuts, greens, creams, pale yellows and oranges blend perfectly giving a warm, cosy effect. Remember to keep shades muted, however; stark or bright colours shriek of disharmony and give the appearance of new cottage living for the chic towny — something to be avoided at all costs.

Below left: *Hearths should be used for real fires.* **Below:** *Create your own work of art, using a 'prodder' to push rag strip through a hessian base. Complete the line, and cut the loops.*

Walls and floors

A simple, refreshing idea is to leave the walls in their bare plaster form, as has been done with the room pictured overleaf. The plaster has been washed with a soft, pale pink and the colour varies according to the dryness of the wall, creating an interesting patchy effect.

Since cottage floors are often stone or tiled an arrangement of colourful rugs is better suited to the style rather than wall-to-wall carpeting. In keeping with the style, you may like to make a traditional rag rug from mixed oddments of fabric. Alternatively, if you have wooden floors, you could try stripping, staining and varnishing them. This way, they look good and save on expense.

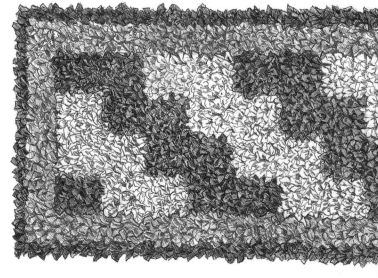

silk shawl — these can still be found at reasonable prices and can look just as effective. The secret is to make sure the fabrics look worn. This is one style where a few moth holes really would not seem out of place. They even add to the character of the style.

Curtains

Curtains are usually simple designs in keeping with the practicality of their purpose — primarily to keep the heat in and afford privacy. Lightweight, small-patterned fabrics probably work best for small rooms and the right length is just below the sill level, in order to avoid a sense of swamping by excessive amounts of fabric. Such luxury would be out of place in a country cottage.

Fabrics and coverings

Fabrics offer the widest scope for individuality. This room has a definite Indian feel to it, with one of the most unusual aspects being the blue and cream appliqué hung centrally across the ceiling. It looks dramatic and produces immediate focal interest.

As for the furnishing fabrics and coverings, these are an adventurous mixture of colours which work well together. The loose plain covers of the comparatively modern sofas and chairs are enlivened with a bold display of patterned cushions and the embroidered rugs draped over the armchair both complement and finalize the arrangement. If you do not have access to, or the finances for, these particular embroidered extravaganzas, you might use other family heirlooms; a piece of lace, a Paisley shawl, or perhaps a

Furniture

Materials such as wood, brass and iron are a key elements here. The practicality of traditional country living would not permit anything else. Therefore, chrome or synthetics should not be considered for your scheme. Cottage furniture was always made from whatever the cottagers could find and cheap, hard wearing designs were the prerequisites.

The rather formal proportions of this room limit the amount of traditional pieces that you might expect to find in a smaller home. Nevertheless, the dark oak chest in the corner alcove is typical of cottage furniture, with its traditional style and highly practical purpose. Alternatively, old chests with hand grained wood finishes

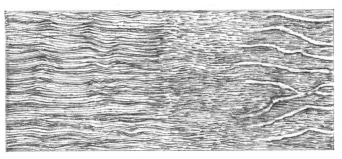

would be most suitable. Another example is the wall bookcase which shows how perfect a plain piece of furniture can look if you incorporate the right accessories. In this case the orange and green books stand out from the darkness of the surround, and the piece provides both a decorative feature and practical storage.

The sofas, although modern in design, are plain enough to conform to the look and the draped covers give them the necessary lived-in appearance.

Above left: *Light, bright chintzes are good design choices for coverings, while gingham checks and tiny floral prints suit smaller rooms.* **Left and below:** *Grain an old chest youself by applying a light coat of glaze (eggshell and turps) to wood. Drag a dry brush over it lengthways to create a ripple effect. Blur the lines with a soft dry brush and then draw roughly parallel heart wood lines on to the glaze with the sharp edge of a cork.*

The kitchen

Space in the traditional country cottage is usually sparing, and there are generally only one or two bedrooms. Rooms, therefore, particularly those downstairs, may have to serve several functions. The sitting room may double as a workroom or study while the kitchen is most likely to act as a dining room and an alternative living room.

Unless it is very small, there should be room for a table and chairs, to allow company for the cook and to keep the general lived-in air that is so essential to the style.

Furniture

Furniture must be genuinely old, and not reproduction. The fashion recently has been for stripped pine furniture but stained wood is also appropriate. The choice of light or dark wood depends very much on the amount of natural light available in your home. Dark furniture in a dark house, for example, will make the rooms overbearing and the cosy effect will be lost.

Remember this too with permanent fixtures such as beamed ceilings. If they have been left in their natural unstained condition, you should leave them well alone. If the beams have been darkened, you could paint the exposed ceiling off-white or cream to 'give height' to the room.

Right and far right: *Rooms are cluttered with useful furnishings. Wooden chairs, tables and kitchen dressers draw the room together. The chintz bedroom curtains create a romantic mood against the plain white bedcovers.*

96

trays make excellent space savers because they can be suspended from the ceiling — a space which is often hugely under-utilized.

Bedrooms

In this bedroom, the overall country effect is rather understated, the iron bedstead being the most ornate piece of furniture in the room. To reflect the true country cottage style, you could give it a more eclectic feel. Coloured patchwork, or hand-embroidered scatter cushions with old lace trimmings would be one way of doing this. Also, instead of sticking to one chintz pattern for all the fabrics, why not mix two or three different ones together, picking out a single colour from the original design and expanding it for different accessories and finishing touches.

Storage

A dresser is ideal for storage. In a strange way, the more it becomes overburdened, the more pieces it seems to take. This style suits the open display theme because the look is busy and works well with the lived-in atmosphere.

It is also the perfect answer for the compulsive hoarder who hates throwing anything away.

Kitchen and living room worktops should also be used for open storage with remaining equipment hung on the wall surfaces. Butcher's

Prettify it

Many a plain wooden bed can be prettified by a simple coat of paint and a posy of flowers. Choose colours and motifs to suit your overall scheme, keeping to the softer, natural shades of hedgerow flowers. Either paint freehand or stencil motifs to both ends of the bed, see page 62 for stencilling. Complete the effect with a bright quilt.

Pictures and frames

Another way to stamp your own personality on to individual rooms is by the use of pictures. Water colours of the local countryside are appropriate, as are old family photographs in black and

white or sepia. Keep the frames plain or, if you already have gilt frames, repaint them in a dark colour. Flower pictures are another good option. In fact any country scene works well. But do not fall into the large oil painting or hunting scene trap; these are much too formal for this style. Embroidered samplers needlepoint pictures and pressed flower arrangements would add a homely touch, so essential to the style.

Right: Pictures in an assortment of frames are ideal. Mix samplers, dried flower scenes and landscapes.

Above: For a strong cottagey feel, stencil flower designs on the bed ends and add a patchwork quilt.

Collectables

Any individual collection prettily displayed will make a country home more appealing. Basketware and chinaware, which are essentially country crafts, are two obvious choices for the style. Baskets offer a decorative quality but they are also useful for storage. They can house greenery, dried herbs, fruit or even overflowing larder tins and still liven up the space. China is equally versatile. Plates can decorate the wall space and larger platters look impressive on dressers. They take away what could otherwise become an overly bland mass of wood.

Old jars, tins, transfer printed pottery, jelly moulds and treen are worth investigating and collecting. They add to the eclectic and the general lived-in look reflecting times past when so many utensils were part of the everyday English Country Cottage — a style of timeless comfort, created with love and care.

Dried flower arrangements

Without country cottage flowers, the style would be incomplete. If you do live in the country, you could grow your own flowers and foliage. What could be more in style than to pick and arrange flowers from your own garden? Otherwise, dried flowers can look exquisite all the year round. Keep to the original colours adding brighter yellows, whites and blues and making sure the arrangement remains casual. Disarranged and overfilled jugs or small baskets is the look to aim for. Forget anything you ever learnt about strategically placed individual blooms, oasis or cut-glass crystal. You'll have much more fun with this idea and gain tremendous satisfaction from your country-style creations.

Mirrors

For whatever style, mirrors are an invaluable and versatile way of enlivening a room. They can be used to enlarge space and proportions, to reflect light into a dark area or, at their most basic, to act simply as wall decorations. Obviously, what type of mirror you choose depends on which room it is planned for. The mirrors in the main picture are traditional and ornate. The rectangular shape over the mantelpiece is particularly effective, as is the square alcove mirror. They both cover a fairly large area and reflect the interesting display at the opposite end of the room. Mirrors for a traditional, less formal room should be plainer in design though not necessarily in shape. Mirrors framed in dark wood are an alternative to gilt frames, and they have the bonus of being cheaper to buy. They can also be repainted, should you tire of the original colour. Pine or pastel painted frames would be ideal for a cottage bedroom or bathroom.

Lamps and lighting

Overhead lighting is too harsh for this style which needs to be soft and shadowy. Old gas and oil lamps are ideal but these are becoming more and more difficult to find. Alternatively, you may prefer wall- or freestanding uplighters – the plainer the design, the better – to throw flattering light from walls to ceiling. For a particularly old-fashioned feeling, you could even return to the original candlelight. The straight, decorative styles of brass or china candlesticks look equally wonderful as table lamp stands. Shades should be plain in design, although small, patterned fabrics would make interesting contrasts, especially if the main background colour and general tone of the room is plain. If you want overhead lighting, look for a subtle brass hanging which will look impressive, even if you choose not to use if for full lighting.

Left: Display wild flowers with home-grown dried garden flowers and stand in bright floral jugs.

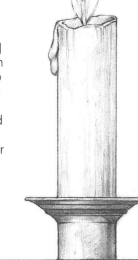

Below: *Buy a modern metal version of the candlestick, paint it gold then sand to give an older look.*

FRENCH PROVINCIAL

The distinctive style known as Provencal (which takes its name from the region of Provence in southern France) has long been admired and imitated by designers and decorators throughout the world. In the process it has become more widely interpreted as the French Provincial Look. The secret of its success is that it s demonstrates a faultless marrying of furniture, furnishings and *objets* from previous centuries with those of the present so that a charming, harmonious whole results.

The style can be adapted equally well to a simple country cottage, a grand château, a town house or a flat. But it is epitomized in the cottages of Provence, colour-washed in warm shades of terracotta pink and chrome yellow, their wooden shutters boldly painted in contrasting shades of green or blue, quickly sun-bleached into softer hues.

Behind windows curtained in ornate filigree lace are low-ceilinged rooms with exposed beams, and floors of cool glazed ceramic tiles or polished wood. Here and there a casual rug or carpet adds texture, complementing rather than concealing the main flooring.

Furniture tends to be chunky and robust; nevertheless the curvy lines of chairbacks and legs have a certain grace. Sometimes, chairs are painted yellow, blue or green — and further decorated with motifs. These may be hand-painted or simply stencilled. Seats are usually of rush, softened by cushions encased in traditional Provençal fabrics.

This style is very much influenced by the countryside and its climate. Provence, for instance, has a hilly terrain, with clay soils, and a landscape still only partly tamed. It is also alternately sundrenched or windblown. Hence the tiled floors for coolness and the shutters to afford protection from both sun and the mistral wind.

Sturdy, lasting materials such as crisp cotton and local faience ware, hand-moulded and painted in the characteristic ochres, reds, white and blues are clearly more appropriate here than fine china, silks and satins. Totally unpretentious, it is a style that is universally popular.

It is also easy to copy on the slimmest of budgets and one that may well outlast others that cost many times as much to achieve. It is not a great deal of money that one needs, but rather a sense of proportion, balance, colour and mood.

Kitchen comforts

All of the qualities which form part of the Provençal style are present in the kitchen shown overleaf, the heart of a French country house. Here, it is customary to eat and entertain as well as to cook, so there is a good sized table covered with a Provençal paisley cotton tablecloth, sunny yellow washed walls and a practical brown and white tiled floor. A positive *batterie de cuisine* is displayed on open shelving where it is immediately to hand. Herbs and spices in pots and jars, glazed pots for terrines, pâtés and potages are also close by. A formidable selection of well-honed knives is ready for use on the butcher's block wedged between two large cookers, one stainless steel, the other an antique cast-iron range, not unlike a modern hard-fuel cooker.

Although the general effect is one of cheerful clutter, all is arranged for maximum efficiency, comfort and visual appeal.

Kitchen craft

All of the elements previously described are easily copied or adapted. Another way to display pans and general cooking utensils would be to hang them from meat hooks placed over a length of narrow curtain rail or dowelling, fixed to the wall.

An old shelving unit, painted white or blue and either wall-mounted or free-standing makes for more efficient storage than conventional, custom-built, deep units. China, glass, cookware and ingredients — plus, of course, cookery books — are then all easily to hand and visible, adding to the cosy, lived-in look.

Smaller utensils such as wooden spoons, scoops, whisks and strainers can jostle for space in crowded earthenware pots, or fan out in a wider wicker basket on top of the unit. They could also be arranged decoratively on wall hooks — wooden spoons would look effective displayed in this way.

Fine fabrics

Still the most famous source of French country fabrics is the seventeenth-century Souleiado mansion in western Provence. From here came the most coveted hand-blocked cottons available and though nowadays they are mostly machine-printed, the craft of hand-blocking is still practised. Many designs still in use today were first introduced two hundred years ago.

The superb quality of the cotton fabric (woven with an incredible 150 threads to the square inch) is matched by that of the designs and the range of colourways varying from boldy beautiful to more subtle and restrained.

This family concern has been owned by the Demerys since 1912 and in more recent times they have substantially expanded the

Above: *Gleaming pots and pans hung from a wall-rail, ready to meet any culinary challenge.*
Right: *World-famous Souleiado prints combine traditional patterns in new ways.*

range. While still using the original designs and traditional colourways of red, blue, green and yellow, variations have been introduced, including grey-green and apricot. They have also combined several original designs such as stripes, paisley and posies to provide an even greater range.

Sometimes the fabrics are finely quilted, to be made into the traditional Provençal quilts. These also make splendid tablecloths, wall-hangings or, hung above a bed, striking bedheads.

So great is the appeal of these Provençal designs that similar ones are now available from several major textile manufacturers.

Lace is also much used, not only for curtains, but for bedspreads, cushions, lampshades and to decorate shelving. Long strips with either a scalloped or V-shaped edge are tacked or stapled to shelf edges, where their crisp whiteness is the perfect complement to collections of pottery and glass.

The ubiquitous banquette *is more comfortable than it looks — and very accommodating without taking up valuable space.*

Country style pottery

Faience is produced locally in many country regions of France. This earthenware pottery in simple, functional shapes is transformed by coloured glazes in green, ochre, terracotta, blue and white. Designs vary from unpretentious borders of tiny flowerheads to ornately swirling, marbleized patterns. Others are in clear, plain colours — perhaps with an embossed pattern in the form of flowers, fruits and birds.

Sometimes, plates, dishes and bowls may also be leaf-shaped. Collections of this attractive earthenware are displayed on open shelving, side tables or walls.

Again, it is fairly easy to find similar ware in pottery

On the shelf, a covetable collection of faience ware. Plates in round, scalloped and embossed leaf shapes, others marbelized in swirls of colour or bold geometric designs.

departments of larger stores, or even certain street markets. Or you might try your hand at hand-painting or marbling plain white plates.

Fundamental furniture

The most characteristic French item of furniture is the armoire. Large-scale and handsome, often with beautifully carved panelled doors, it is invaluable as a bedroom repository for household linen and bedding,

The ubiquitous banquette *is more comfortable than it looks — and very accommodating without taking up valuable space.*

or it can be used as a wardrobe.

In the eighteenth century, when the production of these pieces was at its height, each of the various regions had its own characteristic carved motifs. For example, Provence favoured romantic designs of doves, entwined hearts, angels and garlands. Burgundy favoured geometric designs and Auverne used stars and diamond shapes. These armoires can still be found in England as well as in France, and good reproductions are sold in the United States.

Traditional side buffets were also fairly sturdy and capacious, but equally pleasing to the eye, thanks partly to the lovingly built-up patina on the wood.

Until it became scarce, chestnut or locally grown honey-coloured walnut was used for the more handsome pieces of furniture. Pear wood was also popular, often artificially darkened to look like ebony. Chairs were made from willow, while the larger rush-seated armchairs and *banquettes* capable of seating two or more were made from walnut, beech or mulberry.

Tables, like beds, were simple and functional. However, smaller side tables were often more elaborate.

Many kitchenware items, too, were fashioned from wood: containers for the storage of bread, flour and salt, for example, were as decorative as they were practical. However small or utilitarian, no piece was considered too unimportant for embellishment.

Playing it cool

This rustic window recess complete with old stone sink and shelving is typical of country cottages, not only in the South of France but in other rural retreats, so you may be lucky enough to have one already. If not, you can improvise. All you need is a window wall with a window recess. Apply a coat or two of pale emulsion and install an old stone sink, mounted perhaps on two low walls of brick (erected for the purpose), and then either plastered over or simply emulsioned to match the wall behind. If you have a collection of decorative tiles, this would be an ideal place to display them. Do not worry if they are unmatched – in fact, the effect would be so much better.

Tiles are very much a feature of the French Country look. Apart from their wide use as flooring, they are very much a part of the French bathroom – sometimes completely covering all available wall space. They are also used on kitchen

Above: The special beauty of ordinary objects made significant by the clear Provençal light.
Right: *A marble side-buffet coolly displays the good things of life.*

worktops, around sink areas and in window recesses, not only on the ledge, but around the entire recess. This is a very practical idea should you wish to site a row of plants there. To embrace the style, choose large pots of bright red geraniums, pelagonias or double begonias.

Marble is another cool surface much favoured for this country look and ideal for a side buffet, as shown opposite. With its narrow overshelf, this is a particularly fine example, but you could use an old marble washstand in the same way. Unless the wooden base is in very good condition, why not paint it white to match the marble top – or even try marbling the wood? Notice the way the glass cake stands on which fruit is displayed, and the drinking glasses complement

the cool marble surface. The niche below has been used as storage for vegetables and herbs.

Romantic bedrooms

Bedrooms tend to be simple, uncluttered and restful. This very typical *chambre à coucher* has plain emulsioned walls and exposed old beams. A number of framed, embroidered samplers, a musical instrument and highly decorative wall-sconces provide the interest. The small, yellow-painted metal bed is covered with a traditional cotton quilt.

On the circular bed-side table, covered in an embroidered cloth, stand an antique oil lamp, an oval hand-mirror and a charming posy of field flowers and

lavender sprigs, all composed into an appealing still life that further evokes the French Country style.

The ubiquitous side-table may be of wood, iron or wicker, usually covered, as here, with a pretty cloth – so it does not have to be a priceless antique. Any table of appropriate diameter and height will suffice.

In typical French style, the small wall niche by the door has been used to house a decorative jug and cup. If you like the look, mount a small open-fronted cupboard or box on the wall and paint it to match.

The ceiling beams can also be faked. You may be lucky enough to find throw outs if major house-renovation is taking place in your area; but if not, you can buy suitable timbers at a local wood merchants. If that sounds like too big an undertaking, you could simply nail thin strips of plywood across the ceiling joists at regular intervals, so that they stand just proud of the plaster surface, and paint them to match the ceiling.

Plain emulsioned walls are often finished with a decorative paper border around the ceiling, doors and windows. The same borders can even be used to form fake panelling. A wide variety of frieze papers is now available at decorating shops, or you could devise your own border using an appropriate stencilled motif.

So French, and pretty as a picture, a shapely jug 'framed' in a niche.

French country gardens

In terms of decoration, the exterior of a French country house is distinguished by its style just as much as the interior. Walls are often colour-washed in earthy shades of reddish-pink or chrome yellow while wooden shutters and doors are painted in strong greens and blues. Both windows and doors may be outlined in white, or bordered by stone panels or blocks set into the plaster as a complete framework. Plain doors and shutters might be decorated with studs or large-headed nails, and door furniture such as handles and hinges tends to be rugged.

Garden ornaments vary from simple earthenware pots flanking doorways and overspilling with geraniums, marguerites and sweet-smelling lavender, to extremely ornate ones decorated in bas relief showing flowers, fruits, cones or lattice work.

Wall-mounted earthenware gargoyles are often seen and, more appealing perhaps, small figures of cherubs may be positioned beside a pathway or door, or half concealed in a patch of greenery.

Other ornamentation may be of cast iron – particularly lamps mounted by doors, windows or gateways. Again, these vary from the most simple of oil-lamps to highly ornate, antique ones. Even an old birdcage, wall-mounted and filled with trailing plants, would add to the style.

Wrought iron is popular for gateways, balustrades and balconies around first-floor windows. Garden furniture, too, may be fashioned from wrought iron which lends itself to elaborate scroll designs that make pleasing silhouettes when set near a white-painted wall.

Rattan is also favoured for garden furniture, and the more splendidly ornate pieces also appear in bathrooms and bedrooms.

To complete the garden scene, there are sculptural plants and shrubs such as the *Althea rosea* (hollyhock), and the impressive *Fatsia japonica* spreading wide its massive, seven- to nine-fingered leaves, a fig tree, or a vine, grown in walled patios.

A handsome armoire is much prized. Used here to store household linen tied around with ribbon – French country style.

useful food storage.

Rush or cane-seated chairs with plain wooden back struts are fairly commonplace in street markets or smaller antique shops, especially if you are prepared to buy odd ones and team them together. The French often use unmatched chairs, so this would add to the overall look. Unless you can do the re-caning yourself, check that the existing seating is sound. Any imperfections in the wood can be disguised with a coat of paint and a stencilled motif along the back and down the legs.

Starting with stencils

The word 'stencil' comes from the old French *étinceler*, meaning to sparkle, and has been used as a decorative painting technique from the twelfth century.

If you are using a stencil for the first time, choose a simple motif. You can buy books of stencils ready to cut out and use, or you can easily make your own. Simply draw your chosen motif freehand on to stencil paper or trace suitable designs from magazines or postcards. Then transfer the tracing on to the stencil paper. Before cutting away the design (with small, pointed scissors) make sure there are sufficient 'connecting bridges', otherwise the design will fall to pieces. For making your own stencils, see page 62.

Buy paints and brushes from an art shop where you can get advice if you are at all

Capturing the style

If you have the necessary capital you may be able to buy an armoire from a good antique shop specializing in large items of furniture. If not, you can achieve a similar effect by converting an old wardrobe of generous proportions and, preferably, with twin doors – though this is not absolutely essential.

Remove any internal fittings, such as clothes hooks or rails and instead fit narrow battens at approximately

45cm to 61cm (18in to 2ft) intervals down each side and across the inside back to support shelving of the required length and width. If the exterior is shabby, paint it and add a colourful stencil or hand-painted motif to the panels. Finish by lining the shelves with a small-patterned Provencal print paper. Try storing your sheets, pillowcases, and towels tied around with plain or patterned ribbons and finished with a bow. This

typically French custom is very pretty and practical; it helps keep like with like and makes it easier to find items quickly.

As a substitute for a side buffet, you could adapt a suitably curvaceous sideboard. On the wall above it, you could mount a shelving unit to house your most attractive pieces of pottery and glass or a collection of ceramic figures, glass jars filled with sea-shells, or trailing plants and books. The sideboard will also provide unsure about which materials are suitable for the surface you have in mind. Always make sure that the surface is clean and dry, and secure the stencil with masking tape. Take care not to overload the brush and remember to clean it thoroughly with each change of colour.

After stencilling on to a wooden surface, always protect the design with several thinly-applied coats of clear varnish, ensuring that each one is thoroughly dry before applying the next.

Stencils can be used not only on furniture, but on walls, floors, fabrics and ceramics, so, for the enthusiast there is plenty of scope for further decorative finishes in the French country style. It is a good idea to try out your stencil design on a piece of card or hardboard before embarking on the main project.

Collectors' corner

The French love to display their treasures on side-tables, mantels, shelving and, of course, on the walls. Therefore, any or all of the following ideas will contribute to a general French country look.

Basketry is a traditional French craft, and because basketware comes in so many shapes, sizes and patterns, it is often used for decorative as well as more functional purposes. For instance, in a small coastal village it is not uncommon to see fishing baskets, the main basketwork reinforced with heavier bands of whaling, hung on the wall by a window. Alternatively, you may prefer a collection of straw hats, either wall-mounted or perhaps adorning a bentwood stand in the hallway.

Another very popular idea in France even today, is the wall-hung sheath of wheat, grasses or dried flowers – particularly lavender, which is widely grown there. This custom dates back to the times when a traditional harvest bouquet of wheat or corn was presented to the farmer's wife by harvesters when they brought back the last wagonload to the farm. The bouquet was then hung on the wall for luck (to keep away evil spirits) and for ornament.

Collections of coloured glass or pottery in assorted shapes and sizes are often placed on a windowsill to catch the light, or grouped on a side-table under a lamp, or simply displayed along a mantelpiece – a favourite focal point for treasured *objets*.

Shells, with their wonderful shapes, textures and lustrous surfaces are also very popular – either arranged in a shallow basket set on a hearth, in a pottery bowl, or in a deep and wide glass bowl: a defunct goldfish bowl would be ideal for this. To complete the effect, a row of terracotta pots could be filled with scarlet and white geraniums and arranged on a window sill, or on the steps to the house, and even on top of the garden walls.

A small wall-mounted corner cupboard (open, or glass-fronted) is also very characteristic of the style. Line the interior with a small-patterned paper or edge the shelves with lace or a scalloped, patterned fabric. Alternatively lace-edged handkerchieves or doylies could be overlapped, corner-wise as in the illustration, opposite.

Above: *Curvy pots and jugs are favourite display pieces.*
Left: *Chairs are curvy too, and are often painted or stencilled.*

107

GREEK ISLAND

While Greek classical architecture has long been admired for its purity of form, from the conquering Romans who adapted it through the Palladian and Neo-classical revival, it remains in sharp contrast to that of the rustic style of the islands.

Greek island architecture has been summed up as 'The epitome of architecture without architects'. Its appeal owes little to mainland classical tradition but more to the simple down-to-earth existence of the islanders.

Made from stone hacked from local hillsides, these squat, flat-topped houses with small, shuttered windows provide a cool retreat from the dazzling light and hot sun. Interiors centre around family living – where meals are eaten outside through the long, hot summer months – where the terrace has become an extension of the living space, and relaxation is enjoyed.

From the 1800s the islands have absorbed various influences of style introduced by a wealthy merchant fleet trading via Alexandria, Venice and Odessa, to the extremes of the Turkish empire.

Even today one is reminded of these distant connections by the typical hand-made brick tiles, decorative wood carving, the raised seating area, Venetian-style lanterns and candle sconces, cotton weaving, colourful embroidery and delicate lacemaking.

If you are searching for an 'honest, gritty' style with a hand-made look then the Greek Islands offer plenty of scope – particularly for outdoor living, during hot summer months. Memories of a Greek Island holiday or a colourful postcard may be your starting point or perhaps you will decide to paint your terrace in dazzling blue and white, or with a trompe l'oeil view to capture the beauty of the Greek Island landscape.

Texture and pattern

Greek island interiors rely greatly for their charm on the simple textures created by roughly plastered walls, brick-tiled floors, wooden beamed ceilings and cobbled-stoned courtyards — lit by brilliant light filtered throught lattice-work doors and shutters.

Set against this textured backdrop is the simply-carved wooden furniture of the islands, traditional embroidery, woven rugs and a variety of rush seating and basketware to offer contrasting pattern and colour.

These are the essential ingredients of Greek island interiors which must be appreciated for successful results.

Ceiling to floor

The relaxed style is most imitable, and one that would suit older properties, especially town houses or country cottages with an open aspect. In this bedroom the ceiling is formed by long narrow wooden boards placed above solid timber beams and left in their natural colour. If you are lucky enough to have a beamed ceiling then this is a tremendous advantage. However, should it be a low ceiling, you may prefer to limewash or paint the beams to increase the feeling of height. The Greeks do not think it wrong to paint old beams if they look better that way! The keen enthusiast without a beamed ceiling might consider installing roughly-hewn mock beams simply for the effect.

Walls should be stripped down to bare plaster and any cracks or other defects made good, before finishing with a thin scim or slightly textured plaster. If you decide to use a proprietory product to give the typical rough-plaster finish, avoid the temptation to 'lay it on with a trowel', to make it too much like a relief map. You may eventually need a change of scene, and this is difficult to remove.

A very pretty idea, especially for a bedroom, would be to impress a flower motif into the wet scim (or plaster, if this is needed) while it is still wet, as the Greek islanders do with their tiles (see page 113). The motif could be cut into a large (halved) potato leaving the motif in relief. Use it as a border around the ceiling, door and so on, or as an all-over spot pattern.

To keep within the style, finish the walls with a dazzling matt white emulsion, or you might try painting one wall and/or the ceiling a vivid Mediterranean blue, and contrasting this with a warmer terracotta floor, for example, provided by exposed brick or quarry tiles. For a softer tread, choose warm-coloured Oriental rugs, as in the bedroom.

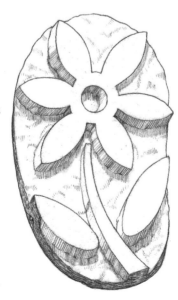

Windows

Windows are small, to keep out the heat of the blazing sun and, ideally, they should be set at least 46 cm (18 in) into the wall, complete with a wooden surround and shutters. In the bedroom, notice the simple carving, showing two panels on the window shutters and three on the door.

Window treatments

Window dressings should be minimal. If wooden shutters are impractical, then simple, natural-coloured roller blinds in a lightly-textured fabric (ratten or Pinoleum) would give the correct cool, spartan look. If curtains are essential, then make them from a lightweight cotton, linen, possibly, muslin or voile in white or natural. You might use printed blue and white fabric. Try to keep to basic checks and stripes. Hang them from a simple pole with brass rings sewn to the top of the curtain heading. Alternatively, the top could be scalloped, castellated, or simply cased and threaded directly on to a fine rod, and if screening is essential for privacy, design this to slip neatly into the window reveal.

Flooring

In addition to being cool and immensely practical, the typical brick-tiled floor of the Greek islands has a special charm. Hand-made from terracotta, each brick is stamped with a daisy pattern — giving a pretty texture underfoot and a nonslip surface.

Flooring can be selected according to the room — in a kitchen, hall or bathroom,

Outline a window with a floral motif impressed in plaster.

Above: *Simple, rustic floor patterns of bricks and terracotta tiles.* **Below:** *circular occasional table and chair have a rough-hewn, honest look.* **Bottom:** *Colourful cross stitch embroidery on linen edged with a typical tasselled fringe.*

you could try an interesting pattern laid in warm red bricks, or un-glazed terracotta (quarry) tiles, or use ceramic tiles with a pronounced Greek flavour. If you live in an upstairs flat where the weight of the real thing could present a problem, you could look for a simulated effect in sheet material or tiles. On the other hand, stripped floorboards give the right flavour of the Greek island style. These can be sealed and polished (not too highly), and softened with a rug – Greek, Oriental, or a simple striped dhurrie would give the best effect. If you prefer to close-carpet, keep to a pale, neutral-coloured, looped Berber-style, and cover with the same sort of rugs as previously mentioned.

Furniture

Greek island furniture is usually free-standing, and has an 'honest' look. In the bedroom, practical items like wardrobes and classic *armoires*, basic sofas and antique chests may be combined with more delicate pieces, such as rush-seated stools, elegant occasional tables, draped bedsteads or four posters, bentwood chairs and lattice screens.

Although furniture may be more difficult to get right – keen DIY enthusiasts should be able to make the squat circular table, with its basically box-like base and arabesque bottom edges (see bedroom overleaf); or any of the other typically shaped tables and chairs, shown here. Make them from whitewood or chipboard finished with a matt or eggshell paint in white or blue.

Latticework is a favourite feature of island furniture and offers great scope for personalizing your scheme. Inexpensive wardrobes and cupboards can easily be transformed by latticework doors. In the picture overleaf, the base of the bed has been enclosed this way but, if it were made with doors, it might possibly double as storage space.

Furniture can often be improvised – search out suitable basketware such as large wicker storage baskets and, with cushions placed on top, they could be used for seating. A bevel-edged piece of timber (polished or painted), for example, may top a pile of terracotta tiles, or a roughly plastered piece of brickwork to form a desk or table.

Four-poster

A draped, four-poster bed is the essential item in any Greek island bedroom. Screened with typically embroidered curtains, this is a gentle distillation of the traditional marriage bed. These were raised on a high platform in the centre of the room surrounded with full-length, heavily embroidered curtains designed with a central 'door' panel.

The bed tends to dominate the bedroom by its height, and similar beds to the one shown overleaf can be bought from many major stores; but an ordinary, wooden boxframe could easily be converted with elegant posts, and a top rail for the curtains. These can be draped around the outside of the bed and loosely hitched to the post with a softer flourish! Old-fashioned, freshly-ironed linen or cotton bedcovers are used with plump pillows and a thin comforter for colder winter nights.

Embroidery

The Greek islands are famous for their embroidery which they generously display on bedhangings, tablecloths, curtains, chairback covers, cushions and pillows. Favourite designs include flowers and foliage, birds, figures and all-over geometric patterns worked in various crossed stitches and pattern darning, usually in vibrant reds, blues, greens and yellows outlined in black. Embroidery is one of the most accessible and inexpensive ways of adding a Greek island look to your room.

Terrace living

Terrace living is a way of life – this is where, during the long summer months, leisurely meals are eaten, family and friends relax in the sun with a bottle of wine, or find the shade under the pergola, and all is well!

Here emphasis is placed on sun, comfort and leisure. As one's eye travels over the distant view and is then arrested by colourful, sweet smelling plants nearby – the effect is breathtaking.

An al fresco *dining area shaded with vine-covered pergola.*

Pantry

Situated between the living area and kitchen, or an inner courtyard or terrace, is the pantry. In this island home, this room serves as a cool store for the kitchen, and

houses general provisions and crockery. It may also be used for other utility purposes such as arranging flowers or ironing.

It displays all the classic ingredients of the style –

rough plaster walls, small, deep-set shuttered windows, the daisy-stamped brick tiled floor, offset by some shiny pieces of local copperware and pewter, and a matching pair of wall candle brackets.

Although white is most frequently used for colour-washing both the exterior and interior walls, softer greens and neutrals give a delicious antiqued effect.

Texture is provided by plaster, brick and wooden beams.

Living area

In addition to low, Egyptian-style settles with buttoned mattress seating and big cushions, a typical living area would probably have also a raised seating area which you approach by a few shallow steps. This is surrounded on two sides by simply carved balustrading, reminiscent of mainland Greek architecture. This would be painted, to match the rest of the woodwork –, and would not be too difficult to construct.

On the other hand, if you are buying upholstered

furniture, look for wooden frames with clean lines, and plain linen or calico covers with a hand-woven look. You may find that a wooden frame, combined with a mattress and cushions, creates the right look – and makes comfortable seating. Alternatively, cane chairs with plump, cotton-covered cushions with tassels at each corner can also create the right effect. Rush-seated, ladder-back chairs are common to most European countries, and should not be too difficult to find.

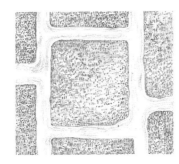

Adapting the style

You can successfully create the style of the Greek islands in your own home, and imagine that you are soaking up the almost eternal sunshine. But remember, the further north you go the colder the light becomes — and frequently the sun is shrouded in a grey mist, so the dazzling whites, blues and greens of the Mediterranean may have to be altered a little to achieve the same sunshine effect. Tinges of yellow or apricot added to the basic colour will help to re-create the correct sunny atmosphere and mood. Use this for the ceilings and walls, woodwork and possibly furniture, but do not forget to use the strong, clear blue, to suggest the brilliant aquamarine sea and sky. For example, in some rooms, you may choose to paint the ceiling, furniture or one wall in this colour — or use it for upholstery or bedding. In contrast to the blue and white, add the rich burnt-orange of natural brick and earthenware for the floor.

If it is not going to be practical to strip walls and fixtures back to the bare essentials, you may prefer to confine the Greek island look to only part of your home, possibly the living area and the bedroom, remembering that a terrace or balcony is essential to the style.

Top to bottom

A simply-constructed pergola, with trailing plants to afford a cooler area and decoration, is important to the terrace.

A sense of permanence is given to this extension of the house simply by its flooring. The essential ingredient here is that it should be stone or flagged, even cobbled, provided the cobblestones are set in a pleasing pattern. A mixture of bricks and smaller flagstones can happily be incorporated into a variety of patterns.

Outside furniture

This should remain fairly unsophisticated with simple, even rustic overtones. Form seating or folding chairs would be in style, while sofas or 'fixed' seating are essential to a look of permanence. Simple fixtures can be built from stone slabs — whitewashed and fitted with loose cushions.

Terracotta pots

An abundant array of sweet-smelling plants and shrubs is as important to the look as sun and sea. Here large pots of varying shapes are arranged and the composition of smaller plants balanced artistically between trailing shrubs, lemon trees and herbs.

Above: *Terrace flooring of cemented flagstones, cobble-and paving-stone patterns.* **Below:** *Terracotta pots for flowers, herbs and shrubs.* **Top right·** *Lanterns for the terrace.*

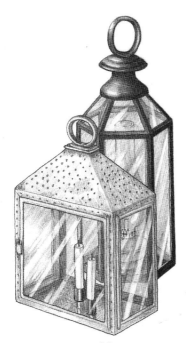

Lamps and lanterns

To complete the effect, you will need oil- or candle-burning outdoor lanterns. These can be hung from the pergola or attached to the wall. Look for large, square or six-sided varieties for an authentic, old Venetian touch.

Provide inside lighting by simple ceramic or wooden table lamps, with plain shades, or wall-mounted candle sconces to throw interesting pools of soft light on the walls, floor and furniture. Forget about wall and centre ceiling lights; these would not be in style.

Faking it

If you do not have space outside, try to adapt part of the living area to look like a sun-drenched terrace. You can achieve this with a *trompe l'eoil* painting to simulate a typical vista. You might even take the illusion one stage further with painted pillars, beyond which the view is seen — and include olive groves and vineyards. An inside pergola would not be too difficult to install. To form a false ceiling, use a simple unpainted garden trellis pinned to struts, and grow vines across it — real or false,

to create a Mediterranean impression. To enhance this effect still further, try to illuminate it softly from above to re-create the impression of sunshine continually slanting through windows or shutters. You could do this with concealed lighting at the top of the window reveal.

Uplighters can be placed behind furniture, or to provide 'glow' through a group of plants and herbs, potted in characteristic earthenware and white-glazed pots, standing on a glass-topped table. If you cannot find a table in style, buy a sheet of thick glass, have the edges polished, and support it on brick pillars, or on a rustic wood frame.

Pantry style

If you are building kitchen or bathroom furniture, make sure it has the traditional rather heavy, panelled look, and either leave the wood natural, or paint it gentle grey, green or soft white in a matt, or subtle lustre (eggshell) finish. Look for bold dressers and large cupboards. For a completely natural look, strip off any old paint or stained finish, bleach

or lighten if necessary, and then seal or wax.

Add internal shutters to windows, fitted into the reveal if possible (you could use louvred ready-made ones), and treat as other woodwork.

Install wooden plate racks from floor to ceiling for storage and display purposes in the dining and kitchen areas; have either open lattice panels or, one glass-fronted and simply-designed display cabinet for china and glass. Search out old wooden or storage chests — or a travelling trunk, painted to look like wood (or drape it with an embroidered cover). A distressed junk shop find might be the right shape, so be bold and paint it white, cerulean or aquamarine blue.

Woven rugs showing Greek key border and star designs.

Cotton runner

The honest charm and practicality of quarry-tiled floors cannot be disputed, but for a softer tread you may prefer to add cheerful cotton runners. Place them in the natural traffic lanes, particularly in larger ground floor bathrooms or kitchen/ dining areas. These days small, cotton runners can easily be laundered in the washing machine and dried fairly quickly.

Choose striped runners in subtle colours and, if possible, with corner fringing to echo the Greek island style.

Accessories

Accessories should be limited to objects such as coffee pots, platters, pretty pottery bowls or jugs of flowers. These should be fresh and wild, or dried varieties; even pots of herbs would add the right flavour.

JAPANESE

The Japanese excel at one-room living; practice over the centuries and a culture based on long-standing traditions, has made them experts at managing small spaces.

Anyone who has stayed with Japanese people and has been given the traditional guest room cannot but be impressed by the sheer simplicity and tranquillity of Japanese style. The floors are covered with sweet-smelling, springy *tatamis* (mats of finely woven sea-grass); the sliding cupboard doors glide open with ease to reveal bedding and a comfortable futon, and the sliding *shoji* screens at the window open up to reveal an exquisite view of miniature landscaped garden. One is loathe to leave such serenity.

However, living in tiny spaces requires discipline. Possessions are restricted; neatness and hygiene are essential virtues to cultivate. For instance, outdoor shoes are always left in the porch of a Japanese home, and then indoor slippers are put on so as not to soil or damage the domestic floorcoverings: a sensible consideration for anyone who wishes to adopt a lifestyle of generally eating and sleeping at floor level.

Nowhere else are you so conscious of the floor and its subtle changes in levels as you are in the Japanese home. Platforms are everywhere: you step up them to sleep, eat and to relax after a meal, but you step down into a tiled bathtub, which is set deep into the floor.

Perhaps the best thing of all about adopting the Japanese style is that you can begin in a small way. The simple act of setting a table and cooking a meal requires that you have to learn about colours, shapes and patterns — becoming, if you like, a collector and connoisseur of pottery and porcelain, because in Japan the presentation of food and drink is a ceremony and an art form in its own right.

Another simple way to begin would be to try your hand at Japanese flower arrangement (*ikebana*), or gardening with miniature trees (*bonsai*). Neither of these fascinating hobbies requires a major outlay. Ikebana, in particular, has long inspired Western flower arrangers to use unusual items like driftwood or well polished pebbles to great effect. And here the necessary understanding of Japanese philosophy and symbolism widens the scope for artistic expression.

While traditional Japanese-style interiors rely on textured surfaces and what may seem at first almost drab colour combinations, today's style favours a 'harder edge'; a monochromatic look of greys and black wood stains with colour accents provided by prints, pottery, cushions and other simple accessories.

Today's Japanese style also relies on modern lighting such as dimmer-switch operated fittings, concealed tracks and some of the smaller and more discreet spot lamps.

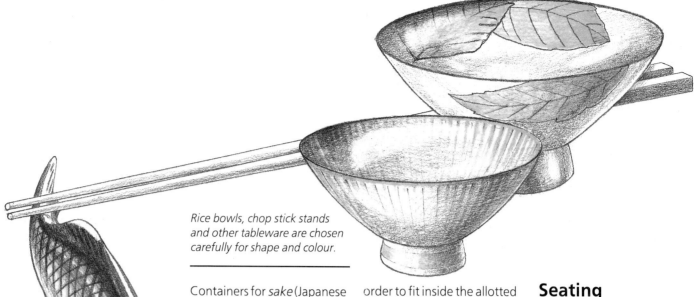

Rice bowls, chop stick stands and other tableware are chosen carefully for shape and colour.

Table settings

Japanese style does not confine itself solely to the interior, it extends to the table and to the meal as well. Food presentation has become a highly sophisticated art form in Japan and has currently inspired much Western cuisine. The cultural influence of *chanoyu*, the tea ceremony, has also had an effect since it was brought to Japan in the sixteenth century by a Zen Buddhist priest, Sen Rikyu. For instance, great attention is paid to the colour and quality of the tea making utensils: shape, pattern and proportion are all considered.

Japanese tableware ranges from the finest bone porcelain through to rich red and black lacquers, mostly used for trays and soup bowls, but there are also beautifully shaped cast-iron casseroles for stews and hot-pots which are available in a variety of shapes and sizes. The table setting here shows some imaginative touches, such as the palm leaf plates for the neat cubes of bean curd (*tofu*), and the thoughtfully provided wooden basket holders for toothpicks.

Containers for *sake* (Japanese rice wine) often come attractively gift-wrapped in squat porcelain jars or simple ceramic bottles. Chopsticks can be either plain lacquer or inlaid with mother-of-pearl, although for simple meals they are usually of plain wood. In Japan it is customary for guests to bring their own otherwise the host will provide disposable wooden ones. Another pretty and hygienic table accessory is the porcelain chopstick holder or stand; these are often made in the form of fish or decorative fruit, and sensibly prevent the surface of a table from becoming marked.

Storage

Space-saving fitted cupboards with lightweight sliding door panels covered in decorative papers were developed centuries ago by the Japanese. From early times a sophisticated, ingenious carpentry was evolved, which meant that the usual problems of sliding track sticking were completely eliminated. Painstaking accuracy in the making and fitting was the key to success but modern sliding track mechanisms make this a much easier job, particularly for DIY enthusiasts. The space inside a traditional Japanese cupboard was strictly regulated – even kimonos had to be carefully folded in

order to fit inside the allotted space.

The *tokonoma*, a traditional wall recess for the hanging of a scroll picture with its small storage cabinet below, has all but disappeared from modern Japanese homes. At one time the *tokonoma* served as a kind of household altar, whereas now it is more likely to contain a television and video. In the picture, shown overleaf, vestigal remains of the *tokonoma* can be seen with a scroll painting and a modern interpretation of *ikebana*.

Seating

Sitting down to traditional Japanese meals used to mean hours of sitting on hunkers, although a low platform was sometimes fitted underneath a dining table so that legs could be stretched. Most Japanese now favour Western-style furniture such as the dining table and chairs shown in the picture overleaf; comfortable three-piece suites and the smart cane reclining chair are now the order of the day in many Japanese living rooms.

Top hung sliding door panels with natural wooden frames can be covered with hand-made papers.

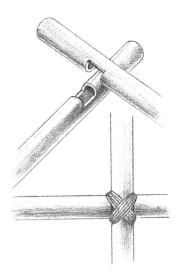

Cross-corner frames are made from bamboo garden canes. Use a fretsaw to cut the notches and a craft knife to shape them. Place vertical over horizontal lengths, lie flat, bind the corners with string. Fix with adhesive.

Prints

Japanese artists like Utamaro and Hokusai have inspired countless European artists from Toulouse-Lautrec to Whistler with their famous *ukiyo-e* or 'floating world' pictures. These woodblock prints depicting genre scenes were the first affordable artworks for the ordinary Japanese citizen. Authentic works now fetch high prices, but pleasing copies are also available. Opinions differ over framing methods, but the conventional way is to use a cream-coloured mounting card with a black frame moulding. For modern Japanese prints, such as the ones here, framing can be more varied: framing kits of glass sheet held by simple metal clips, or cross-cornered bamboo frames with coloured mounts are equally decorative and exciting. Original Japanese prints, and especially those that are valuable, should always be framed under glass and hung away from direct light (including spotlamps) as colours can easily fade, and the scroll fabric is likely to deteriorate.

Ikebana

The Japanese art of flower arrangement *ikebana* is very different from any other but its influence has been so pervasive that flower arranging is now seriously recognized as an art form. In *ikebana* the use of unusually shaped pieces of drift-wood, peeled branches *mitsumata*, rocks and polished pebbles *mihama koishi*, combined with different ways of fixing and positioning according to Buddhist principles gives rise to a symbolic language and gratifies a desire to be at one with nature.

As opposed to Western flower arrangement where the perfection, colour and type of bloom is all important, *ikebana* is concerned more with the flowing quality of the lines. The trilogy of Heaven, Man and Earth are represented by these lines. The central line symbolizes Heaven and rises highest; Man is symbolized by lateral lines placed in front of the centre line while Earth is represented by the shortest stems in front.

Full blooms are rarely incorporated since their perfection soon fades and in the philosophy of *ikebana* symbolize the past, death and dissolution. Young shoots and buds are preferred, symbolizing as they do birth, creation and future promise, and are considered to detract less from the main structural stem and branch lines. This form of artistic expression is very imitable, and for relatively little outlay, will add authenticity and colour to your Japanese-style interior.

This charming Ikebana arrangement for summer combines vine leaves with campanula in a simple pottery container.

Tatami mats

The Japanese were designing with a grid system long before architect, Le Corbusier, used his Modulor. The traditional measurements of *tatami* mats, 90 cm by 180 cm (3 ft by 6 ft), served the purpose very well. It was, therefore, common practice to refer to the size of a room as being an eight- or six-mat room. The subdivisions of walls and windows, including the measurements of the wooden section of *shoji* screens were all made to correspond to *tatami* dimensions. This imposed a regular, linear pattern and a system of proportion which gave a pleasing visual link to the whole interior. The effect has a spiritual beauty and order.

Tatami mats of finely woven sea-grass were once considered a relatively inexpensive floorcovering, but this is no longer the case, and only the better off Japanese can now afford them. The black tape used to bind the edges is sometimes replaced by coloured brocade on more luxurious mats. *Tatami* also make an excellent

New-style one-room living can take place in the tiniest space

platform covering for relaxation areas – as seen here in the bedroom and the dining/living room, overleaf. These panels of compressed rice straw come in slightly different sizes; the traditional mat being 95.25 cm (37½ in) square by 5 cm (2½ in) deep and the larger size 95.25 cm (37½ in) x 120 cm (47½ in) x 5 cm (2½ in).

Futons

In a typical Japanese home where space is at a premium, bedrooms often have to be shared – a potentially difficult arrangement made possible by the use of bedrolls *(futons)*. The Japanese have used *futons* for sleeping on for over 4,000 years; a traditionally made futon consists of three layers of pure cotton wadding inserted through a central opening in the cotton cover; the corners are then stuffed with extra wadding to keep their shape. The central seam is closed by

Shoji screens

Above: *Versatile futons can either be folded and stored in cupboards or act as daytime seating.* **Right:** *Beautifully laid floorboards are highly favoured.*

handstitching and is considered by futon experts to be a stronger finishing seam than that of the base or side edges. It is the central seaming and the firm stuffed corners that are the hallmarks of the genuine futon. There are many Western versions which are not made to these traditional specifications and consequently are less likely to wear as well.

Traditional futons are always 100 per cent cotton and their comfort is calculated by the number of layers; each layer being approximately, 2.5 cm (1 in) thick. A three-layer futon can vary from between 6 cm 7.5 cm (2½ in-3 in) thick, depending on the manufacturer. This seems adequate for most people, but those used to sleeping on sprung mattresses may take around a week to get used to

it. On the other hand, a three-layer futon is relatively easy to roll up and arrange into daytime seating. For more comfortable sleeping a six-layer futon is far superior, but it needs at least two people to roll it up and store in a cupboard (with sliding doors). A slightly costlier compromise is to invest in two, three-layer futons; this would undoubtedly save time and be much easier to manage for those involved in daily seating conversion.

However, in time all pure cotton fillings have a tendency to 'compact' and some futons can feel quite hard, even developing mildew after as little as six months' use. This could well be the result of not airing the futon regularly after sleeping. You sweat over a pint per night into the mattress, and if the bedroom is cold or even slightly damp, it is essential to air your futon two or three times a week — hanging them over a chair, or balcony on a sunny day. Futon bases of slatted wood, allowing air flow, greatly

alleviate the problem. Some of the new-style futons are said to 'compact' less when filled with a mixture of polyester, wool and/or coconut fibre — this also improves the air flow.

While Japanese futons are rolled out of sight when not in use, Western versions are expected to work much harder — doubling as daytime seating when space is tight. Quite a number of slatted bases now exist for this purpose but for easy, daily conversion you should check that your base is hinged and is as light as possible. Most firms selling futons also offer a choice of removable cotton covers, cushions, bedding and furniture in Japanese style. Small, low display tables and upright straight backed *Gaijin* chairs are all important components of what is essentially the Euro Japanese style. A further innovation for one-room living is a blanket chest in which your bedding is stored by day while disguised as an elegant sideboard.

Another essential ingredient of Japanese-style living is the screen, which is used to redefine living space. *Shoji* screens do just this, but they can also do wonders for windows that are overlooked or have a dismal view. *Shoji* papers are delicately watermarked and can be wonderfully flattering light diffusers. Even with the greatest of care, paper surfaces may become damaged but individual sections can easily be replaced with *shoji* paper that can be bought by the roll from specialist suppliers. The panels of the screen hinge together and each section is made up of 28 cm (11 in) squares in two standard panel sizes; six squares by two or eight squares by two. The frames, shown in the picture here, are in black stained pine, but a natural finish is also available from specialist furnishing shops. Used as free-standing room dividers the traditional Shoji screens are vulnerable to the slightest knock, so it may be more practical to have the panels installed professionally, as seen in the living room opposite, using special sliding door fixings.

Lacquer

It would be impossible to describe here the numerous types and techniques used in lacquer work. Traditional lacquer is still one of the most time-consuming crafts in existence — as many as forty coats of resin may be applied to a single piece and prices are correspondingly high. But today, industry employs various man-made lacquer substitutes and the finished products are reasonably priced and harder wearing. Widely available in tableware and small objects such as make-up boxes and small chests of drawers these accessories can add exquisite touches of brilliant colour and rich pattern to otherwise plain surroundings.

Textiles

Brocades in three different patterns were often used to frame the edges of scroll paintings *emaki*, and brocade patchwork quilts are still a very highly prieed possession. Bold, handblocked printed fabrics feature largely in the brightly coloured cotton squares *furoshiki* that every Japanese uses for carrying packed lunches, books, sewing and knitting things, for example. There is also the traditional folk-weave cloth — *kasuri* — which resembles a small-scale ikat weave — usually in dark colours. It epitomizes Japanese style, generally being used for utility clothing — notably that of fishermen.

One way to discover old and, possibly, original Japanese fabrics is to hunt round old clothes shops. Antique kimonos that are too fragile to wear can be transformed into wonderful wall decorations by simply slotting a bamboo pole through the sleeves, approximately 5 cm (2½ in) in diameter by 182 cm (6 ft) long. To hang: wind lengths of nylon thread (fisherman's line) round the ends of the pole and attach these to wall-fixed eye hooks.

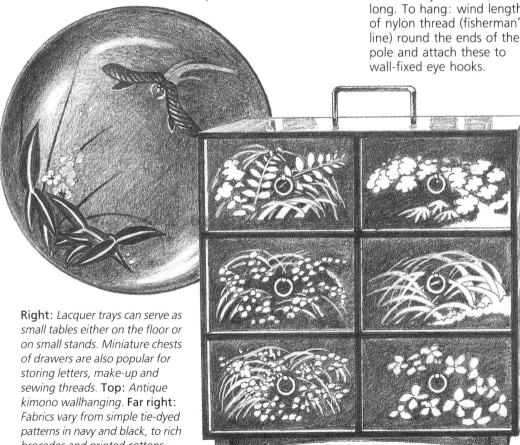

Right: *Lacquer trays can serve as small tables either on the floor or on small stands. Miniature chests of drawers are also popular for storing letters, make-up and sewing threads.* **Top:** *Antique kimono wallhanging.* **Far right:** *Fabrics vary from simple tie-dyed patterns in navy and black, to rich brocades and printed cottons.*

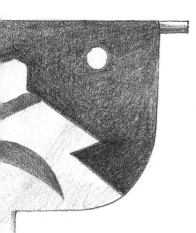

Gardens

If you have a small garden or can adapt a small area, as seen from your windows, you can cultivate a Japanese-style garden to complete the effect.

Gardening reached Japan from China and, as with *ikebana*, the rules are formalized to illustrate a philosophical point. Most Japanese gardens are extremely small, often measuring no more than one or two square metres, the contents being little more than a single tree, two or three bushes and a large stone. The gravel is carefully raked, and enclosing it all will be a high boarded fence. Yet the total effect seen from the inside of a room looking out is one of space, and the feeling of closeness with the garden (almost coming inside the house) is further emphasized by the sliding windows and shutters.

Bonsai

The art of *bonsai* – '*bon*' meaning pot and '*sai*' tree, is also thought to have come to Japan from China. Some liken it to Western topiary as both crafts demand much patience and skill. In Japan *bonsai* are usually left outside on a verandah, and are occasionally brought in for a short time before being returned outdoors.

It is possible to grow your own *bonsai* from seed but it is easier to start with one already established at a specialist nursery. *Bonsai* trees can also grow quite naturally in rock crevices on exposed cliffs for example – so it is not an entirely unnatural form. Success lies in choosing an example where the miniaturization is kept accurately in scale; leaves and fruit should be suitably small in comparison with the trunk. A common failing is that leaves are barely less than natural size so the effect is completely lost. Because the trees are not shaped by genetic changes only branch and leaf size can be made smaller- not the fruit and flowers.

Great attention has to be paid to regular pruning, lighting and temperature in the first years. The choice of container is also important; these are mostly of pottery with unglazed interiors and in subdued colours so as not to detract from the tree. Shapes are generally shallow except for 'cascade' style *bonsai* where a deeper pot is used.

All pots must have large drainage holes and for something as special as *bonsai*, it might be worth your while seeking the help of a local craft potter.

Rules for the appearance of *bonsai* pots can be summed up approximately as follows: the height of a shallow pot should not be less than the width of the tree trunk; the diameter of the pot should not be less than a third of the (visible) height of the tree. Too small pots will make a tree look cramped, whereas too large pots will swamp it.

A bonsai tree of a pleasing shape and perfect proportions. Choose containers in subdued colours and simple shapes.

MODERNIST

The 1920s saw the culmination of the revolution in art, architecture and design in Europe which finally overthrew 400 years of artistic tradition established in the Renaissance. Known, as the Modern Movement, it had its roots in the ninteenth century and the struggles of ardent social and artistic reformers to reconcile men and machines, art and industry.

In the early 1920s two separate groups of men and women, one in Weimar in Germany, the other in Paris, were dedicated to designing in a manner appropriate to the new, functional, machine-based age, as if no other styles had preceded them. The two groups produced work which was astonishingly similar in style. Tubular steel-framed furniture, glass-topped tables, uncompromising geometric forms, and buildings whose interiors and exteriors were remarkable for their absence of ornament. Stark industrial shapes and materials burst upon a public immersed in the excesses of Art Déco and Jacobean Revival and it was immediately dubbed 'Modernist'.

It says a great deal for those pioneers, who had little contact with each other at the time, that many of the things they made two generations ago have the fresh look of contemporary designs today.

An ardent enthusiast of the style is designer/shopkeeper Joseph, whose calm, austere Modernist flat is filled with classical designs by many of the original members of the *Union des Artistes Modernes* (founded in Paris in 1930, and greatly inspired by Le Corbusier).

In Paris, the clientele tended to be rich and famous; whereas at the Weimar Bauhaus, the school where painters, sculptors, craftsmen, architects and designers all worked together under the inspired direction of Walter Gropius, the clients were from industry, eager to use this new, creative energy.

Of the two groups, the Bauhaus has had by far the greatest influence. It had a highly developed philosophy which was largely taken to America after 1933 when the National Socialists had closed down the school and many pupils and masters fled the country as political refugees.

One of the widest influences of its philosophy can be seen in any fitted kitchen today. Standardization of storage units for mass production was first developed at the Bauhaus by Marcel Breuer in the 1920s.

Putting on the style

It may look easy – this is all part of the effect – but before leaping into Modernism one should be aware that the components need to be put together with much thought and care, and with respect to the correct apportioning of shape and space. While.the dangers are that the style can easily become impersonal and dull, its delights, on the other hand, are that it can provide the most peaceful and cerebral background to a hectic city lifestyle. It should make you tidy too! Being a chic city look, it is, of course, at its best in a modern apartment block.

Obviously the ideal way to plan the Modernist style is first to get rid of anything that could possibly hint at a previous order of things, as Eva Jiricna has been able to do here in Joseph's central London apartment. It is stripped of everything bar the decorative effects of daylight and the neutral texture and colour of the walls and floor.

To prevent the greyish oatmeal of the walls from giving an overall bland effect, they have been painted with a special outdoor paint. This is a mixture of fibre, paint and adhesive, and gives a fine crunchy texture which holds the light. Here it has been sprayed on to the walls, a technique which calls for a certain amount of skill to get the right density.

Light reflecting off any type of evenly-textured wall covering adds richness and depth to the overall effect. It would be quite in keeping with the spirit of the times to cover your walls with either a fabric, like hessian or straw cloth, or a paper with a simulated woven surface. The workshop at the Bauhaus

designed wallpapers with single coloured textures and simple slub weaves which were adopted by industry. Some of the memorable walls of the period must have been the matched parchment panels or the golden split straws glued vertically side by side, as devised by Jean Michel Frank for his rich Parisian clients. Such effects can be bought by the roll nowadays from almost all wallpaper stores. The keynote is austerity, with single-colour neutral walls, flush from floor to ceiling.

Looking outwards

Glass was a tremendously exciting material for the pioneers of Modernism. In Paris, Pierre Charreau designed the Maison de Verre (1928-31) with its glass brick walls and steel columns. The

development of new load-bearing techniques which took all the weight of a building from the walls meant that architects could use glass where it had never been used before. As light now flooded the interior, so the new strikingly simple shapes of furniture could be seen like pieces of sculpture. In keeping with the style, their window treatments were spare and uncluttered. Here, in Joseph's apartment, the finest sliver-thin Venetian blinds shut out a dreary city-scape whilst allowing the light to filter through. And, for night time, trim-looking Roman blinds provide privacy.

Such was the excitement with plate-glass, with its large greenish-tinged sheets of a smooth uniform quality, that it was used in the 1920s for the first time in any quantity for table tops. The thick

plate-glass and steel-framed table, shown overleaf, is one of Le Corbusier's classic designs. At the same time, Marcel Breuer of the Bauhaus was working on designs like the nest of tables below. The originals, with chromed steel frames and lacquered wood tops in different colours have been copied and reworked so many times (and often with glass tops), that you can find their counterparts in many furniture shops today.

Below left: *The clean uncluttered lines of Roman blinds are ideal for Modernist windows. Fabrics with small all-over patterns or plain colours are best for their softly pleated folds.* **Below:** *Copies of Marcel Breuer's nest of four tables (1926) fit happily into today's modern interiors.*

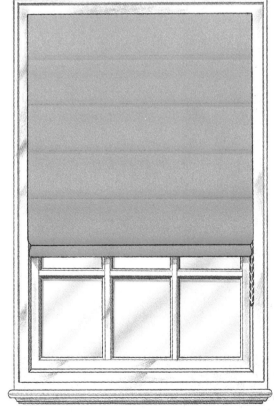

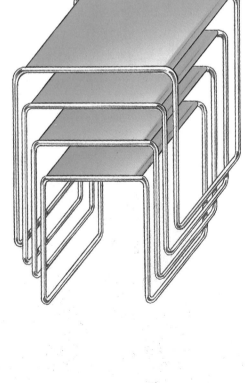

Lighting up

With so many shiny surfaces, lighting must be carefully thought out so that the reflections do not dazzle. The extravagent Fortuny lamp, shown overleaf, with its reflector dish turned to the wall provides indirect light with minimal dazzle. Recessed spot lights also give good background lighting, and are easily controlled with dimmer switches.

Students at the Bauhaus turned out some stunning light fittings which are again widely copied. Most good lighting departments offer a range of Bauhaus-type lamps — an essential ingredient of the style.

Left: A selection of light fittings designed by the Bauhaus (1920s) and present-day Habitat.
Below: A 1930s-style print 'Exposition de Meubles Contemporains Français' by Athena. Bottom: Square-shaped sofa upholstered in a plain-textured fabric.

Comfort

Despite the 'bare bones' look of so much metal tubing, comfort is a considerable factor and this large, luxuriously squashy sofa covered in black hide is typical of the boxy shapes of Modernist upholstered furniture. Slimmer, sleeker, contemporary versions of the cube-style sofas which originated at this time, are readily available from better furniture stores.

Display

Having the right background for your Modernist furniture is just as important as choosing the pieces themselves. Walls, like floors and windows, require the least fussy treatment to give the effect of smooth, uninterrupted lines and the maximum feeling of space.

A fairly large, single picture or print displayed on one wall, as in the picture overleaf, provides an attractive focal point, and suits the Modernist style much better than massed groups of smaller pictures or other collectables, which would give an eclectic look.

The cost of the picture shown, of Celia Birtwell by David Hockney, may well be too high for most of us, but the principle behind the choosing, framing and placing is important. Notice how the subject and treatment complement the entire room.

There are several print companies who produce excellent Thirties-style prints, and providing they are simply framed with lots of space around them, they will add colour and character to your Modernist interior.

Good design does not date

Looking towards the other end of Joseph's apartment, you can see the dining area, and here it is interesting to note that even though these contemporary chairs, table and rugs were first produced about 60 years ago, they have, today, a freshness of line – and a timelessness! The reason Eva Jiriĉna, who decorated Joseph's flat, chose these pieces of furniture is because she believes as 'first generation modern designs' they are still the best: very few people making modern furniture today do it with such dedication and attention to detail. 'God is in the detail',

extolled Mies van der Rohe (the last director of the Bauhaus) whose Barcelona suite of chromed steel and leather (1929) is still lovingly reproduced and is a best seller, to the most sophisticated, design-conscious people.

These reproductions are perfect for the most ardent Modernist. Constructed from uniform factory-made components, albeit of the highest quality and finished by hand, they can be produced today exactly as they originally were with their own vitality and perfection of form. These pieces of furniture can be expensive, but because the quality is

superb, they age with dignity. International design companies with offices in all the major cities make and sell this kind of furniture. And the people who buy are those who are aware of our twentieth-century design heritage.

Making it affordable

Over the past ten years or so, much cheaper versions of this furniture have begun to appear in the High Street. Design-conscious shops like Habitat have pioneered the trend. This clever copy of Marcel Breuer's Wassily chair (1925) – the first bent steel-

Above: *Light and space enhance the pure sculptural qualities of modernist furniture.*
Right: *A Bauhaus solution to a baby's cradle.*

tube chair ever made (at the time, Breuer had been contemplating the lightness and strength of a bicycle frame) – is sold by Habitat for less than half the price of the variation sold by Form International, but then the price is reflected in the quality of chrome and leather. Nevertheless, these mid-priced variations put such designs within the reach of many more people interested in the Modernist style.

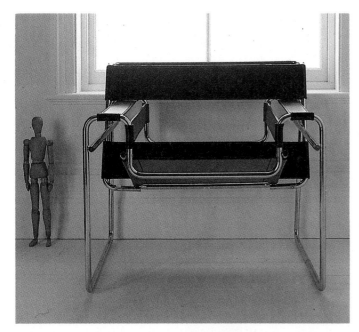

have as much fun with them as any Bauhaus student might have had wrestling with colour and form exercises.

Space-age look

Joseph's kitchen shows the same obsessive attention to detail as the rest of his apartment. The accoutrements are made from stainless steel; an excellent material which suits the Modernist ideal. The effect is of pure machine aesthetic with a spare, space-age look. Notice also the clean lines of the tiled floor. Here, other flooring such as wood or cork would simply not be in style. On the other hand, as these tiles are relatively expensive, you could achieve a similar effect with smart vinyl tiles.

An important finishing touch, however, is the black grouting to sharpen the edges of the white tiles. This produces a grid pattern that suggests an interesting illusion of space, within a small area. The whole Modernist effect is enlivened by a simple bunch of colourful anemonies.

Top: A modern copy of a Marcel Breuer design for a tubular chair (1928). **Below:** Exact spacing makes ordinary utensils aesthetically pleasing.

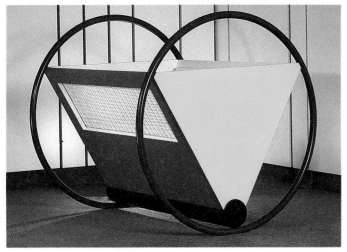

Colour and form

The sombre colours of the Eileen Gray carpet, highlighted with flashes of white, show a perfection and restraint which is both very French and modern-day Minimalist. At the Bauhaus, however, it was usual to experiment with much more colour. There students were encouraged to explore the possibilities of the three primaries, red, yellow and blue, in relation to the forms of the circle, triangle and square. This cradle, designed in 1922 by Peter Keler, was developed from an exercise given by Walter Gropius to his students, and a modern version is available today.

Enthusiasts decorating on a low budget (and for whom even a High Street look-alike is too expensive) might be inspired to innovate by the simplicity of this cradle. Metal framed chairs and tables can often be found in second-hand shops, usually in need of re-chroming (which is expensive) or re-covering. These can easily be given a new lease of life by stripping and redecorating with a primary palette. For storage, you might look for square wooden wine boxes. These can be sanded down, colour-stained and varnished, before screwing them to the wall or, alternatively, using them as floor units or tables. You can

Pattern

A very decorative and yet practical device much used in the 1920s and 1930s was the hinged screen. Eileen Gray (the Irish designer whose lacquer screens of this period are now collectors' pieces), also designed the rugs and wood-framed side chairs in Joseph's apartment, of which these are modern copies. The rug designs in particular set the fashion for abstract patterned rugs which was to last until the late 1930s. These were often the only element of pattern in a room. Really striking modern rugs with much the same spirit are now being recreated. Rug-maker Helen Yardly, whose rugs like this are gallery pieces, says she's making them 'to go with all the Mies van der Rohe type furniture which is in fashion again.' The

wheel is turning full circle.

Using the three primary colours, and the three basic shapes, the square, circle, and triangle, students at the Bauhaus created some brilliantly colourful and highly distinctive geometric patterns for textiles and ceramics. This furnishing fabric, called 'Bauhaus', is produced by Liberty, London, and has been one of their most popular fabrics for ten years or more. Based on a tapestry woven in 1927 at the Bauhaus, it must have appeared extreme and daring 60 years ago. So much so, that the National Socialists who closed down the school in 1933 said such designs were 'abnormal and un-German'. The same charge was levelled against the crudely colourful pottery known as Weimar Ceramics,

Left to right: Helen Yardley's hand-tufted rug is a brilliant evocation of 1930s abstract pattern. Hand-knotted rug designed at the Bauhaus (1924). Liberty's 'Bauhaus' printed furnishing fabric.

which was also produced in Germany up to 1933 and was directly influenced by the Bauhaus.

For many people, this colourful tableware typifies 1930s design. In England its echo can be found in pottery by Doulton, Clarice Cliff, Shelley and others. All are now collectors' pieces, but can still be bought at quite reasonable prices. Nothing prevents a Modernist interior from becoming too selfconsciously stark more than a collection of these cheerful pieces of pottery.

Shape and ornament

Modernist artefacts in metal, ceramic and glass were, as you might expect, simple yet shapely with no extraneous ornament. Through Joseph's elegant metal mesh screen you can glimpse a round glass bowl with lilies in it. This simple outline, like that of the jet black glass jar on the floor, is important to the Modernist look. Fussy little vases, or indeed, anything fussy is 'out' and a single sweeping, shapely statement is 'in'. That goes for flowers too. Photographs of the period almost always show big vases with just one kind of flower in them; yellow daisies, scarlet gladioli, bunches of blossom, large chrysanthemums, and most highly favoured of all, the Madonna or Arum lilies.

Buying the best

The single most widely-recognized product from this period is undoubtely the metal-framed furniture. The impact of the Bauhaus and Le Corbusier on the mass market has meant that no canteen or club house has been without its share of stacking metal chairs. However, many people thought them too institutional for their homes. Now that such attractive copies are available, these classic designs are being reintroduced into contemporary Modernist homes with great style and flair. Habitat's Bauhaus side chair and armchair are reasonably priced, in comparison to Joseph's beautiful Mallet Steven's dining chairs, which would cost a great deal more.

If you are rich, and you like perfection, then you should consider Mies van der Rohe's Barcelona (1929) collection of two chairs, table, stool and day bed. The most famous piece is the chair (below). The balance and proportions of this design are faultless, as are the materials with which is made – thick, flat, chromed steel for the frame and deep cushions covered in hide. Sit on one of these pieces and you'll be spoiled for ever for anything less! For most people, this would be a real investment, but then, no serious modernist interior would be complete without a contribution from Mies van der Rohe, a genius architect/designer, and the last Director of the Bauhaus.

Above: *Bold, beautiful pottery from Weimer ceramics (1933) epitomizes the Bauhaus ideal. Its hard-edged geometric pattern is softened by a spray technique unique to this period. From Tilman Buddensieg's collection shown at the Victorian and Albert Museum, London, 1986.*
Right: *Modern vases currently available from Heals, London.*

Modernist comfort plus. Mies van der Rohe's Barcelona chair with its chromed steel frame and hide cushions.

Fortunately both glass and ceramic vases, which can be used either sculpturally or for holding flowers, are the height of contemporary fashion, and would add a flavour of the style. They can be found in High Street home-furnishing shops at very competitive prices. Some of the 'spatter-and-crackle' glazed modern pottery jars make attractive show pieces and are not too expensive.

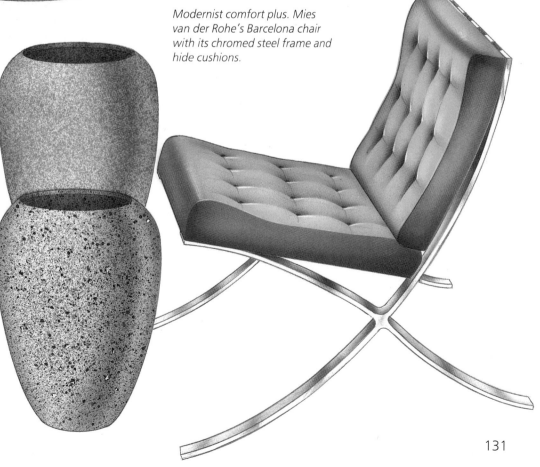

ART DECO

The years between the end of World War I (1918) and the Depression (1929) saw the most remarkable surge of creative energy in the decorative arts in France. Unlike England, where arts and literature reverted to a very traditional style (Liberty's mock-Tudor building is London's great monument to this period), France was positively encouraged by the state in the form of the Ministry of Arts to re-establish its reputation in the *beâux arts*, but in a contemporary style. The *nouveau riche* were keen to spend and to invest their wealth, and there was no shortage of clients for the cabinet makers, potters, weavers, metal- and glass-workers whose combined creative skills produced this outburst of cultural vitality. The 1925 Paris *Exposition Internationale des Arts Décoratifs et Industriels Modernes* established the Art Déco style.

As this was an international exhibition, each country displayed its own form of Art Déco. England triumphed especially in pottery with designers like Susy Cooper and Clarice Cliff whose plaque overleaf epitomizes Déco. But it was a mite-sized contribution compared to what was happening in France. Art Déco was applied to all forms of design from clothes, (always regarded by the French as an important branch of the decorative arts) to bathrooms, a great novelty in the 1920s.

The characteristic swags of highly stylized flower clusters, with their flattened geometric faces and the attenuated, rounded forms of Neo-classical figures, were well established before the war. As were the colours: rich reds, blues, purples, pinks and chrome yellows, inspired by the Russian ballet which had taken Paris by storm in 1909.

The craftsmen who survived the terrible years of war had traditional skills and the influences of the Directoire and Consulate periods are quite discernable, especially among the more important furniture designers. This marvellous chaise longue is a superb example of the way in which French designers of the period interpreted their history.

Assembling the style

One of the great features of this period was the art of the interior designer. Several large French department stores had their own ateliers working under the direction of distinguished designers like Paul Follot, for example, at Pomone (part of Bon Marché), who was also a lecturer in the government-run school of decorative art. Here clients could commission a total decorative scheme, which might include anything from specially printed textiles to individually-made chairs, rugs and vases. The distinction between fine and applied art began to merge, artists had become interior decorators and vice versa. Even the great cabinet-maker Emile-Jacques Ruhlmann was involved in the origination of interior designs for his wealthy clients. Working in the tradition of eighteenth-century cabinet-

makers, but in a more simple, streamlined style, Ruhlmann created furniture whose shapes and finishes were to become legendary. Few could copy exactly his exquisite workmanship in the luxurious rare materials he used; beautifully grained woods like burr-walnut or macassar ebony, lovingly inlaid with shagreen, ivory, lizard skin or tortoiseshell. This vignette of a Ruhlmann interior of about 1925 shows several characteristics of high Art Déco; the suggestion of rich colours, the tassled cushions, the edges of the curved divan and cushions piped in a contrasting colour, the stylized blossom painted on the walls and the simple shape of the low, round table, the edges of which would probably have been banded with ivory.

Besides designing wonderful pieces of furniture in unusual woods, like the

Ruhlmann cabinet (now in the Brighton Museum, Sussex, England) the *ensemblier* would direct his designers to create splendid rugs and fabrics for both walls and curtains. This rug, also from Brighton Museum came from the atelier run by Poiret Martine. Probably designed by about 1920, the plum, pink, green and yellow flowers tend to verge on the folksy. These rugs are now collectors' pieces, like the rug (on the previous page) in the Paris apartment of designer Emmanuelle Khan. They are hand knotted, so if you are sold on the idea of having one (and they would make excellent focal points in any sitting room, or bedroom) you could make up your own design and hook it in turkey rug wool. *Ensembliers* liked to put them on either a smooth parquet floor or on top of a neutral coloured wall-to-wall carpet.

Finding furniture

If you look carefully there are still lots of Déco-ish pieces of furniture around in England. Most of it was made in the 1930s, which was when the French style began to have a wider influence. A lot of it is big, and in terms of sheer quality it is good value, especially if you think of it in contrast to laminated fibreboard, which is what constitutes so much modern furniture and which has no historic status or second-hand value. If your house or flat pre-dates the 1930s, you might consider a Déco scheme and experiment with one or two bigger pieces of furniture. The beautiful sweeping curves of the chaise longue are now being incorporated into modern sofas and these designs are worth tracking down for their sheer style. Old sofas bought as auction can seem exciting, but they can have all sorts of

Artist Raoul Dufy's brilliant prints designed for Bianchini.

already subjected to the ruthless geometry that was to become so popular as decoration in the 1930s, and is more often than not banded with Art Déco.

Art Déco

The essence of the style is appropriately summed up in this bronze medallion

Above and below: *The exhibition medal and Dunand's vases show contrasting decorative and classical aspects of the period.*

designed by P. Turin and struck especially for the 1925 Paris exhibition. All the main features are here. The flowers, the exaggerated limbs and drapery of the young girl are very classical in inspiration, while the clouds are faintly Chinese. A few craftsmen like Jean Dunand, with his superb vases in hammered metal, with damascened patterns in gold and silver, were to explore the simplicity which was to come – and yet he was also completely at home in the highly decorative world of the early 1920s. The shapes he used were as an essential part of French interior as, for example, the frosted glass vase in the Khan's apartment. While original Dunand vases are now fabulously expensive, there are available several modern pottery versions that cost a few pounds and evoke a wonderful feeling of Art Déco style.

hidden costs attached to them: refurbishing and restoring is an expensive undertaking. If you do decide to reupholster an old sofa, velvet or some sort of velour would be appropriate, and of course, you should have lots of cushions.

There were many different sources of inspiration behind the essentially decorative nature of this period. One was China, as can be seen in the Khan's sunlit rug on page 132. The formalized landscape shapes correspond closely, albeit on a much larger scale, to the carefully shaded colours of Chinese silk embroidery. Another was African art, which had already been discovered by the Cubists. The artist Raoul Dufy, who in the 1920s was far better known for his avant-garde textile designs than his scenes of society life, worked first for Paul Poiret, the couturier, who also owned 'L'Atelier Martine', an atelier for interior decoration. Before the war, he employed Dufy to design fabrics for both dresses and furnishings. Later Dufy went to Bianchini et Ferier where he produced stunning designs like *La Jungle* with its elephant and leopard motifs. There is no hint here of the severe, abstract geometric style which was so soon to replace many figurative and floral themes. But in *Les Moissonneurs*, another Dufy design, the figures of the harvester and his horse are

Far left: *High Art Déco interior designed by J. Ruhlman, 1925.*
Left: *Richly decorative rugs typical of those produced at the Atelier Martine before 1925.*

Be bold with backgrounds

In the 1920s the profusion of paintings which had been such a characteristic feature of the interiors of the generation before was swept away. In vogue were bold, decorative schemes such as murals or large painted panels which could be taken in at one glance. Paul Poiret's Atélier Martine favoured flower and foliage themes; in 1927, for instance, a private dining room on the prestigious liner *Île-de-France* had fantastic marquetry walls decorated with lush tropical foliage. A few years earlier a Poiret-Martine scheme for a bedroom with dark-toned walls displayed a windblown, blossom-covered tree in light colours with flowers scattered on to a second wall and over the ceiling. This inspired a well-known London Art Déco dealer to copy the idea for his London flat, which you can see here. If you have a large expanse of bare wall, this is a relatively inexpensive way to achieve the Déco feel. Most libraries should have two or three reference books covering this period. Choose a suitable design, copy it on to tracing paper and square it up to scale on the wall. Small test pots of emulsion are useful for experimenting to get the right colours. For a design similar to this, with repeated flower motifs, you could cut half a dozen simple blossom shapes out of dense foam sponge and use them as printing blocks.

Other forms of introducing background decoration included exquisite lacquered screens. Jean Dunand, also a metal worker, executed some of the finest pieces and this gleaming, gilded panel with

the outstretched horse's head, now in a private English collection, is typical not only of his versatility, a trademark of so many designers in this era, but also of the classical references in so much of what they did. The horse could have just stepped down from the Parthenon save for the lines being a little too smooth and rounded, and it also has a more mannered and elongated look.

Select sculpture

In addition to the fine artistry of Dunand, many other sculptural objects abounded. The most famous were bronze

Above: *A free-style mural based on a design by Poiret's Atelier Martine.* **Below:** *Gold satin and bronze of high French Art Déco.*

and ivory figures of women, often based on the Greek goddess Diana, the Huntress. They featured in a variety of different guises, from lamp-stands to exquisitely modelled leaping or dancing female forms. For a wider market, pottery and porcelain manufacturers made figures of bears, dogs and doves, again all sharing simple, smooth lines that can be seen in the dog and the scarlet polar bear. The bronze family grouping here is a beautifully expressive piece, and very much bridges the divide between Déco and modern sculpture. These opulent gold satin chairs are in themselves monuments to the luxury of the period, with the carved swag decoration on the sides and stylized leaf decoration on the front frame. Happily, manufacturers are catching on to the fact that not all people want to sit in upholstered boxes and these subtle curved shapes are making a comeback. Look out for the pretty *bergère* style armchairs and sofas with shell-shaped backs.

Opalescent glassware

No discussion of this period would be complete without reference to René Lalique and his glass. An exceptional craftsman, who had achieved fame as a jeweller in the early 1900s René Lalique saw clearly the possibilities of combining old craftsmanship with modern machine technology. His vases, bowls and lights, boxes, clocks and plates all mirrored the changes and novelties of the age. Having worked with precious stones as a jeweller, he developed techniques in the actual making of the glass

which made it quite jewel-like both in colour and density. He would then ornament the surface in such a way as to make the decoration look carved. Natural forms like birds, flowers and figures all formed recurrent motifs. The time to collect Lalique was 20 years ago, but if you really like Déco, it's worth trying to get at least one authentic piece. As well as being a pleasure to own it will never lose its value (from £300 upwards, depending on the design.) Lalique's appeal is such that there are one or two galleries in every international city that deal in his work.

Lalique's success naturally meant that there were many imitators of his style. In England, Joblings brought out a range of frosted glass novelties which they called Opalique — a clever name, considering they were copying Lalique's milky blue opalescent glass! Such glassware is typical of its time,

and is the kind of thing that can still be found on market stalls and in secondhand shops at affordable prices.

Top: *A beautifully carved and gilded horse's head by Jean Dunand.* **Below:** *A René Lalique vase in opalescent glass.*

Pottery

Because Art Déco, in its purest form, was the product of superb craftsmanship, original pieces are likely to be expensive and relatively rare. However, since it was such a decorative style, it was easy to copy and in England it was the pottery designers who first embraced the style, exploiting it with flair and originality. The name that first comes to mind is one of the most innovative potters of the period, Clarice Cliff. While a great many English designers languished in a sort of Tudor gloom, she and a handful of other potters were remarkable for injecting colour and ingenuity, into their designs. This Clarice Cliff teapot is a fascinating example of high Art Déco. The flat flower and spiral motifs in yellow, bright orange and green, on a Modernistic shape display the individual components. Various angular shapes and geometric patterns which are often included in Déco really have their roots in cubism and the Bauhaus.

The firm Carter, Stabler and Adams, also known as Poole Pottery, were one of the few firms attempting to show

English Art Déco pottery is an unmistakable hybrid combining the rich colours of the Russian Ballet, formalized clusters of flowers and leaf swags with the restraining influence of modernism. This typical selection shows a comparatively modest teapot and plaque in dazzling jazz-age colours, by Clarice Cliff. And the refined matt pink jar with plum tones, turquoise lustre and gilded leaves, is by Susie Cooper.

contemporary designs at the 1925 Paris exhibition. Their wares, like those of Susie Cooper, really caught the colourful, light and spontaneous spirit of the time. This Susie Cooper vase, now in the Victoria & Albert Museum, London shows the figure of a fawn, a recurrent motif in French work. Fortunately there is still available a lot of pottery of this period. Some of it is rather highly priced, but do not be put off – individual items with characteristic decoration can be picked up fairly cheaply, and the sort of vigorous freehand decoration which went into this work makes each piece an object of art in minature.

Metalwork

An art which is almost lost to us today, but which was an important feature of the time is that of the metal worker. One of the most celebrated craftsmen, Edgar Brandt, was able to produce wonderful designs in copper, iron, brass and other metals; his gates, radiator cases, tables, chairs and screens seemed like large scale pieces of jewellery. Replicas of his famous *Cigognes d'Alsace* (1923) in wrought-iron and bronze were installed in the lifts in Selfridges, London. Quite apart from the fact that all this delicacy of detail had been achieved in such a tough material, the panels tell us a great deal about Art Déco and the debt it owed especially to Chinese and Japanese art, as any one can see who has visited the Toshiba Gallery of Japanese art, at the Victoria and Albert Museum, London. The spirals, the soft padded looking clouds and the sun-burst suggested behind the octagon of flying birds are a good starting point for any decorative scheme, for choosing fabrics or stencilling a border on a wall, perhaps. Some of these panels are now

on display in Brighton Museum, Sussex, which also houses a delightful collection of decorative art from the 1920s and 1930s and should not be missed by anyone wanting further to explore the possibilities of this period.

Light fantastic

While the sort of skills required to make a Dunand screen or Brandt panel do not exist anymore, among the most widely copied objects are light fittings. The more geometric, Modernist wall lights have been in fashion for five or six years now, but if you want to make a statement that is part sculptural, part Art Déco, go for one of the 'lady' lights. A few years ago these lady lights were viewed with horror and disdain and were unbelieveably cheap: nowadays, the original Déco lamps are expensive. Some contempory copies are very good, like this Diana lamp made in resin and brass. Big bowl shades for ceiling fittings, with mottled or marble finishes were made in huge quantities, and considering what they cost to hand-make today, they are reasonably priced.

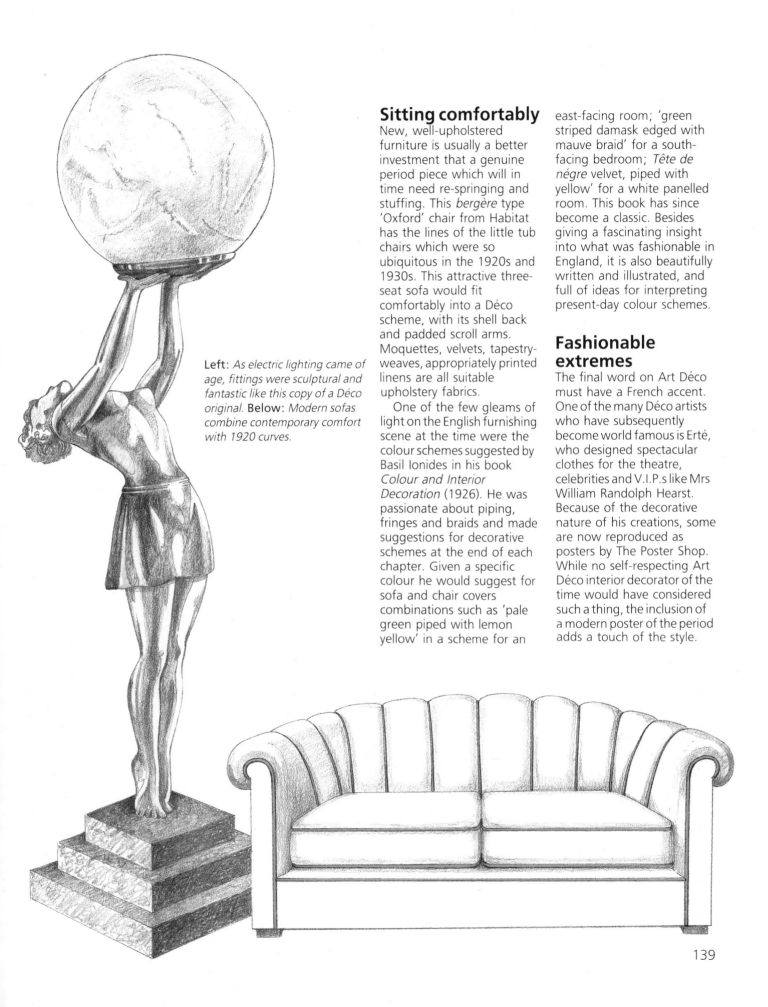

Left: *As electric lighting came of age, fittings were sculptural and fantastic like this copy of a Déco original.* Below: *Modern sofas combine contemporary comfort with 1920 curves.*

Sitting comfortably

New, well-upholstered furniture is usually a better investment that a genuine period piece which will in time need re-springing and stuffing. This *bergère* type 'Oxford' chair from Habitat has the lines of the little tub chairs which were so ubiquitous in the 1920s and 1930s. This attractive three-seat sofa would fit comfortably into a Déco scheme, with its shell back and padded scroll arms. Moquettes, velvets, tapestry-weaves, appropriately printed linens are all suitable upholstery fabrics.

One of the few gleams of light on the English furnishing scene at the time were the colour schemes suggested by Basil Ionides in his book *Colour and Interior Decoration* (1926). He was passionate about piping, fringes and braids and made suggestions for decorative schemes at the end of each chapter. Given a specific colour he would suggest for sofa and chair covers combinations such as 'pale green piped with lemon yellow' in a scheme for an east-facing room; 'green striped damask edged with mauve braid' for a south-facing bedroom; *Tête de négre* velvet, piped with yellow' for a white panelled room. This book has since become a classic. Besides giving a fascinating insight into what was fashionable in England, it is also beautifully written and illustrated, and full of ideas for interpreting present-day colour schemes.

Fashionable extremes

The final word on Art Déco must have a French accent. One of the many Déco artists who have subsequently become world famous is Erté, who designed spectacular clothes for the theatre, celebrities and V.I.P.s like Mrs William Randolph Hearst. Because of the decorative nature of his creations, some are now reproduced as posters by The Poster Shop. While no self-respecting Art Déco interior decorator of the time would have considered such a thing, the inclusion of a modern poster of the period adds a touch of the style.

BOHEMIAN

The Bohemian style grew out of the creative hot beds of Chelsea and Bloomsbury, flourishing between 1910 and 1930. Its highly colourful image of artists and their studios and the unconventional lifestyles that surrounded them, is hallmarked by the extravagant decoration of fireplaces, vases, tables, chairs and every other household object, not so much to make them easy on the eye, but rather to transform them into works of art.

The Bloomsbury set, among whom were Virginia Woolf, Duncan Grant, Vanessa Bell and Roger Fry, were all luminaries of the wider revolution of literature and art at the time. It was this group of artists who extended their creative talents to the homes in which they lived and so carried the Bohemian ethos into the field of domestic design.

Roger Fry, for example, was at the centre of avant-garde art in London before 1914. He had a crusading enthusiasm to seduce the conservative Edwardians to the sympathies of the Post-Impressionist painters through domestic design. By opening the Omega Workshops in 1913 Fry married the Arts and Crafts Movement and Modernism; the result was new, untried colour in the form of painted walls and fabrics, cushions, lampshades, decorated furniture and ceramics, all much patronized by the celebrated Bloomsbury Group.

If Fry was the high priest of the Omega look then the temple was certainly Charleston Manor, Sussex, the home of Duncan Grant and Vanessa Bell from 1916. The house has now been restored as a national record of the movement. It was regularly visited by the Bloomsbury set and many artists of the day during World War I and afterwards. There you can see the style given its fullest expression; no surface or object has escaped the touch of the artist's brush.

The Bohemian style is currently undergoing a renaissance, albeit with some revisions. The murals of dusty dreams; pastel sketches of struggling gods, and now even witty trompe l'oeil in punchy primary colours are once again the signature of consciously unconventional and adventurous young people. For the confident connoisseur of shape and colour, the effect is artistic and undeniably individual.

One of the joys of this style is that it is not expensive to create. It is, however, an elusive one and you will need creative energy and audacious ideas to control and combine a variety of styles against this backdrop of extrovert and witty paint magic. The effect is thrilling.

Art unfettered

Wall paintings are the accessible and inexpensive way to 'Bohemianize' any room. These murals are the basis of the Bohemian style and it is the essence of these that must be appreciated if the effect is to be successful. You may have to employ a professional painter with sympathetic tastes to help you develop your ideas, but this is not essential.

As with all painted decoration, the charm of painted pattern is that it is completely tailor-made for the room. You can use it discreetly or go completely over the top with the dazzling, bold shapes and Fauvist colours associated with the Bloomsbury style. The secret is to combine drama with deft use of material and thus create an orgy of original paintings. With simple, bold colours and emphatic textures you can develop a look that is eclectic yet peculiarly English.

Pattern

In the breakfast room shown on the previous page, the backdrop of warm pastel decoration flows around the walls and over fabrics (even the lampshades are painted), so that the furniture becomes almost incidental. Cotton curtains, a table, a couple of chairs and a standard lamp make the room dance with pattern and light. Pattern upon pattern, colour against colour; the effect is optically stunning – even in a medium-sized room. This is full bodied, lusty work, a heady mixture of abstract and romantic. As Jim Smart, doyen of paint finishes, is fond of saying, 'A room that has been properly painted needs no furniture'.

Above: *Typical Bohemian wall-painting designs exhibiting qualities of sensual irregularity.*
Right: *For your fabrics try simple abstracts or follow the figurative motifs and stencilled leaves as shown in the sitting room on page 144.*

Artistic fabrics

Plain cotton can be dyed or painted with fabric paints and used for curtains, cushion covers or simply to drape over pieces of undistinguished furniture. If you choose abstract designs you can let your imagination run riot. Painted curtains provide a theatrical backdrop with deeper colours of lilac, blue and peach, dramatized still further by the use of black to offset the colours.

Take inspiration from 1950s Africana by painting large symbolic coffee beans that jump right up to the dado rail or from Post-Impressionist artists such as Matisse or Mire. Or you could emulate the look of the six Omega-printed linens; one of these was named Pamela – after Fry's daughter – and was a riot of blue, pink, purple and black, not unlike the colours

seen in this breakfast room. For those who are artistic a figurative design, such as an ardent Apollo flying after Daphne, or a female nude gathered about with a cloak, would be fun. Continue the same theme over cushions and even rugs laid over bare boards.

Omega furniture

Deriving its charm from an extravaganza of colour, the Bohemian style has an almost tongue-in-cheek approach to design; a revolutionary levity. The table looks like a superior junk shop find and can be made from plywood and broomsticks, painted with anonymous black eggshell and varnished with a satin finish.

The tubular chairs are reminiscent of designs by Marcel Breuer *circa* 1928, and the folding table reminds me of one by Hassenpflug of the same year. These exciting designs of the 1920s were wide open to every kind of experiment and advance in their search to create dramatic spectacle, and for this reason furniture of this era is perfect for the Bohemian look. Tables with a central cylindrical leg and square foot were popular with the Omega set as were dining chairs with lacquered, gilded, or painted frames. Bohemian-style painting blends the furniture into the surroundings by continuing the rampaging wavy lines, blobs of colour and abstract designs over the lamp shades, tables and even across the floor.

Typical lyrical themes are waterlilies with perhaps a central square filled with random dots and dashes, or even a geometrical arrangement of pointed and

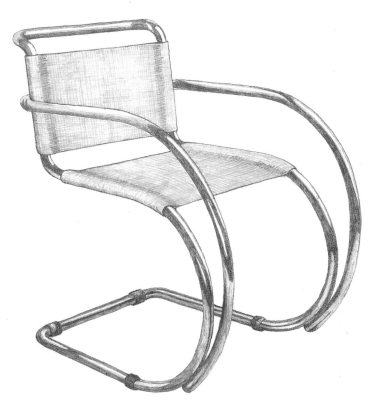

rounded leaves. Note the bowl of fruit on the table, with the 'lost' orange – a still life study with all the characteristics of the Omega style.

Lamps

Wooden lampstands like this one, were indicative of the Bohemian look, in fact, in 1913, they were one of the earliest types of household goods to get the Omega Workshops treatment. They were usually painted in four or five colours, each with a unique decoration of abstract marks – dots, squiggles and triangles. The bases of these table lamps were characteristically simple in shape and handpainted in the same geometric style to be seen on the fabric designs, often with cross-hatching. The colours are yet again vital and bold.

Chairs of bent tubular steel, by architect designers such as Marcel Breuer or even Mies van der Rohe, provide a stark and shocking contrast to the complex whirls of paint and fabric.

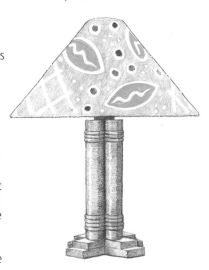

The device of squiggles, exotic colour combinations and fantastic shapes is highly effective when brightly illuminated.

BOHEMIAN

Stencilled sitting room

When painting or stencilling this type of look it is best to pencil lightly where you propose to place your motifs. The best paints to use are fast drying ones to obviate smudging. Artists' acrylics dry almost instantly and the colour range is enormous, but many professionals also choose to use signwriters' paints as the colours are richer and the paints less 'plastic' to use. They also dry very quickly. If you want to speed up the painting operation still further you should use aerosol paints in cans as recommended by professional stenciller Lyn Le Grice.

Simple does not have to mean naive. Old textiles are a rich source of suitable motifs including heraldic designs, lace and paisley patterns. Textile designer Cressida Bell (grand-daughter of Vanessa) sometimes incorporates the fleur-de-lis with the Charleston motif of a giant sponged comma and painted sprays of white flowers. Often the simplest ideas are the best, and this is very true of stencilling. A leaf shape cut out of plastic foam and dipped into matt vinyl emulsion is perfect for a swirling shower of leaves. If you use this idea, you can vary the direction of the prints, spiralling and overlapping them into random or all-over repeat patterns. Continue to use the sponge after the paint has begun to run out, for an attractive faded effect. You can even add your own squiggles to the leaves with a gold felt-tip pen.

For making your own stencils, from card or acetate, see American County style, page 62.

Reflected glory

This room is dominated by the fireplace which is surrounded by stencilled paint work in the form of blue and orange leaves. The colours are vibrant, the textures breathe and the patterns look dashed on, but all with that apparently casual vitality which amateurs do not always pull off.

Using a mirror above the fireplace is a clever idea as it serves to double the effect of the painted sculptures and ceramics and brings the amorous gods cavorting down from the walls and on to the mantelpiece.

Below it the plain cane chair imparts a distinctly Fifties flavour and style with draped painted linen cover in

three colours; this time a combination of airforce blue, ochre and terracotta. The design incorporates circles with internal cross hatching and classic Omega lattice work designs which are repeated on the walls; dots, diamonds and zigzags.

Colours for the Eighties

Interiors, being self-expressions, should be constantly changing, absorbing new enthusiasms and individualisms, so if you are going for more of an Eighties-update of Omega, abandon the subtle colours of the original look for the new vibrancy of bold primaries. Even if you cannot quite

The completed effect is one of fabrics and walls overwhelmed by freestyle paintings, together with an undertone of frenzy. The mantelpiece is littered with fascinating memorabilia.

accept the resurgent nostalgia for Bloomsbury, Fry's observation on the potency of colour and its ability to transform still stands: 'Our artist may be able merely out of contrast of two or three pure colours applied in simple rectangular shapes to transform the room completely, giving it a new feeling of space and dignity or richness.'

Fauvist fabrics

The school that produces decorative fabrics redolent of the saturated Bohemian interiors of Vuillard or Bonnard includes such textile designers as Sarah Campbell, Susan Collier, Lillian Delevoryas, Natalie Gibson and Annagrete Halling-Kock. Their designs seem thoroughly appropriate for intimate rooms in which the objects are gathered, not as trophies of culture but for their associative qualities. The influence is nostalgic and escapist.

Collier Campbell's rich and varied textiles make them, as here, immediately recognizable. The fabric covering the sofa, for example, has all the power and immediacy of the Fauvist painters. Collier Campbell's fabrics, like many of the textiles of this contemporary group, appear to have been conceived and expressed as paintings rather than as designs – a theme that fits very well into the rationale of the Bohemian style.

Update with trompe l'oeil

For a real show stopper, murals and trompe l'oeil are hard to beat. Not since the Renaissance have so many clients commissioned so many wall decoration and show pieces. A mural by one of the famous muralists such as Ian Cairnie or Lincoln Taber would certainly be an international status symbol. But you do not have to be a millionaire to achieve originality. The Eighties solution is, by comparison, cheap and cheerful and less onerous than you might at first think.

This child-like, but amusing windowscape, from the flat of textile designer Susan Collier, of washing hanging out in the garden on a windy day, is not a difficult one to draw, and the potential for great individuality and colour is endless. The motifs include birds and bees, and simplistic dragonflies, butterflies and a dove, bright handkerchiefs, tea towels, curtains and pelmet. The painted bay tree seems to be flowering out of the colourful jardinière in front of it.

Looking closely you will see that there is nothing new in this room – in fact the sofa and tiny wicker Hansel and Gretel chairs have definitely seen better days, but the overall effect is still one that is dazzlingly warm and bright and definitely Bohemian. The dark red velvet upholstered frame chair adds a touch of fading grandeur, while the shelving holds a vast array of artistic paraphernalia, including handpainted plates in zany orange, red, green and blue, with a simple still-life design matching a huge plant pot on the aged jardinière.

The Bohemian bedroom

The bedrooms of the Bloomsbury set were intimate interiors, often French in flavour, being filled with Cézanne watercolours and figures by Matisse. They were strongly reminiscent of the tones and timbres of Provence, with its tiled floors and the slightly rustic, painted peasant furniture.

In one of the bedrooms at Charleston Manor (see picture opposite), even the window recesses were painted with still lifes, trompe l'oeil flowers and vases, cross-hatching and sun symbols. There is a great restfulness about the soft, slightly faded colours of the room.

Generally the look is one of

a few handsome personal objects, set against a restrained background, but look a little further and you will see how richly artistic the room really is, with its unreserved feeling of romanticism.

Top: *Susan Collier's living room brings the look up-to-the-minute with bright primary colours.*
Above: *The softer interior of the bedroom shows a more authentic Charleston effect, echoing the styles of admired artists of that earlier period.*

Backgrounds

You may find that to update the Charleston Manor look with bright primaries is a little hard to live with. But if you do decide against its faded pastels you could, for example, try a cerise or rose-coloured background softened with stencilled paisley patterns. Stencilling matt colour on to a shiny base is an effective way of achieving a damask effect which is a lovely texture for a bedroom.

For an alternative Bohemian paint effect, use broad stripes in clear, gentle colours, such as aquamarine and apricot, to create a striking background.

Ceramics

Fry and the other Omega Bohemians disliked the contemporary pottery of the time and wanted to revolutionize this form of art, which they held to be the most intimately connected with lifestyles.

The pottery you choose should be seen as they saw it, as a form of sculpture, and displayed accordingly – perhaps as on this mantelpiece (see Reflected glory), beside an original ceramic by Quentin Bell (son of Clive and Vanessa). Laura Ashley has recently produced

_____

Ceramics are very much a part of the Bohemian look. Copy a favourite theme of Duncan Grant's – a swimmer negotiating choppy waves.

a collection of his original ceramic designs based on those of the traditional Bloomsbury artists.

Alternatively, look for Far Eastern, early Italian or Arabic styles with sumptuously rich glazes. Or find something in buff-coloured earthenware covered in a white tin glaze and further hand-paint it in Bohemian colours. Vary the colours you use, but try to complement the colouring of the fabrics and walls. The fundamental aim is to destroy the past accretions of taste by creating something quite unorthodox and artistic – so let yourself go!

For decorating vases and jars use lines, circles and interlaced bands, or take

inspiration from post-Impressionist paintings and sketch elegant ladies with parasols; a nude swimmer negotiating choppy waves, for example, or Duncan Grant's favourite – a goldfish in blue water with a circle enclosing hatched diagonal lines.

Painted furniture

Painted furniture is currently in vogue and enjoying a tremendous resurgence of popularity. People find that painted pieces fit especially well in the colour – and texture – conscious interiors of today. Paint is also the perfect camouflage for less distinguished furniture. Hand painting is the ideal way to cut your teeth on the whole business of decorative painting; making full-scale

projects simpler and less daunting through experience.

A large wooden bed would be the perfect piece on which to let your painting fall. You could embellish both the bedhead and foot, decorating them with romantic images of Morpheus the god of Sleep!

For the hint of sophistication of which the Bohemians were so fond, you might like to add a chinoiserie table or a piece of Italian gilt glass, a table, chair or faïence from Avignon or Piedmont, even a French ebony or ormulu cabinet. But always buy with your mind on the shape, colour and visual impact of the object rather than on its connoisseur value or fashionable chic.

Fire screens and panels were very much part of the Omega style as they provide large ready-made areas for a variety of brush strokes and design ideas. If you can find a really decorative screen with an arched top, preferably antique or archaic-looking, try to incorporate the arch into your painting. Flowers and leaves in great profusion, a ring of female dancers or the popular lily pond design (after Matisse, 1912), for example, are all charming and would make marvellously successful images.

Charleston Manor lives on – a style of great vigour and charm has re-entered the mainstream of English taste.

Create your own original design for screens and panels in Fauvist colours.

Above: *A bedhead is the perfect place to exhibit your artistic flair. Look upon it as a large, blank canvas and reveal your true Bohemian colours!*

FIFTIES

By the 1950s Le Corbusier's 1921 dream of a house as 'a machine for living in' had come of age. Modern architects strongly influenced by him had created, all too successfully, houses devoid of ornament and bleak, boxy apartment blocks. Interiors were given interest and individuality by the way in which they were furnished. For this reason the Fifties look is one that you might like to go for if you live in a modern flat or on a post-war housing estate. Second-hand furniture shops all over the country are bulging with Fifties products — from palette-shaped coffee tables to moulded plastic chairs. Therefore, this is a good time to 'get in' on a style which is much more interesting than it might at first appear.

World War II meant that in England and much of Europe, the 1940s were dominated by extreme shortages. Furnishings, like many other things, were controlled by government regulations and were necessarily spartan in style, Utility furniture being all that was available. The effects of such restrictions lasted well into the 1950s.

In America, it was a different story. Being freer from the constraints of war, designers like Eero Saarinen and Charles Eames (see page 157) were able to develop further the ideas and techniques pioneered by Chrysler in the 1930s, while researching for military purposes. Techniques involved in the bonding of wood, rubber, metal and glass and the casting of aluminium were used to develop one of the most characteristic of all Fifties features — moulded plywood furniture, made with a light frame of bent steel rod, usually featuring splayed, tapering legs with pointed feet.

A third, equally strong influence came from Scandinavia where the Nordic love of wood and other natural materials, including plants, was welcomed in post-war England by a nation who had hitherto been starved of any such novelty. The better architect-designed houses featured large plateglass windows and open plan interiors — a relatively sparse, functional style that opened up a whole new concept of display, especially for pottery, glass and plants. New and exciting houseplants tended to bring the outside indoors — a craze that has continued today.

With the ending of wartime restrictions, the late 1950s saw luxury and novelty re-enter the mainstream of interior design.

Preliminaries

Long, low lines amid open-plan spaces, with the absence of architectural ornament, save bare wood and brickwork, are such intrinsic features of the style that if your rooms have high ceilings with decorative mouldings and classical architraves, then a conversion to the true Fifties style would not be possible without major structural alterations. On the other hand, you could create a colourful flavour of the style by making a collection of easily grouped items like pottery or glass.

Back to basics

For best results in achieving a Fifties flavour, start with the walls. Ideally they should be stripped of picture rails and mouldings with shallow skirtings. Before choosing the colour scheme observe how and where the natural light falls. If you have a big picture window or patio doors (see picture overleaf), you will need a paler shade around the window, to offset the light casting the wall in shadow. Popular colour schemes included cream and white, dove grey, duck-egg blue, lemon yellow, sage and every shade of pale to mid green, and oyster pink, in egg-shell finish. Bright colours like garnet red, golden yellow, maroon and cobalt were mixed with plenty of white or cream. Interior designers put tremendous emphasis on the study of tonal values and the way in which different shades of colour were able to make rooms seem higher, lower, wider, longer, thinner or fatter. Frequently, one or two walls would be papered and the others painted in a colour picked up from the pattern.

Elements of pattern

Walls of glass call for bold patterned fabrics yet simple window treatments, using poles or discreet tracks for hanging the curtains. This tropical jungle print with its juicy, grey-green leaves and accents of black and orange on a lacquer red ground shows the strong contemporary African influence, which included all sorts of leopard, tiger and zebra skin prints (see page 152). In England this was sparked off by the brilliantly coloured cottons produced by the Manchester Calico Printers, destined for the African market, and seen for the first time by the public at the Festival of Britain in 1951. After 12 years of drab utility the colour and vigour of these patterns seized the imagination of the public.

If your windows are not big enough to take a large, zany print or a simple Scandinavian-type weave, you could copy a very modish device of the time and paper one wall *only* with a striking pattern and pick out colours from it to echo in paint, curtains, loose covers, accessories and flooring.

Scandinavian looks

One of the most attractive aspects of the Scandinavian influence was the abundance of plain and natural wood surfaces, like the frame of the chair shown overleaf used as a decorative finish in its own right. Oiled or polished wooden floors were enhanced with rugs. Turkish and Persian rugs have never been out of fashion, and the lifting of post-war restrictions led to a flood of newer designs being imported, like this Bokhara-style rug. Notice how it has been carefully chosen to complement the curtain design.

Later, the Scandinavians began to export their shaggy-pile rya rugs which they produced in a superb variety of shaded, jewel-like colours and with more abstract swirls and geometric patterns as the decade progressed. You could snuggle deep down into these rugs as you curled up in front of your open flue fire and listened to Rock 'n' Roll records. Rya rugs were such a novelty that they stayed popular with the English until the early 1970s.

Another important feature, using the natural wood finish, was the open tread staircase supported on uprights of light wood or metal. These can easily be installed in most types of homes.

If your house has small rooms and you would rather live in a large open-plan space it is a feature you can copy. With professional advice, walls can be knocked down, which will create a new sense of light and space, amid angular forms of peculiar beauty.

Printed furnishing fabrics, left to right: Heal's Calyx by Lucienne Day; Story's Neptune by F. C. Rice; linen from Liberty.

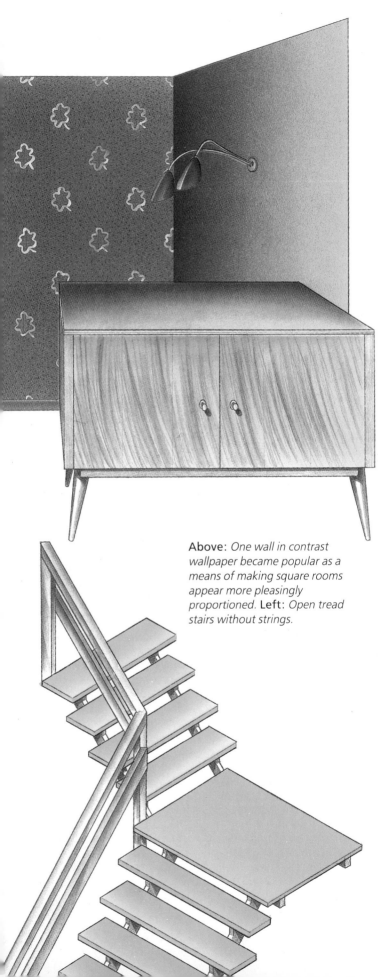

Above: *One wall in contrast wallpaper became popular as a means of making square rooms appear more pleasingly proportioned.* **Left:** *Open tread stairs without strings.*

Definitive styles

Nothing brings the 1950s more quickly to mind than a chair with a moulded plywood seat of vague anthropomorphic shape with splayed steel legs. The archetype, in this country, must be Ernest Race's Antelope chair, designed in 1953. Tables shared many of these same characteristics, the best examples having plywood tops, often with upswept ends or amoeba-like in shape, and balanced on sharply angled tapering legs. However, because some forms of design in the 1950s took up where the 1930s left off to a certain extent, certain items such as this radiogramme reflect a definite Thirties Odeon look.

Embracing art forms

Contemporary 'modern' art found its natural home in these airy open-plan spaces. Abstract objects, like this metal tube and wood sculpture with its large oval 'head' complement the setting admirably. With a little inspiration, you could easily create your own version; collections of large, smooth pebbles with interesting striations, and driftwood, curiously wrought by the elements can perform a similar function. Arrange them with close attention to light and shade, shape and form.

Prints by influential artists of the time like Jean Miro, Dubuffet and Ben Nicholson, are available from many museums and art galleries. Alternatively, a radical late 1980s print with a 1950s feel, from one of the many talented young printmakers working today, would be equally suitable. Remember when selecting your print that, for an authentic look, the tones should suit your overall scheme.

For the serious collector try to find a piece of good studio pottery. In England, pieces by Hans Coper and Lucie Rie (see

Lucie Rie bowl, 1953.

illustration below) would still make excellent investments. Their beautiful stoneware bowls and vases in soft natural colourings are classics of the style and command fairly high prices. For a less expensive alternative, you may prefer the look of the poppy head vase to evoke the 1950s look.

Planting in

In a changeable northern climate, it would be cruel even to try to keep a cactus of this size (see page 146) in anything but a hothouse. However, as more homes had central heating installed, so the craze for semi-tropical plants increased. 'Quaint, attractive little plants' enthused a journalist writing in *Good Housekeeping* in 1958, so along with rubber plants, cheese plants and philodendrons, a collection of cacti is almost essential, and happily, any number will grow quite well on a sunny windowsill.

The Fifties mix

While many of the endeavours of 1950s designers and architects were sincere and excellent, they were obsessed by functional and technically efficient solutions for living. Human nature, being what it is, however, is quirky and seldom as rational as we should like it to be. Ironically, lots of the things which are now being collected by Fifties enthusiasts are the very objects which caused the then counsellors of good taste to shudder. The

Design Council, London, which opened its showroom in 1956, would never have accepted many of the things that make this North American apartment such fun and give it tremendous character.

Organic modernism

The owner has had no qualms about mixing a collection of delightful Jan Arp-style mirrors – notice their free form – with a pair of modern

triangular tables butted at an angle to create the illusion of a sloping surface. The mirrors and the shapes of the chairs are all part of what is called 'organic modernism'. A good example of this type of design is the glass-topped table with its free-form sculpted legs, made by Japanese sculptor Isamu Noguchi in the 1940s for American furnishers Herman Miller (see overleaf). While in the 1930s form was dictated by the unrelenting lines of the machine, by the 1950s designers were in

Above and right: *Updated with Disneyland pastels this is the 1950s look at its most engaging, young and witty. Radios, mirrors, rubber plants are findable and affordable. Shined up, these rooms prove that nostalgia need not look dowdy or kitsch.*

revolt against it. Instead they looked closely at the shapes of nature for inspiration. The curved abstract forms and triangular shapes which resulted became a style labelled 'Contemporary'.

This vignette shows a functional drinks trolley bearing a dazzling array of chromeware and an engaging wall plaque, reminiscent of Tcheliteler's famous blue lady.

New materials

The manufacturing of plastics developed apace during the war, especially in the aircraft industry. The curved form of the moulded shell is characteristic of the moulding process which has been used as a feature in the casings of these radios shown opposite. Vast mass-production lines and the comparative cheapness of the finished products meant that a fashion element could be introduced. The plastics industry boomed. All the things we now take for granted, such as plastic bowls, plates, cups and saucers, gradually appeared on the market – there is a collection of them here, on the windowsill (see dining room). There were also brooms and buckets, and as the decade progressed the colours got brighter. Stacking chairs were made with moulded plastic seats and to begin with the original plywood shapes were copied (see dining room).

The next most important point is to get the colours right; choose yellow, slate blue, persimmon and black and you've got something which says 'Fifties'!

Stainless steel products, chiefly kitchen utensils and tableware, were mass-produced for the first time. If you hunt around secondhand shops and flea markets you could also make up a most interesting collection of china and glass.

Tea and coffee services, for example, in white and a single contrasting colour: black, maroon, yellow or sage green were often enlivened with a fine linear pattern. This sparkling collection of stainless steel ware (see trolly detail) makes a beautiful, if expensive, display. But you could start more modestly and practically with a small collection of cutlery, trays, dishes, and pots and pans. Many of the designs first sold over thirty years ago are still available in the shops.

Storage

No Fifties interior would be complete without its complement of modular storage units, either fixed to the wall, as shown here in the bedroom, used as a room divider, or in the kitchen. The idea was probably first conceived at the Bauhaus in the 1920s (see page 125), but it took a generation for the idea to reach the market place. It was, and still is, one of the best solutions for storage problems.

Pottery and glass

The whimsy and flavour of any period is often to be found in pottery and glass, and the Fifties are no exception. The little elongated pod-shaped vase (see bedroom) is a typical example, with its ebony glaze and decoration of bright lines and dashes. This and the kissing-couple wall plaque (see trolly detail) are an instant evocation of the 1950s. It would be possible to make up a most interesting collection of similar items, for example, colourful jugs, sugar bowls, cups and saucers or plates. Imports of really beautiful glassware from Scandinavia and Italy fired the imagination of the general public who, with growing appreciation, demanded more colourful pieces purely for ornamentation.

Windows

If you wish to pursue a purely functional decorative theme in the space you inhabit, and your windows are not overlooked, then the white security grille as seen in this apartment may be the answer. On the other hand, what would be more typical of the period, and less expensive, are Venetian blinds with wide slats, either in white or in a colour chosen to tone with the walls. Alternatively, pinch pleated curtains in an abstract or figurative design, set in panels, would be most appropriate. Pinch pleat tapes were available for the first time in 1958 and immediately became fashionable. This made curtain making so much easier and curtains for large, popular picture windows could, more easily, be made at home.

Lighting

Lighting and fittings underwent a minor revolution. Previously sturdy table-lamps and wall lights were now adjustable, or at least made to look as if they were. Lamps seemed to sprout long, prehensile enquiring necks with insect-like heads, similar to the red, spun steel shade with its flexible stem (see bedroom

overleaf). Designs ranged from the angular aspect of a praying mantis, to the more starkly practical, such as the Anglepoise, which was and still is very efficient. The hinged Anglepoise lamp first appeared in offices and factories well before World War II, and by the 1950s was in wide use in the home. If you are adopting the Scandinavian look using the softer wood, wool and weave approach, you might feel happier with simple wooden table or standard lamps on a tapering base with a triangular-shaped shade. For the central ceiling light, you might try one of these most elegant pleated paper 'umbrellas' which you could easily copy in parchment.

As fluorescent tubes began to light up the kitchen, 'streamlined efficiency' and 'labour saving' became the watchwords of the day.

Keeping tidy

Robin Day, one of England's most distinguished post-war industrial designers, won a prestigious award in America for his unit/modular storage (which can be seen in the Victoria & Albert Museum, London). This concept of being able to add to variable units of storage including shelves, glass display areas, drawers, drop fronted desks and/or drinks cabinets was entirely new, and is still a brilliant idea. Variations on this theme became common and were enormously practical, especially in those houses and flats that were designed without fireplaces and their accompanying recesses – which had, hitherto, usually been converted into cupboards. Freestanding units with open shelves can be used to demarcate dining and living areas while retaining the

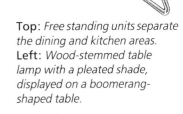

Top: *Free standing units separate the dining and kitchen areas.*
Left: *Wood-stemmed table lamp with a pleated shade, displayed on a boomerang-shaped table.*

maximum feeling of light and space – also to display your collection of plants, Henry Moore-inspired pebbles, wire sculptures, African carvings and abstract figurative pottery. In the kitchen, units and work surfaces were laminated with 'wipe-clean' Formica, while shelves were lined with stick-on Fablon, and quite clearly, the death knell had been sounded for scrubbed pine kitchen tables and venerable dust-catching dressers.

Fine furniture

Finding the real Fifties furniture is not a great problem, but you should first train yourself to distinguish between the good and the junk. With better furniture, you will notice that a great deal of technical skill will have gone into its structure, and in determining the distribution

of mass; the balance of a chair seat, for example, and its relationship to the frame and legs. One of the masters of this particular art was Charles Eames – and a laminated rosewood-and-leather armchair of his with a matching ottoman on a cast aluminium base was sold for £410 at Christie's spring 1984 sale in London. Harry Bertoia, another master of the period, designed these wire chairs (on opposite page) which are beautifully abstract, sculptural shapes of wire and welded steel rods. Both designers were extremely influential and their ideas widely adapted.

Always look for a good finish, whether it is wood, plastic or metal; check the joints, see that the plywood is not split or cracked and that the upholstery is in good shape. In Britain, Ercol made high quality revamps of the

classic beechwood Windsor chair. As the decade progressed more wood finishes were used – oiled teak, rosewood, afromosia, beech. As the long low look established itself furniture shapes became plumper and more comfortable.

Eating and drinking

Some of the best stainless steel cutlery was designed for Old Hall by Robert Welch who, interestingly enough, trained as a silversmith. In 1958 Old Hall introduced this tea service called 'Heirloom' and the complete set with tray cost 10 guineas. If you cannot buy a similar tea service, then you could look for secondhand originals.

Stainless steel offered many practical advantages. It was made with either a mirror polish or satin finish, and to maintain, required nothing more than rinsing and polishing with a soft, dry cloth. And as the rage for stainless steel continued; side dishes, tureens, condiment sets, eggcups, napkin rings, toast racks, candle holders and coffee sets followed. Cooking pans and dishes were designed for the first time as 'oven-to-table' ware, and every household had its

quota of these dishes in ceramic, oven glass or cast iron. During the 1950s, boomerang tables similar to the one shown opposite, sold at Liberty, London for 2 guineas. Original boomerang and palette-shaped tables do occasionally turn up at salerooms, but either design could quite easily be made at home by DIY enthusiasts – creating an authentic focal point essential to the style.

Glass

The smartest contemporary glass that came from Scandinavia and Italy was often totally non-functional like this enormous glass bottle with its elegant stopper, but the shapes were new and exciting, and in wonderful patterns and colours. Italian glassmakers tended to produce designs with glorious splashes of turquoise, blue, lacquer red and yellow, while the Scandinavians had a cooler approach, preferring smoky, subtle tints of green, blue or grey. Towards the end of the 1950s Italian glass mosaics were used to decorate walls, the tops of coffee tables and yes, even plant pots. The effect was vibrant, energetic and expressive!

Signposts

We are barely a generation away from the Fifties, and for this reason the period is comparatively thinly documented. But you will find that some of the best sources of reference are 1950s films and magazines, and designers' and architects' year books, which you can see at your local library.

Nostalgia for 1950s and Rock 'n' Roll lives on!

Far left: *Wire chair, from Harry Bertoia's collection (1952), which included a high-backed armchair and a neatly padded dining chair. These are still produced and are available from specialist furniture stores.* **Left**: *Stainless steel tableware designed by Robert Welch for Old Hall.*

HI-TECH

The Hi-tech style is an approach to architecture and interior design which makes its priorities the materials, finishes and actual components of industrial and technological processes. The assimilation of these manufactured items seems to many an appropriate way to greet a modern world; more in tune with the spirit of the times than the recreation of past epochs and styles. If you feel attracted by this style, then you are unlikely to be the sort of person who has collected piles of possessions, and dusty old things at that, and you are therefore probably intending to live in a limited space, neatly and cleverly adapted to your needs. Equally if you have a collection of comfortable, sagging old sofas and are determined not to be parted from them, then this is not really the style for you.

This room represents a fairly extreme version of Hi-tech. Most of us and, indeed most designers in the style, start off with solid masonry and the limitations of a traditionally built house. Not that that need be a deterrent to achieving an up to the minute effect. All you need is the imagination to transform a series of four-square walls into something special and restraint in organizing your possessions to fit into the space available.

Here in a house built by an architect for his own family the rooms follow the discipline of the grid which is represented by the placing of the principal supports or columns. The Hi-tech look is emphasized by the space frames of the ceiling, which look rather like a smart new industrial shed or warehouse, even an airport. This is because we are not used, in a domestic setting, to see so plainly the elements of the construction. They are very much the same as they would be for those kinds of buildings – if on a far smaller scale, since they have been scaled down to suit a domestic interior.

The roots of Hi-tech lie in the expression of the components' 'honesty' and the idea, shared by the modern movement, of form following function. This gives flexibility, as well as a stark and functional look which tends to prescribe the way you live, rather than the other way round.

Uncluttered space

The essence of the style is crisp, bright and clean. Black and white, chrome and silver, primary colours and sharp edges are all part of the hi-tech feel. In this kind of interior, shown overleaf, you have to live neatly with no visible dust or piles of old magazines. Cupboards are walk-in, and the stairs, which can be seen in the far corner here, are of the metal spiral type, which uses far less valuable floor space. A generous feeling of uncluttered space is also characteristic of this style.

There is a liking for plenty of natural light, of which this house has ample since the walls are basically glass and then screened, in this case with banks of Venetian blinds. Orderliness is the order of the day, since if you get the angle of the blinds wrong, the house would be completely transparent by night.

Furniture must follow the spare nature of the style; and should be placed carefully and symmetrically – random and informal grouping will merely succeed in making the room look untidy. Here modern classic designs are used, with comfortable, neutral-coloured sofas for relaxation.

Floors

To offset the spare and carefully chosen objects in a Hi-tech interior floors need to be either hard, easily – cleaned surfaces, such as tiles, sanded wood, or studded synthetic rubber, or carpeted using very inconspicuous colours such as neutral, beige or grey. The effect of rather spartan simplicity has to be maintained in all details and so a highly-coloured or patterned floor covering would not contribute to that. A cheap and inventive finish is to install a hardboard floor and then paint it with several layers of extremely hard-wearing lino paint to provide a matt surface. If the same colour, for example cream or white, is chosen for the walls, it makes a very good background for a strongly defined Hi-tech scheme.

Lighting

Fittings should be discreet, and targetted with care. Recent ranges of Italian uplighters and adaptable desk or table lights have been an inspiration to lighting manufacturers and much cheaper versions are now widely available. Lighting is sufficiently important for it to be the first consideration when furnishing a room; you get the lighting right, and in a bare Hi-tech setting it is all the more important, then the rest follows. Mirrors can be used to good effect to

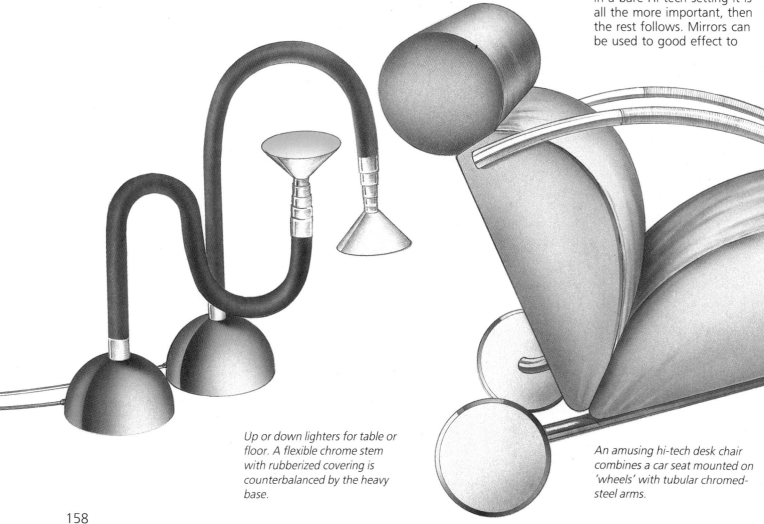

Up or down lighters for table or floor. A flexible chrome stem with rubberized covering is counterbalanced by the heavy base.

An amusing hi-tech desk chair combines a car seat mounted on 'wheels' with tubular chromed-steel arms.

complement existing lighting and, of course, to provide as much illusion of extra space as can possibly be managed.

Windows

Hi-tech rooms benefit from generous windows and a good deal of natural light and dictate the simplest, most functional of window coverings. Either absolutely plain drop blinds or Venetian blinds (often with a satinized or metallic finish) are the best choice. If your house or flat is not overlooked you may decide to dispense with blinds, at least in living rooms, since a deep black night can be as good a backdrop as anything.

Furniture

The Hi-tech interior calls for relatively little furniture, but it should be well-designed and the best you can find. It

should accommodate good modern design – many 1930s reproductions are excellent for the style; it will certainly not be improved by floral sofas or anything with a suspicion of clutter about it. Low pieces, simple tables of the Japanese kind, classic leather or pleasantly textured fabric seating, a very simple wooden based bed or futon, all would look good.

A functional trestle table with a set of moulded plastic or wire chairs would serve equally well. The cleverest people will manage to find very mundane furniture, perhaps being thrown out from an office or even industrial use, and by revamping them turn them into something exciting. Sprayed with a black lacquer paint, for example, the cheapest, dullest piece will take on different properties. Another method is to stove-enamel metal objects, again a way to utterly transform the ordinary but serviceable, into eyecatching pieces with high style.

A standard industrial spiral stair adapted with perforated risers and checker-plate sheeting steps.

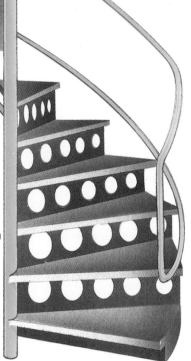

Materials

The Hi-tech look uses glass, steel, rubber and synthetics, and does not have much space or place for wood, soft fabrics and never a suspicion of either old gilt or new brass. The only exceptions lie in subterfuge – the recovering, respraying or enamelling of unacceptable finishes to bring them up to the pristine level required for such a setting.

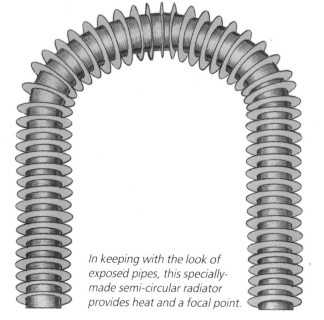

In keeping with the look of exposed pipes, this specially-made semi-circular radiator provides heat and a focal point.

Heat and power

Radiators come into their own in the Hi-tech interior. Self explanatory in their function, they can be sited without disguise and can be used either horizontally or vertically to give the required emphasis. Similarly details such as electric power points can be made prominent, especially now that you can buy spiral flexes in brilliant colours to draw attention to them. For extra warmth, there are neatly designed multi-fuel stoves which can fit well into the Hi-tech house, without introducing an unwelcome note of folksiness.

Mobile storage

Storage in the Hi-tech house is likely to become a feature of some importance. Sometimes an entire room is given over to providing a walk-in cupboard, serving the needs of the entire house or flat, but for things which are needed to hand, such as books and records a mobile storage unit such as this one is ideal. For storing clothes, a

Stainless steel hospital equipment is almost de rigeur in a Hi-tech interior for holding hi-fi equipment. Its shiny looks attune perfectly with slatted blinds.

metal swimming pool basket rack would be suitable. Like the interior on page 160, the component materials are very industrial in image, if not in

fact. These shelves consist of a simple steel grid, which has been left open-sided except for shelf ends where books or records are stored. Fixed shelving, often looking very much like the storage in a depot for car parts, tends to follow the same look. In fact, the architect here has also used old warehouse shelving, resprayed, for shelves elsewhere in her flat.

Kitchen economy

The kitchen in this house which, significantly, has been designed by a woman architect, for her own use, is highly economic in its use of space. The design is much aided by the use of complex, exposed shelving arrangements all made accessible by a staggered layout. The surfaces here are as industrial as you can find:

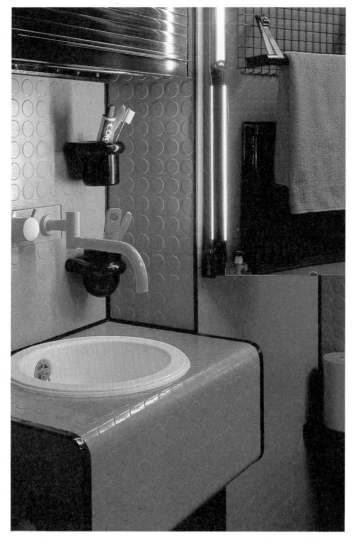

Left and above: *Pirelli rubber flooring wraps around walls and units making a practical foil to accessories. Italian enamelled brass taps are a Hi-tech must.*

studded synthetic rubber, more often associated with floors in airports and art galleries, is here used to cover walls, the splash back and the work surface. Colours are bold, and set against black shelves, these primary shades help to draw attention to the kitchen utensils, all on permanent display on their racks or hooks. Since everything in the kitchen is on show, notice that even the utensils have been carefully chosen both for colour and design. The extremely limited space available suggests this very dense arrangement but the same ideas could well be expanded into a far larger space, to equally good effect; in which case the shelving might not be so densely stacked, but the stores should be neatly displayed.

Bathroom plus

The bathroom, in the same house, is even smaller than the kitchen, measuring just 1.52 m × 1.37 m (5 ft × 4½ ft). The same materials are used as in the kitchen; the tough synthetic rubber surface that will not scratch, chip or prove difficult to keep clean. Notice that the same colour scheme has been chosen, which helps to give a sense of space and unity.

Shortage of room has led to a 'galley bathroom', with folding mirror and towel rail that can be folded back over the basin when not in use – simple and yet inexpensive ways of maximizing the potential of restricted space.

Taps, toothbrushes and holder and all fittings are, as in the kitchen, brightly coloured and neatly designed objects in their own right. It is in a confined space like this that carefully chosen sets of implements or fittings are essential – otherwise the tiny room would look chaotic and very far from Hi-tech.

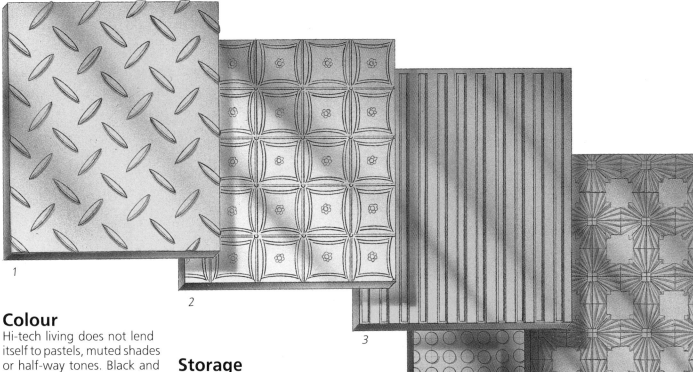

1

2

3

4

5

Colour

Hi-tech living does not lend itself to pastels, muted shades or half-way tones. Black and white, or red and black, or any combination of either monochrome or primary shades look good. The use of steel and matt black or satinized finishes in many of the objects or furnishings designed for a Hi-tech setting also suggests that these colours and textures are most suitable. If you are trying to achieve the look, without the kind of expenditure that designer-made furniture implies, then respraying and ingenious DIY touches can help you to get it right.

Surfaces

As pointed out in the section on flooring, the use of industrial and hardwearing materials is important. Many of the materials used as flooring appear elsewhere; for example, the studded synthetic rubber used widely in the kitchen and bathroom illustrated. However, natural materials such as ceramics or slate can look extremely well as kitchen surfaces, and do not detract from the functional look that is required.

Storage

Hi-tech living is uncompromising. If you want to store unsightly things (perhaps the furniture you grew fond of in another style?) the best plan is to either give over a small box room entirely to storage so that it need not be seen, or else build a walk-in cupboard for the purpose. It could be under the stairs or off a passage. Other items, books, papers or files, can be stacked on metal shelving — for although neatness is essential in the Hi-tech house, a certain degree of everyday busy-ness can be visible — the evidence of industry at home? A good way of achieving storage space as well as the impression of a bigger room is to have mirrored doors; when closed they magnify the area quite dramatically. Another way round the problem of storage is to try and find furniture that combines a series of drawers or unused space; for example a bed may conveniently disguise a generous area of unused space, ideal for keeping bed linen and towels out of sight.

House plants

The discipline of the Hi-tech interior suggests that some relief is needed and often a choice of bold plants, with strong and unusual foliage, can bring just the necessary touch of life. Plants have become very fashionable in the conservatories of many Hi-tech offices and commercial buildings, and the kind of palms and exotics that are used to soften those environments look well in a domestic setting — given enough space so that they don't overwhelm the occupants. Of course if your

Non-slip rubber floor covering: (1) runner in deck plate design; (3) (5) embossed stripes and circles available in tiles and runner; (2) (4) pressed tin wall or ceiling sheeting.

house or flat actually has the space for a conservatory you can add a simply designed greenhouse and provide the same effect, seen from further away. Not all conservatories are extravagant Gothic or Victorian reproductions and such an extension can also provide a practical heat store as well as an extra room.

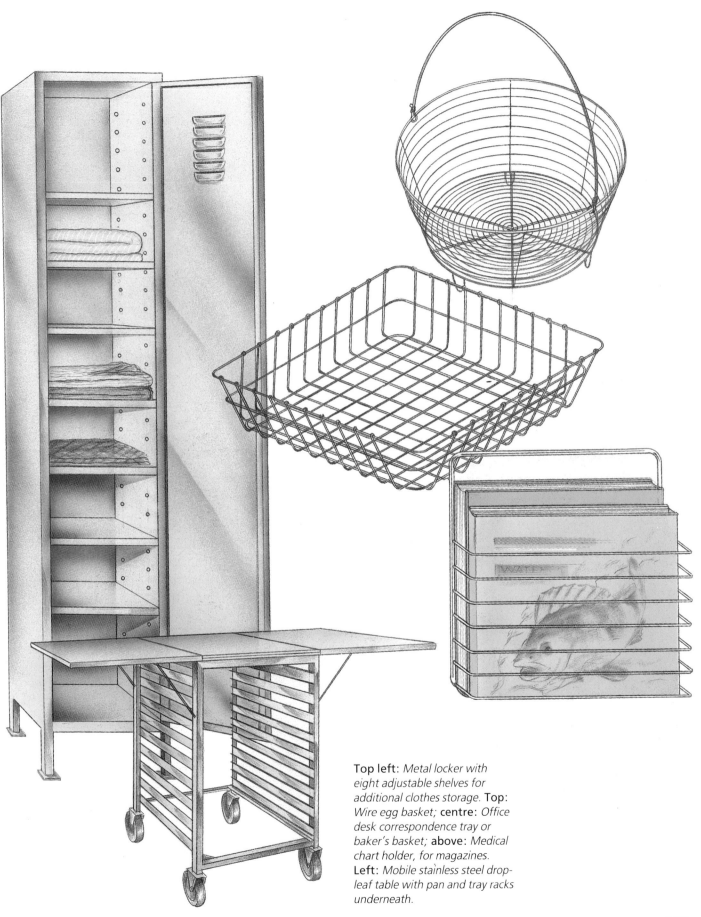

Top left: *Metal locker with eight adjustable shelves for additional clothes storage.* **Top:** *Wire egg basket;* **centre:** *Office desk correspondence tray or baker's basket;* **above:** *Medical chart holder, for magazines.* **Left:** *Mobile stainless steel drop-leaf table with pan and tray racks underneath.*

POST MODERN

The origins of this relatively recent style are difficult to ascertain but it is generally thought to have been sparked off towards the end of the 1960s by the American architect, Charles Jencks. Jencks was then co-author with George Baird of a book entitled *Meaning in Architecture*; its appearance in 1969 caused shock waves throughout architectural circles because Jencks suggested that the driving force of Post-Modernism was a quest for meaning.

It could also be said that the whole Post-Modern movement was in revolt against contemporary 1960s Modernism, which at the time still held sway in America, as elsewhere. By the early 1970s, a few architects were exchanging the 'less is more' dictum of the Bauhaus for the 'less is a bore' declaration of Post-Modern architect, Robert Venturi. Post-Modernists argued the case for the return of architectural ornament. Ornament could express symbolism; it could be a language. Ornament could be fun and provide the fantasy element – something that had been missing from architecture and landscaping for far too long they claimed. Ornament could also serve a visual purpose: the eye tires quickly when it is left to roam over too many blank, empty surfaces; visual accents were needed.

With this in mind architects such as Jencks, Venturi and Robert Stern went back to the past to study the uses and value of architectural ornament. From their studies the architects developed their own personal interpretations of classical Greek and Egyptian styles but the gist of the message was that, given today's technology and materials, attention could now be refocussed on the importance of string courses, mouldings, arches and columns.

A love of symbolism also features strongly in Jenck's garden at his Los Angeles home. Milton's *Allegro* is illustrated by beds of vivid pink, red, blue and white flowers in the pool-side garden at the approach to the house. The house itself, whose dining room is featured opposite, symbolizes the four elements: fire, earth, air and water. The architectural style is that of a conventional ranch with a series of pavilions which are painted in varying shades of blue and mauve. Most of the materials used are simple stained wooden boarding and simple framing. There is a pool built in the shape of the state of California, and nearby is a pergola with path leading from the bright flowery *Allegro* side of the house to the shadowy canyon side with its greenery and here the darker thoughts of Milton's *Il Penseroso* are realized. Here, too, a rustic alphabet designed by Jencks, has quotations from the poem carved on the transom beams of the garage-temple where refuse bins and sewage containers are stored.

POST-MODERN

Dining room

The sun-drenched corner of the dining room at Charles Jencks's Los Angeles house has been cleverly utilized and special windows feature an uninterrupted central viewing panel so that the link with the outside is retained. Note the lack of curtains and blinds, an important aspect of Post-Modern rooms; an unusual small curved, screen in fretwork echoes the intimacy of the round table. Fan-shaped chair backs seem to act as a further screen and the blonde wood is incised with silver tape, which gives an overall effect reminiscent of Egyptian palace and Art Déco furnishing. The floor is of ceramic tiles in two colours. The famous Jencksian stylized stepped palm motif appears in the architrave moulding and the light fitting sconce.

Many features in the room can be simulated surprisingly inexpensively; for example, the marbled finishes on the ceiling, plaster bowl light fitting and serving counter top. Acquiring a set of neo-Egyptian dining chairs on the lines of the ones shown here, however, would mean employing the services of an expert craftsman cabinet maker, but, it is still possible to buy bargains in Art Déco chairs which could be given bird's eye maple graining and lining out treatment. The dining room table top could be a circle of blockboard also grained and lined out, the base being made from an existing table.

Mock details

It is also worth hunting round DIY suppliers for reproductions of old mouldings; many shops now stock these in wood, plastic or polystyrene. Also worth looking for are moulded wood brackets and beading to make fluted legs on furniture. There is an enormous selection of ready-made arches, columns and corbels that could be adapted to Post-Modern style. The same applies to door and window frames, although special designs, such as the large bull's eye, diamond, triangular and semi-circular that feature in Post-Modern detailing, would have to be specially made and built in.

Mouldings

Post-Modern style depends on the use of mouldings to add visual pauses and interest to bare expanses of wall. Specialist DIY suppliers now stock comprehensive ranges in wood, plastic or polystyrene. Some of the simpler cove and bolection mouldings are of the type Post-Modernists use to accentuate architectural detail. It can be difficult for

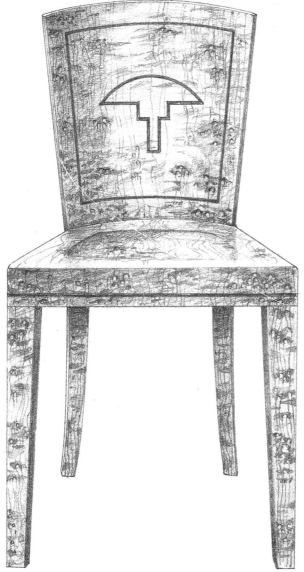

Above: *Lining out creates interest on plain furniture. You can use a fine artist's brush and acrylic paint, a felt-tip pen or narrow self-adhesive tapes for decorating car body work can also work well.*

Right: *Marbling small areas by hand can be done quickly using a sponge to smudge acrylic paints in diagonal lines onto an emulsion-painted ground. With a fine brush, 'fidget' in the veins.*

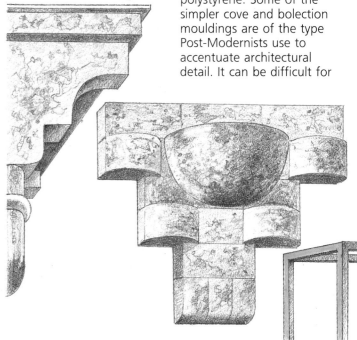

DIY enthusiasts to make accurate mitres in some of the wider skirting board mouldings but most of the other narrower mouldings can be mitred using a framer's mitre block. Charles Jencks has also rethought the mitre problem in some cases, slotting the moulding in at right angles as seen in the bathroom dado mouldings around the basins. Other Post-Modern mouldings, for example, the stepped palm tree around the lighting sconces and architraves, can be cut out of hardboard, plywood sheet or, better still, multiple density fibreboard which can be routed out.

Moulding adhesives are so strong that fixing them in place is fairly straightforward, but in the case of some of the heavier wooden mouldings or where the surface is uneven, it may be necessary to insert panel pins about 15 cm (6 in) in from the mitred corner. This would be the case if you were making the architectural-style clock, as

Below left: *Stepped walls are typically Post-Modern. Create extra interest with frames made from painted mouldings to surround displayed ceramic vases.* Left: *Moulding off-cuts are useful for making clock surrounds.* Above: *Detail of bird's eye maple graining.*

shown above. It is also a good idea to paint the mouldings before actually sticking them to the surface. When fixing moulding, place it on the wall where you want it to go, make sure it is straight, and then draw around it. Sanding the area lightly gives better adhesion but take care not to go over the pencil lines.

When making a fake door panel (see dining room) it is necessary to work out where to fix the bead mouldings first. The beading can then be cut and mitred to fit before being stuck down on to a piece of hardboard and painted over with emulsion to match the walls. Alternatively, you could substitute garden trellis for the squares of moulding.

Bird's eye maple graining

Again, try and obtain a piece of bird's eye maple or study some genuine examples. Practise the effects first on a piece of wood until you get the one you want. Then sand down the surfaces well and paint with a coat of cream emulsion. When this is dry, dilute some burnt sienna artist's acrylic paint in a little water and lightly sponge the surface all over. Then while the paint is still wet, use a professional grainer's mottling brush to simulate the maple grain and 'flirt' in the highlights. The mottling brush takes out some parts of the colour while giving the remainder a soft 'mottled' look. Bird's eye maple

markings are irregular so you will need to soften and blur some areas while defining others with more of the tiny wood knots that make the 'bird's eyes'. These can be applied with a little diluted burnt umber artist's acrylic paint and should consist of a tiny dark spot in a light centre.

Professional grainers apply these knots with a special tool which is hollow in the centre, but spots painted in with a fine brush will be as effective as long as the base paint is still wet. Areas of the wood can then be sponged over with diluted raw sienna, and a graining brush used to add the finishing touches when dry. Finally, apply a clear high gloss varnish for long-lasting protection.

167

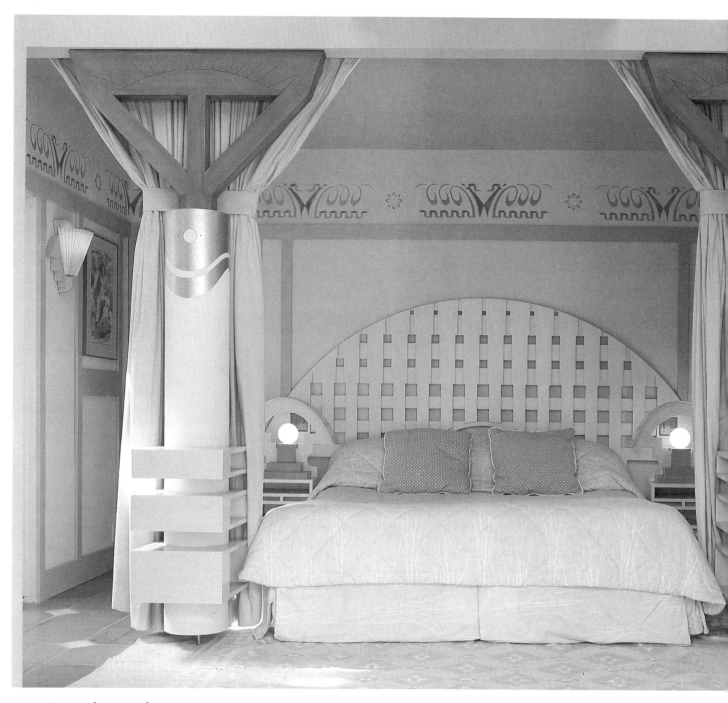

Los Angeles order

This is the master bedroom in the Aer Pavilion of the Jencks's Los Angeles home. The bed gives the impression of a four-poster with its specially designed columns in the style that Jencks has christened the Los Angeles order. Here sunrises are carved in relief on the redwood capitals, while the bases are prevented from looking over-heavy by being slightly suspended above the floor – a central steel support gives the impression that they are almost floating. The stepped base, another Jencksian characteristic, provides visual relief as well as practical storage. More of the Jencksian stylized 'stepped' palm tree motifs are echoed on the bedside table lamp bases and wall lamp sconces.

A specially designed trellis-style bedhead and the white quilted bedspread recall the style of the Scottish architect, Charles Rennie Mackintosh. But ordinary painted garden trellis could be substituted and look very stylist. The floor tiles are terracotta inset with pale grey ceramic tozzettos (inlay tiles). A painted frieze above the bed represents the four elements of fire, air, earth and water. The whole

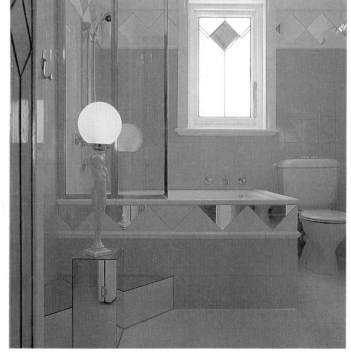

'The shock of the old' is how Charles Jencks first described the effect of discovering classical architecture and ornament. Here, in a bedroom translated in beautifully subtle colours, traces of Egyptian palace entablature can be seen in the wonderfully monumental columns and frieze. **Right:** *As can be seen in these bathrooms, ornament and attention to detail are important. Friezes, lighting, furniture and decorative finishes have meant the revival of old crafts and techniques using new materials.*

Hollywood bowl

Shades of 1930s Hollywood and Art Déco influences are seen in this peach colour scheme and luxurious use of mirror. A frieze of mirror tiles on the walls is repeated again on the sides of the bath. Display stands of mirror glass support a Retro globe lamp fitting. Note the Post-Modern hallmark of unadorned windows – a single mirror tile and some decorative leading.

Hollywood basin

Generous pedestal basins in the 1930s style appear to float on the navy carpet. Note the Post-Modern details: alcoves backed in deep blue glass where a galaxy of perfume bottles seems to be suspended on invisible, fitted glass shelves. Classical details are also cleverly reinterpreted – conventional arch keystones become keystone-shaped mirrors acting as a visual linking device between the circular windows above the alcoves. Dado rail bolection (indented) moulding painted blue accentuates architectural detailing while wall-fixed lamps beam the light ceilingwards and create a feeling of infinite space.

colour scheme is typically Post-Modern and particularly successful: soft greys for the wall panelling and woodwork while the colours in the dhurrie are repeated in the peach curtains and the frieze.

The effect is stunning, tremendously stylish and has great individuality.

Stencilling

It is quite easy to make up border stencils using simple motifs of the kind shown in the bedroom picture. Shops providing photocopies can enlarge your own motifs which can then be traced off on to traditional stencil board or acetate. Acetate film is easier to cut and register when working on border repeats; it also enables very fine and precise lines to be drawn but you will need waterproof ink and a special pen (such as a rotring). The 'bridges' between the cut-out areas should be strong because if they are too thin the stencil will break. Acrylic artist's paints are suitable for small areas and are far less wasteful than buying litres of emulsion paint. Spray-on mount adhesive is useful when stencilling precise motifs which need even application and absolutely clean sharp edges. Using mount adhesive on the back of a stencil rather than drawing pins will allow you to move the stencil easily without making marks. An alternative idea is to stencil a border pattern on to a roll of paper and stick this to the wall, as stencilling directly on to the wall is tiring on the arms. Use a good quality lining paper and stick with a wallpaper adhesive. But if using this method check that the stencil paints are waterproof, such as acrylic. Use a separate stencil for each colour.

Mirror tiles

Mirror tiles are easy to apply to walls as well as ceramic, wood and laminate surfaces. Most mirror tiles come with their own self-adhesive pads for fixing but there are some types that need to be attached with special mirror-fixing adhesives.

Lead strip

Decorative, self-adhesive lead strip comes in various widths and in white, gold or traditional grey to simulate that used with real stained glass. The coloured infills can be painted using special glass paints; alternatively, coloured transparent plastic films held in place by the leading are effective. Both paints and coloured films are applied to the inside of the window and are reasonably resistant to sunlight. Lead strip used in this way also looks effective when the infills are not coloured or when very little colour is used.

Above: *Stencilled borders add colour and visual interest to a room, while (halved) mirror tiles make a smart bathroom feature.*

Right: *Stained-glass windows are a good disguise for windows that are overlooked or have an unpleasant view. Note the mirror tile infill, as used by Charles Jencks in his bathroom.*

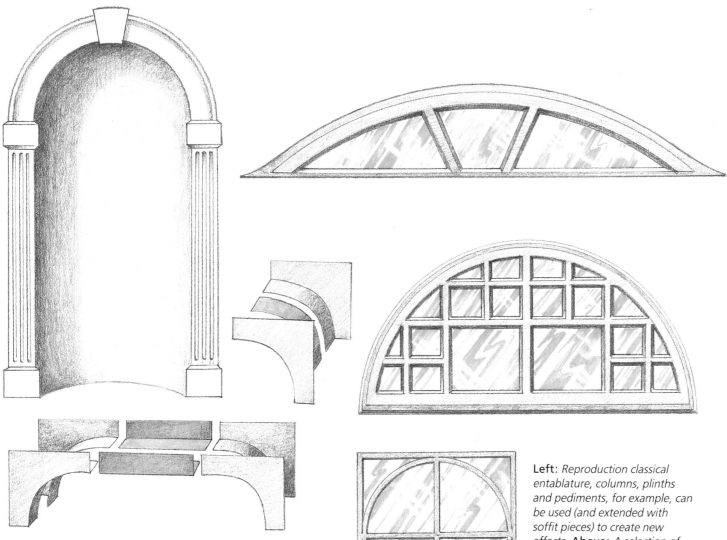

Arches and columns

These now come pre-fabricated in several Greek patterns and are mostly made from glass-reinforced plastic, (GRP); arches may also be in polystyrene. There are a number of sizes to choose from so it is a question of picking the one that best fits the aperture; larger apertures may need a bridging section which can be cut to size; extra soffit pieces can also be used to fill a gap where the wall thickness exceeds 23 cm (9 in). Ready-made styles will not be Post-Modern so they will need replastering to achieve the right look; lengths of plastic drainpipe can be used for small columns, once marbled over no one would ever guess their origin.

Windows

It is possible to build-in extra transoms and mullions on ready-made designs but windows of the type seen in the dining room picture of Charles Jencks's Los Angeles house are specially made to his design. Similarly, round bullseye windows can be purchased ready-made but the cost is higher if you want them to open. Windows larger than 60 cm (2 ft) diameter, as seen in the bathroom pictures, would also have to be specially made. Setting round windows into a brick wall also requires considerable building skill.

Universal symbols

Critics of Post-Modernism point out that deciding on

Left: *Reproduction classical entablature, columns, plinths and pediments, for example, can be used (and extended with soffit pieces) to create new effects.* **Above:** *A selection of Post-Modern windows. Many enthusiasts prefer slatted blinds to curtains – often made up in unusual shapes.*

symbols that signify universal values and spiritual beliefs is not easy. All too often it results in a private language understood only by a few. And the return to yesterday's architectural styles has resulted in buildings of gargantuan, over-blown classicism. Only time can tell what the true implications and outcome of this style will be. But where Post-Modernism has made a positive contribution is in the renewed attention that architects of the 1980s have been paying to architectural detail and decoration.

Interiors and exteriors have seen an increased use of mouldings, alcoves, top lighting and a generally increased awareness of the possibilities offered by old buildings and how they can be adapted in a more sympathetic way, and with greater individuality. As a style Post-Modernism shares something with Art Déco, many of the old cinema façades of the 1920s and 1930s incorporated a light-hearted approach to Greek and Egyptian styles and are now considered architectural gems in their own right.

171

MINIMALIST

This is the look that wins most favour with those who are involved in decision-making. Architects and designers, whose job entails a daily agonizing over the complexities of form, pattern and colour, become Minimalists in their own homes where their idea of relaxed surroundings is interpreted by having nothing around to distract them. Minimalist homes are intentionally bare, clinical and smooth-functioning; a look that is both pleasing to the eye and takes precedence over tactile comfort.

The birthplace of Minimalism was probably the Bauhaus — that great design school founded by architect Walter Gropius at Weimar in 1919, just after the end of World War I. In the early days of the movement, students and teachers carried the idea to an extreme by living on a 'Minimalist' diet: a kind of vegetarian mash without the addition of any spices except garlic. Fortunately, this part of Bauhausian Minimalism did not become as popular as other aspects of the movement, but it was part of the Bauhaus attempt at 'starting from zero'. Indeed, it was this catchphrase together with the pronouncement of Minimalist architect, Mies van der Rohe, that 'less is more', which sums up the aims of Minimalist style.

Bauhaus radicalism was applied ruthlessly to everything from buildings and interiors to gadgets. The Bauhaus architect, Marcel Breuer, actually went as far as designing a Minimalist nursery, in which giant play blocks doubled as infant storage units. And an early Breuer kitchen, *circa* 1922, was designed around a modular system that was considered revolutionary at the time. It was the first fitted kitchen of the type we recognize today and, true Minimalist that he was, Breuer had hidden everything behind uniform cupboard doors.

Unfortunately, the efforts of the early pioneers of Minimalism were generally unappreciated. Utopian schemes for workers' housing failed dismally as occupants complained that the interiors were too clinical. They wanted cosiness and they found the bare interiors difficult to decorate; there was no patterned wallpaper, no curtains or flowery rugs, no fringed lampshades and no mantelpieces for displaying personal memorabilia. Radiator coils were left absolutely bare, there was no upholstered furniture in 'pretty fabrics'; only hard, shiny, uncomfortable tubular steel, leather, cane or canvas seating. The lighter and harder the material used, the better according to the Bauhaus maxim. Scatter rugs were also 'out' and grey and black lino went underfoot.

Design concepts

It is strange to think that what seems to be conventional design nowadays was once regarded as shocking. On the other hand, the famous rectilinear furniture of the Dutch architect, Gerrit Rietveld, still looks as startling today as it did to the stolid burghers of Rotterdam in the 1920s. The Bauhaus-trained architect, Le Corbusier, famous for his 'Modular' grid system which was based on the golden section and for his dictum, 'the house is a machine for living in,' designed a bathroom for the Villa Savoye at Poissy, which had a contoured minimalist ceramic-tiled chaise longue that would take pride of place in any bathroom today. And yet it was designed more than 50 years ago.

Indeed, it is probably because of the Minimalists' ability to rethink design concepts at a fundamental level that any real change has taken place in the way bedrooms and bathrooms are used today. According to many forward-thinking Minimalists, bedrooms will become smaller and will function solely as sleeping areas by being reduced to almost the same size as the bed. The space that would have been used for wardrobe storage, and the extra space gained from the reduced-size bedroom will be used as a

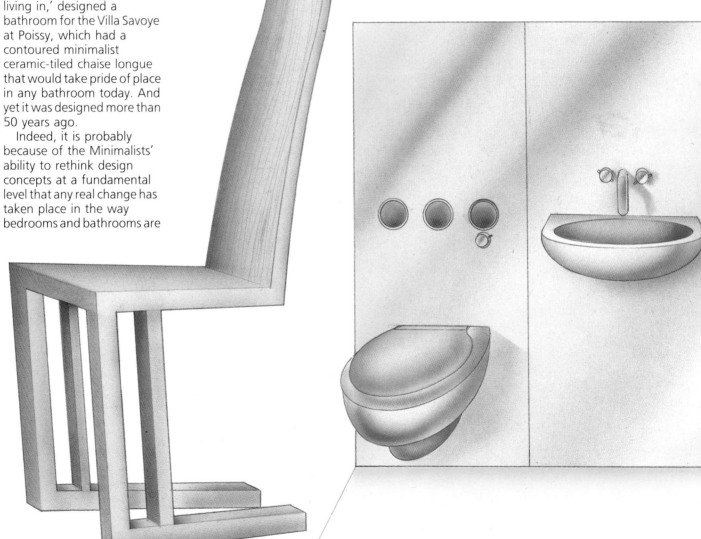

Left: *Eighties minimalism. This cantilevered chair designed by Nicholas Mortimer looks elegant but offers few concessions to comfort.* **Below**: *Quick-assembly laminated panels in the bathroom take a wall-hung basin and w.c.*

laundry-cum-valet or 'grooming' room.

This would be a far more hygienic arrangement for the washing, ironing and storage of clothes than the current practice of using the kitchen. The bathroom of the 1990s will also have to become larger if only to accommodate such extras as a minimalist wall-hung bidet which, in current terms, means adding an extra two metres of space to the average five square metres.

However, Minimalism is a

style that is expensive to achieve successfully. It relies to a great extent on perfect craftsmanship and expensive materials: marble, stainless steel, ceramic tiles and expert spray-on finishes are not, as a rule, cheap. But budding design students who are also good at DIY can achieve Minimalist style on a budget by using re-cycled materials and building clever storage-cum-seating platforms. The guiding principle is that no electrical wiring or plumbing must show. This usually means expensive chasing work; channels have to be gouged out of existing walls; the offending wires or pipes laid and the surfaces expertly replastered. The easiest way round this problem if you want to achieve Minimalist style is to do it all beforehand – preferably at the building stage. Alternatively, if you are converting an existing room, one solution is to build a complete shell within the existing four walls, and for this quick-assembly partition wall systems can be useful.

High sleeping

The raised sleeping platform of the bed, shown overleaf, was built in plywood and then covered with industrial metal flooring of aluminium sheet. The textured, raised surface can be easily cleaned by wiping it over with a damp cloth. Electrical outlets are neatly inset into the platform at the foot of the bed and covered by a stainless steel flap when not in use. The platform also houses all the unsightly wiring as well as providing extra storage. Access to this is by means of trap doors. This type of floor must be earthed to comply with safety regulations and this is a job best tackled by experts. An elegant standard, uplighter lamp fitting appears to light the whole room but other concealed lighting is also making a discreet contribution. The D-shape cut-out area of the platform provides a storage niche for a television set or flower display.

The bed, specially designed in polished aluminium, could also be considered as a piece of free-standing sculpture in its own right.

The only concession made to its original purpose is the white cotton bedspread with its pretty white scalloped edge. The silver Venetian blind sporting extra-slim slats is a very Minimalist feature. The only colours that are allowed to intrude on what is essentially a monochromatic scheme are the primary red, blue and yellow teamed with black on the Rietveld chair. This chair is not intended to be comfortable, its function is purely to provide visual contrast.

Left: *Minimalist cabin-style door made in aluminium sheet has a rubber edging strip to improve fit and reduce noise.* **Below:** *Artist, Piet Mondrian (1872-1944) embraced minimalist ethics in his abstract grid paintings.*

Left: *Cool, uncluttered calm is of the essence in the living room.* **Above**: *No messy bathmats are allowed to feature in the bathroom!*

Black and white

Severe, rectilinear Minimalist living rooms can still make some concessions to comfortable seating: soft furnishings with a 'hard edge' can be chosen for this purpose. Here, the sofa matches the grey of the occasional tables placed in the foreground and at the side. The narrow, Minimalist black and white stripes of the mirror frame are cleverly echoed in the pottery plate. The white ceramic floor tiles set in dark grey grouting make a pleasing grid pattern and provide a wonderful, light reflecting surface. Anyone who wants to make a dark basement lighter would be advised to lay a white ceramic floor like this. It is worth shopping around for white ceramic floor tiles as some DIY super stores are offering a variety of inexpensive ranges. Minimal maintenance with a damp sponge and hot water are all that is needed to keep them sparkling bright.

A single, severe standard uplighter beams its light on to the ceiling giving the illusion of infinite space above. Other background lighting is provided by means of tiny concealed, ceiling-fixed downlighters which are suitably discreet and unobtrusive. All the lighting here can be operated on dimmer switch controls so the atmosphere can be altered to suit the mood.

In Minimalist living rooms, television, hi-fi, video and books – no matter how well designed – are hidden away. Wall units similar to the type in the dining room picture are appropriate. Some of the more recent German designs also possess a chameleon-like ability to change from a sober flush-fronted bookcase to a fully equipped bar or TV and video unit at the flick of a switch. For those contemplating building their own hi-fi equipment into storage units or platforms would be wise to check its suitability with the manufacturer, as special models do exist for building into enclosed situations.

A wall crammed with paintings is anathema to Minimalists. One at a time is

convenient space-saving and inexpensive ways to provide this bathroom essential. Nautical touches are apparent in the porthole window and net magazine holder that stores sponges and soap. A stainless steel wall-fixed towel holder meant for the kitchen does a neat space-saving job and holds the Minimalist occupant's obligatory black (or white) bath towel. Top lighting is neatly concealed behind a false ceiling which acts as a baffle and diffuses the fluorescent light downwards. A laboratory storage jar houses a loofah, back brush and sponge.

Eating in style

This dining room is a Minimalist's dream, with nothing but the barest essentials on show. The open expanse of laminate topped table is relieved by a vase of tulips heads hanging *au naturel* and offering an exaggerated spot of colour against the starkness of the surroundings. And if you are wondering what lies behind the anonymous wall of storage units, neat rows of drinking glasses and tableware is the answer. The doors on units like these operate on magnetic touch catches, which mean that no handles are needed. DIY enthusiasts should take care when fixing them to pick the right catch for the door weight and to ensure accurate alignment.

Kitchen economy

Complete uniformity is what kitchen Minimalists look for. These clean line German units with D-shaped handles have been designed with

the rule. Objects are given similarly selective treatment, the opaque glass vases here need no flower arrangements since these would detract from the perfection of their form.

Bathroom chic

This is a bathroom designed on true Bauhaus Minimalist principles. With all these hard surfaces no concessions have been made to tactile comforts, although the soft beige tones of real marble counteract too much sterility. Having floors and walls clad in marble also means you can splash away with impunity — no need for untidy shower curtains and screens. Minimalists also realize that running a shower from mixer taps is one of the most

Minimalists in mind. Sinks and hob units should present no visual interruptions on the worktop surface; they should match in colour and, have no mounting plates to ensure that they appear integral to the worktop. No colourful casseroles or folksy pottery adorn this kitchen. Saucepans are kept to a miniumum: these shiny stainless steel saucepans have built-in steamers so a three-course

Top: *Maximum storage for minimalist tableware.* **Above**: *Clean lines give the ideal effect.*

meal can be cooked to perfection — with minimal effort. A centred services column above the sink carries plumbing and electrical wiring.

Slimline Venetian blinds screen the Minimalist cook from the untidy world outside.

Finishes

Stainless steel may seem an unconventional choice for a bath (see page 177) but it has been in use for some time now in hospitals. It is also possible to find stainless steel w.c. fittings; public conveniences are sometimes fitted with these as stainless steel is regarded as having better vandal-proof qualities than ceramic. Stainless steel wash basins can be made from small, circular sinks inset into a countertop. Stainless steel wall tiles are available and a stainless steel edging strip gives a smart, tough finish around architraves and for kickplates on built-in kitchen storage units.

Although stainless steel is heat-resistant and non-corrosive it is not scratch-resistant. This does not matter for flooring but a stainless steel bath and sink may benefit from occasional polishing with a non-abrasive cleaning paste.

Minimalists also take for-granted the fact that w.cs. bidets and basins should be wall hung wherever possible and cisterns should be concealed; this saves floor and wall space and looks so much neater. Pre-plumbed laminate panels are also something Minimalists prefer so that piping can be instantly hidden – useful if you are building a completely new interior in an existing shell. Even taps can be Minimalist: a plain chrome, or enamelled pipe is the ideal, fussy embellishments are out.

To some extent Minimalism is the precursor of the 1990s. Not least because it extends to the way electronic gadgets and appliances are styled. The spirit of Minimalism embraces both an amusing approach to design, such as the folded metal clock above, and electronic remote control where computers and all technical developments in this field will eventually lead

to change in the design of our homes and the way we want to live in them. What was once a dream of a few far-sighted European architects back in the 1920s has now become a reality.

Electronics

For instance, tomorrow's sleeping platforms such as the one shown on page 173, may well contain control panels for operating the rest of the home. Heating, security, bills, recipes may be summoned up at the push of a button.

Alternatively, control panels could be installed in the headboard, although Minimalists might decline to see a visible control board; in which case there would probably be some camouflage panel – Minimalists do not like to see their electronics on show. But eventually the bed itself may disappear – by day it could sink down into the platform out of view while

Left: *Taps by Vola have clean sculptured lines; sinks are moulded as an integral part of the worktop.* **Above:** *Clocks boast smooth surfaces devoid of numerals; dials tell the time.*

the platform is used as a daytime office.

Household chores are already made easier by Minimalists who think nothing of using the most sophisticated equipment. Microwave ovens, which can cook food in seconds, will be a normal feature alongside traditional cooking gadgets that are so well designed they cannot easily be improved upon. Energy-saving is another attraction of electronic gadgets. Today's (and tomorrow's) dishwashers and washing machines are more economic to run and less wasteful of heat energy; they are also quieter running and easier to set. Minimalists do not mind

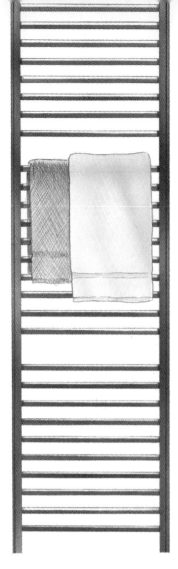

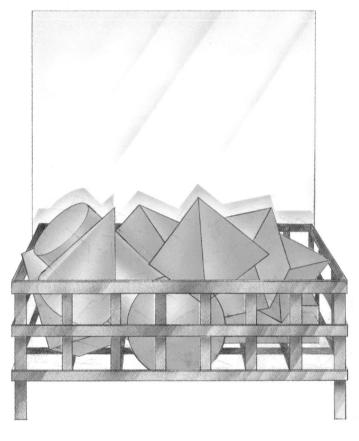

Far left: *Today's radiators are designed to be on show; narrow ones can run along a skirting or up an architrave. This example doubles as a towel rail and as efficient bathroom heating.*

Left: *Fireplaces can still be focal points in minimalist interiors without compromising aesthetic principles. The Geolog gas fire is the first of its kind to provide a modern solution.*

paying over the odds for these extra advantages; in fact, it can be money well spent as some computerized electronic appliances can now diagnose their own faults, making inconvenient, costly visits from service engineers less likely.

Heating, ventilation points

The hard surfaces, which are such a feature of Minimilism, encourage a tendency towards condensation. To combat this unpleasant side effect Minimalists spend a good deal of money ensuring that good insulation, ventilation and heating are included at the outset of construction. Windows streaming with condensation do not enhance the clean uncluttered impression of this style. The installation of double glazing is essential and as a precaution the minimalist invests in the best

sealed units available. Minimalists may even have roller blinds specially fitted inside the double glazed units.

When considering the effects of heating on hard surfaces, underfloor systems, whether electric or waterborne, work particularly well with ceramic and marble floors and are very popular in Scandinavian countries. Discreet radiator grilles can also be inset face upwards in floors under a window to counteract any down draughts. Once the method of heating has been chosen, the next step is to ensure adequate ventilation; Minimalist living depends very much on this as a hidden asset. Minimalist kitchens and bathrooms feel airy and pleasant with no unpleasant

smells and this demands frequent air changes – around 3 to 4 in each hour is considered comfortable.

It is probable that future ventilation systems will comprise a ducted core built into the home with the function of warming cold air as it comes into the home and then distributing it to the different areas, while simultaneously extracting the stale air. In hot weather the system will work in reverse.

When it comes to kitchen ventilation, a wide variety of appliances have been designed with Minimalist kitchens in mind and are readily available. There are, for example, ovens which combine integral extractor fans, and hob units that also have powerful extractors to

suck offending cooking smells downwards through low-level ducting to an outside wall. Although more expensive than conventional cooker hoods, these hob fittings are well worth the extra expense because of their improved efficiency and space-saving features.

Small bathrooms can also be ventilated successfully with electrically operated, ventilated, louvre appliances, some of which also incorporate a light. Louvred windows are useful in lavatories and kitchens as ventilation can be controlled without causing unnecessary draughts.

But not all Minimalists agree that every source of heat and light should be hidden from view. Some yearn for fireplaces and feel the need to look at a flickering flame. A white ceramic tiled surround is acceptable within the confines of Minimalism while a fireback of heat-resistant glass makes a change from traditional black cast iron. Even Minimalist gas-logs are different from conventional logs – the fire cement can be moulded into geometric shapes such as tetrahedrons, spheres and cubes which glow from a specially designed sand blasted and polished iron basket.

CREATIVE SALVAGE

The style of Creative Salvage, and the present interest in recycling scrap material and turning it into decorative art forms of unusual and exciting furniture designs can be traced back to the beginning of this century.

Dada, the forerunner of this style, was an art movement (of continental origin) created by, amongst others, Marcel Duchamp and Francis Picabia in New York. A revolt against what they saw as the smugness of the art world's attitude to artistic creations, it involved the use of household objects assembled in such a way as to render them useless, turning them instead into new and controversial art forms. It was a disillusioned, cynical movement brought about by the effects of World War I and was an artistic comment against established values.

During the comparative affluence of the 1920s and early 1930s, the interest in this particular art form and design subsided as the more sophisticated monochromatic and Art Deco ideas took over. Fashionable society wanted geometrical lines, so, while designers still used modern materials and metals, the shapes were sleeker, simpler and more considered.

It was not until after World War II that the theme of recycling came back into practice. At that time it was no longer part of an anti-establishment stand which reflected market and cultural values, it was a necessity. The upper and middle classes were forced to discover and resort to their own form of recycling because of the shortages caused by the war. Thus they transformed parachute silk into wedding dresses and curtains into coats and were drawn into the development of their own recycling style.

In the furniture design field, Creative Salvage was once more used for utility purposes. The design of furniture made from orange crates was applauded and encouraged, at least while the shortage of raw materials existed. After that, a society eager to return to its former level of luxury was glad to disgard such an idea borne out of deprivations.

The receptive 1960s with its cultural ideology, its hippie-ethnic look, gave way to the materialistic 1970s. All in the design world was slick, sleek and, some would consider, antiseptic and cold. The era of mass-produced, mass-marketed furniture had arrived and there was little interest in individuality. Comfort was in conformity.

Now, however, the wheel has turned full circle and Creative Salvage is back. As with the punk movement, its roots are in rebellion. The hard edge of the design is softened by the use of fabrics and colour and, like the character of the 1980s, it is a style for the individual who is courageous, confident and daring.

Black, white and grey

The Creative Salvage style is ideally suited for a high-rise town apartment or a warehouse loft conversion. In its purest form, the colourless theme of black, white and grey blends well with the stark concrete lines of the buildings outside but for those who need colour in their homes to compensate for the lack of outside city colour, the idea adapts well.

Developing the style

It is important to remember that although some of these furniture designs are made from scrap metal, the overall effect of the style is not junk. Overcrowding is out. Rooms should be kept uncluttered and fairly spartan, allowing the decorative points of interest to show in the furniture. In the bedroom, shown on the previous page, there is a Minimalist mood with the bed, table and campaign chair being the only large objects in the room. All of them are strictly functional. It is only the decorative pieces on the marble-topped table that add a display point and have no apparent use. Interestingly, the ornate silver pieces contrast well with the style's imposed sparseness and lighten the heaviness of the furniture. The Creative Salvage style is one that can be sophisticated enough to incorporate old valued pieces into the thoroughly modern room.

Left: *Modern sculptural metalwork can be softened by incorporating antique heirlooms or old-style designs. These decorative objects are also practical – another necessity for the style.*

Ceilings

The beamed ceilings here are painted over in a dark colour not only to emphasize the contrast of light and dark, but also to give the optical effect of drawing them downwards and thus reducing the height of the ceiling. This room with its near floor-length windows and high ceilings is light enough to take the dark colour but if you are decorating anywhere smaller, a lighter shade would be better. If you wish to make a special feature of the ceiling, use gloss paint which will complement the hard metallic gloss of the furniture. Otherwise, to draw it down and yet keep it unobtrusive, use matt or eggshell paint.

Flooring

The hard, spartan theme is further emphasized by plain varnished floorboards and bare undecorated walls. If you have boards that are in good condition or where only one or two need to be replaced, then varnishing is an immediate option. If they are not good enough to be displayed in their natural state, try colour-staining or painting them. You could either keep close to the natural colour or be more adventurous and go for a complete contrast. Whitewash (rubbed down to give a limed effect), off-white paint or pastel colours would be suitable.

Walls

This style is perfect for those on a limited budget because you not only avoid the expense of covering the walls with pictures, but you need not repair already visible faults. Here, the plaster marks have been left unpainted. Peeling plain wallpaper would have the same effect and provide a break from an otherwise overall blandness. If you are unlucky enough to have a perfect finish, you can achieve a similar effect by painting a part of the wall in a different, or darker shade from the rest. Another interesting way of livening up a plain wall is to add surface textures. You could do this by lining it with newspaper applied in an abstract way, and then painting or colour-washing when dry. The effect is different but still appropriate to the style.

Left: Curtains in disarray allow for creative indulgence and look wonderful. Materials should be light and reflective. Below: An ornate simple chair contrasts with metal clothes rail draped with leftover fabric. Below left: Line walls with newspaper and then paint over to give an unusual textured effect.

Softening the line

To avoid the room looking too bleak to inhabit, some form of softening should be introduced. In this bedroom the soft touches are the curtains and bedlinen. The curtains, hung with apparent nonchalance, trail several inches on to the floor in keeping with the non-conformity of the style. Alternatively, the lower edges of the curtains can be arranged and kept in place by inserting fabric-covered weights (continuous length) into the hem.

The lace-edged pillows and disarray of plain white sheeting soften the low-level areas. To extend the idea a metal clothes rail, which could double as a screen, might be draped over with muslin or voile when not in use and serve both a practical and decorative function.

Dining in style

Although the idea of material swathed extravagantly from ceiling to floor may seem impractical in most rooms, the dining room is one place where such impracticalities can be overlooked. In many homes the dining room is often used less frequently than others and is, in most cases, the place where you can be most experimental while causing the least damage and expense.

Dining rooms may be rarely used but they still need great thought and planning, particularly when it comes to furniture. Chairs with unupholstered seats may look good but they are uncomfortable to sit on for any length of time. This can be compensated by adding cushions of course, which will soften the hard edges and keep them suitable for the room's main purpose - that of entertaining hospitably.

Draping fabric

If you cannot handle the thought of such expensive carpeting as in the style pictured here, an alternative would be to keep the flooring bare and drape material loosely over the chairs, leaving the table plain by way of a contrast. Alternatively, if you want to change the mood of the room or even its general usage, a quick and stunning idea is to dress the windows with asymmetrical draperies. Soft fabric could be loosely draped around a pole or tacked to wooden blocks above the window frame.

Table decoration should be kept simple. Old heirlooms such as single candlesticks make a striking impact against the background of flimsy fabric and solid metal.

However, remember that even small details like the colour of the candles are crucial to the style. For example, deep grey, purple or white candles would look stylish, red ruins the effect.

Highlighting your features

Lighting is sometimes thought of only at the last moment. In a dining room this is of even greater importance. If the lights are too bright they will detract from the atmosphere created here while the modern form of overhead lighting would be entirely wrong for the style. The only exception would be if you had some sort of chandelier hung from higher than average ceilings. Otherwise, something like the horseshoe candelabra pictured here would be a good choice. By day it is a decoratively elaborate showpiece encased

Above and right: *The furniture for this style is made mostly from scrap metal. These designers learnt to weld the work themselves, but if you are not up to that standard seek out your own local welder and suggest original designs for him to carry out.*

in snippets, muslin or voile. By night, its white candles will throw flickering shadows across the room.

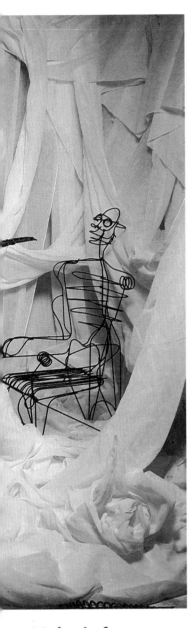

Above: *Table displays are carefully considered. A candelabra adds a suitably romantic look. Similarly, the loosely knotted tablecloth gives a completely individual effect.*

unconventionality of this idea is demonstrated by the loose knot tied at the bottom of this ornate table covering which turns a traditional theme into a carefree gesture. The old fashioned candlestick contrasts strongly with the modern table lamp, while the only wall hanging is an arrangement of dried leaves. It is the unlikely mix of these objects which creates the interest, not the individual pieces.

Make it fun

As far as the furniture construction itself is concerned, the art school graduates who made these pieces insist that it is possible for laymen to make them themselves with home welding kits. However, if you have doubts about trying it out, find a welder who would be able to interpret individual ideas for you. The materials here were found in scrap metal yards, but the designs came out of the shape of the original findings. The single chair consists of a truck mud flap for the seat and reinforcement rods for the legs. Before you try out something quite so adventurous, it would be worth experimenting with something more abstract, a corrugated iron sculpture, perhaps, or a jagged edged mirror. Remember that it is the element of individuality that counts more than the perfection of the work. In fact, perfection is merely in the eye of the beholder, a state of mind.

Still life

As mentioned earlier, although the style is based on recycling unwanted objects, haphazard junk and untidiness has no place here. Every detail is thought out carefully, even down to the corner table display. The

Adding colour

If you want this softer effect overall then the quickest way to achieve it is generally by adding colour. The off-white of the ceiling and the pale green of the wall is interrupted by the warmth of the orange cornices. The woodwork of the skirting boards matches the cornices. You will find it best to stick to a maximum of three harmonious colours, if they are to be used close together, otherwise the effect will be busy which would be wrong.

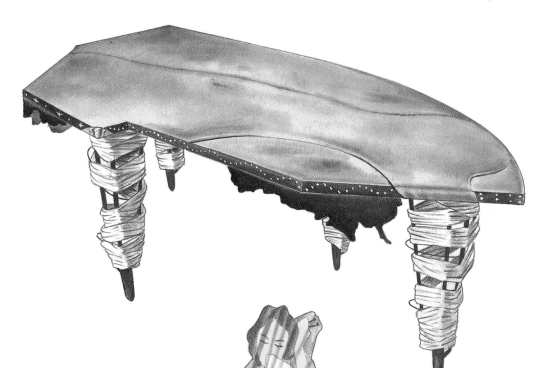

added to bare floors. If the room is large enough for partitioning, a screen collaged with oddments of fabric or paper would make an interesting focal point, and a practical piece of furniture. The hard metal furniture can be compensated for by something on the lines of simple cane chairs. These can be sprayed black to give a hard edge but remain, essentially, comfortable.

Upholstered furniture

If you already have upholstered furniture you can make loose plain covers to conceal and destructure the shape. Or tightly upholster one chair in an elaborate but unconventional way. The stud buttons, for example, may not be in line or the creases between the buttons not quite eased out.

The individual touch

One of the charms of this style is that individualism is everything. Provided you stick to the basic rules, whatever you do will be right. It is also perfect for the truly unhouse-proud. Exposed radiators - especially the old fashioned kind - should be painted to stand out from the wall and such things as electric wiring should be left to hang safely but undisturbed where they were installed. Novelty for the Creative Salvage style is not only fun, it is a necessity, and a cheap way of furnishing a new home. A piece of chipboard covered with leather off-cuts makes an interesting tabletop and bandaged reinforced leg rods make the table a piece of visual fun. As the style began as an anti-style statement, nothing is too absurd. Dustbin lids make good plant stands; pieces of corrugated iron cut to size make window shutters. These also can be papered or painted in style. If you can imagine it, you can have it.

Above, left and below: *Make your own or add to existing furniture. This leather table, by Bill Amberg, shows what imagination can do. Corrugated sculpture is interesting or try less-traditional upholstery.*

Sitting more comfortably

The one room where the simplicity rule can be relaxed is the sitting room which, because of its frequent usage, needs comfort as a prerequisite for its design. Plain or abstract-style rugs in soft, muted colours can be

Wall hangings

This is one place where you are likely to want some sort of wall hanging even if you do favour the minimalist approach. An interesting idea is to use old picture frames painted the colour of the wall so that, when hung, the picture stands out leaving the frame as background interest only.

Windows

Other important points in the sitting room are the windows and how they are covered. If your room needs natural light, then sheers or semi-sheers like calico, muslin, voile, net or lace will make good curtaining fabric. For a stunningly simple display try draping the fabric over a plain wooden pole and gathering up each side with string. If you prefer the traditional method, drape the fabric over the floor to keep within the nature of the unconsidered style. Should you require privacy then you could cover your windows with hand-decorated shutters made from corrugated iron.

Central focal points

As for the central focal point, many houses or apartments still have some sort of fireplace in situ. Depending on the age of the piece it could either be left where it is and painted to fit with your own ideas – 1930s and 1950s tiled fireplaces look stunning in black or white – or changed for something extreme such as a stone monument. As for what fills the space on the mantelpiece, this is where your personal creativity can really get to work. Glass candlesticks with wax drips still in place or empty wooden picture frames with wooden chair legs placed side by side make dramatic contrasts. Cracked china or terracotta and even the odd half-empty wine bottle can find its way up there without embarrassment. Artistic rebellion, radical chic, recycling minimilism, and extreme individuality is what Creative Salvage is all about. It's a fascinating combination.

Mantelpieces should be used for more than the odd candlestick or photograph. Cracked or jagged pots and vases look well-placed. So does a half-empty wine bottle. Even wooden chair legs can be decorative if they have interesting curves and shapes. Here, cheap is classy.

INDEX

USEFUL ADDRESSES

Neo-classical

Clifton Little Venice
3 Warwick Place
London W9
Tel: 01-289 7894
Architectural relics

Haddonstone Limited
The Forge House
East Haddon
Northampton NN6 8DB
Tel: 0604 770711
Cast stone architectural embellishments

Hodkin and Jones
23 Rathbone Place
London W1P 1DB
Tel: 01-636 2249
Fibrous plaster mouldings

Georgian

Roger Board Designs
273 Putney Bridge Road
London SW15 2PT
Tel: 01-789 0046/8
Period panelled rooms in antique pine, oak and mahogany. Carved pine mantlepieces, libraries, bookcases, staircases

J H Bourdon-Smith Limited
24 Mason's Yard
St. James's
Duke Street
London SW1Y 6BU
Tel: 01-839 4714
Antique silver (Georgian)

Colefax & Fowler Chintz Shop
149 Ebury Street
London SW1W 9QN
Tel: 01-730 2173
Chintzes, cottons, voiles and wallpaper based on 18th- and 19th-century designs

Regency

The Antique Textile Company
100 Portland Road
London W11
Tel: 01-221 7730
Regency chintzes, embroideries, Paisleys

Hallidays
28 Beauchamp Place
London SW3 1NJ
Tel: 01-589 5534
Reproduction carved mantlepieces

Through the Looking Glass
563 King's Road
London SW6 2EB
Tel: 01-736 7799
Antique mirrors

Warner & Sons Limited
7-11 Noel Street
London W1V 4AL
Tel: 01-439 2411
Reproduction historical furnishing fabrics and wallpapers

Gothick

Cole and Son
18 Mortimer Street
London W1A 4BU
Tel: 01-580 1066
Reproduction Gothick hand-printed designs for wallpaper and borders

W G Crotch and Son
119 Fore Street
Ipswich
Suffolk
Tel: 0473 50349
Fibrous plaster mouldings

Soho Design Limited
1-5 Poland Street
London W1V 3DG
Tel: 01-439 7654
Modern stacking chair

Victorian

Acquisitions (Fireplaces) Limited
269 Camden High Street
London NW1 7BX
Tel: 01-485 4955
Original and reproduction cast-metal early Victorian fireplaces, brass grates and fenders, fire irons and coal buckets

Faverdale
Darlington
Co Durham DL3 0PW
Tel: 0325 468522
Victorian-style conservatories

Elizabeth Bradley Designs
1 West End
Beaumaris
Anglesey
Gwynedd
Tel: 0248 811055
Cushions: Berlin woolwork needlework kits

Lunn Antiques
86 New Kings Road
London SW6 4LU
Tel: 01-736 4638
Antique and modern lace: tablecloths, bedspreads, cushions, curtains and bed-linen

Nineties

The Art Tile Company
c/o Pot Clays
Brick Kiln Lane
Etruria
Stoke-on-Trent
Staffordshire ST4 7BP
Tel: 0782 29819
Ceramic tiles

Goddard and Gibbs Studio
41-49 Kingsland Road
London E2 8AD
Tel: 01-739 6563
Stained glass restoration and commissions

Arthur Sanderson & Sons Limited
Sanderson House
52-53 Berners Street
London W1A 2JE
Tel: 01-636 7800
Coordinating fabrics and wallpapers, including a range of hand-printed wallpapers reproducing designs by William Morris, Walter Crane, Lewis Day and Owen Jones

Christopher Wray
600 King's Road
London SW6 2DX
Tel: 01-736 8434
Original copies of Victorian, Edwardian lighting

American Country

Crane Kalman Gallery
178 Brompton Road
London SW3
Tel: 01-584 7566
Furniture and accessories

Hermitage Rugs
Shaws
Newcastleton
Roxburghshire
Scotland TD9 0SH
Rag rugs to commission

The Patchwork Dog and the Calico Cat
21 Chalk Farm Road
London NW1 8AG
Tel: 01-485 1239
Patchwork quilts

Wilchester County
Stable Cottage
Vicarage Lane
Steeple Ashton
Trowbridge
Wiltshire (Mail order only)
Candle wall brackets and chandeliers

Biedermeier

Rupert Cavendish
561 King's Road
London SW6
Tel: 01-731 7041/01-736 6024
Furniture, wallpaper, fabrics and accessories

Watts and Christensen
54 Cambridge Street
London SW1
Tel: 01-834 3554
Furniture and accessories

Gustavian

Karl's
6 Cheval Place
London SW7
Tel: 01-225 2625
Swedish 19th century furniture

The Stove Shop
1a Beethoven Street
London W10 4LG
Tel: 01-969 9531
Restored antique stoves

Sasha Waddell Associates
22 North End Parade
North End Road
London W14 0SJ
Tel: 01-603 0474
Furniture and fabric

English Country House

Laura Ashley Limited
The Decoration Collection Corner
71 Lower Sloane Street
London SW1W 8DA
Tel: 01-730 1771
And branches throughout the country
Fabrics, paint, wallpaper, bed linens and lampshades

General Trading Company
144 Sloane Street
London SW1X 9BL
Tel: 01-730 0411
Country house accessories

Glorafilia
The Old Mill House
The Ridgeway
Mill Hill Village
London NW7 4CB Tel: 01-906 02123
Needlepoint designs

English Country Cottage

Amazing Grates
61 High Road
London N2 8AB
Tel: 01-883 9590 6017
Fireplaces

G Austin and Sons Limited
11-23 Peckham Rye
London SE15 3NX
Tel: 01-639 3163
Furniture, antiques